MACON

The Center of Georgia

MACON
The Center of Georgia

by Tracy Maurer

Corporate Profiles by Maryann Bates, Cindy Sams, and Barbara Thompson

Featuring the Photography of Ken Krakow

Produced in cooperation with The Greater Macon Chamber of Commerce

Community Communications, Montgomery, Alabama

CREDITS

Community Communications—Book Division
Publishers: Ronald P. Beers
James E. Turner

Staff for *Macon: The Center of Georgia*
Publisher's Sales Associate: Bill Koons
Executive Editor: James E. Turner
Managing Editor: Candice L. Strickland
Design Director: Camille Leonard
Designer: Ivy B. Harris
Photo Editors: Candice L. Strickland and Ivy B. Harris
Production Manager: Corinne E. Cau
Sales Secretary: Annette Lozier
Editorial Assistant: Emlyn Saunders
Proofreader: Connie Sessions
Accounting Services: Sara Ann Turner
Printing Production: Frank Rosenberg/GSAmerica

Community Communications
A Division of LWT Communications Inc.
Montgomery, Alabama

James E. Turner, Chairman of the Board
Ronald P. Beers, President
Daniel S. Chambliss, Vice President

Photography on this spread by Ken Krakow.

CONTENTS

A Center of Attraction from the Earliest Times

Nestled beside the Ocmulgee River, Macon's lush forests and rolling hills attracted settlement long before written history. The fruitful fields and mild climate sustained some of the earliest known North American cultures and eventually piqued the interest of European explorers. After Hernando DeSoto arrived, the location grew in importance as a trading post and treaty meeting place. Macon became a thriving city, and, spared the ravages of the Civil War, created its place among Georgia's premier communities.

Growing Downtown and All Around

The determined efforts of the Greater Macon Chamber of Commerce, in cooperation with the Macon Economic Development Commission, the Downtown Council, local government, and state officials, have brought a multitude of new businesses to the area. The planned $50 million revitalization of downtown is quickly generating renewed interest in this historic part of the city. As easy distribution paths provided by Macon's central location bring more businesses here, the resulting influx of people to the area is producing a boom in home construction, service sector, and retail businesses.

The Industrial Economy Takes Off

Five major industrial parks serve heavy to light manufacturing, high-tech operations, and warehouse/distribution facilities in the area. Some trace their history to the textile mills while others developed when Macon established military units here, especially Robins Air Force Base and Warner Robins Air Logistics Center. Employing thousands of civilian and military personnel, the base helped spur Macon's "Aerospace Alley" and a multitude of government operations. The area's leaders continue to work toward expanding the industrial economy, predicting considerable growth well into the next century.

A Healthy Service Center

Like most of the country, Macon's economic focus has shifted from agriculture to manufacturing to service and retail sectors. The health care industry dominates Macon's service sector, with six hospitals serving patients from across the state's mid-section. The central location makes doctor visits, consultations, and hospital stays convenient for everyone. Banking, insurance, and other "back-office" industries evolved with the health care firms and employ thousands of people here. Retail growth has also exploded throughout Macon.

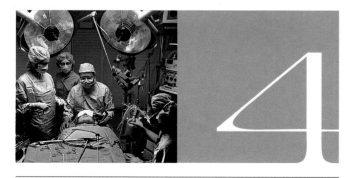

A Smart Approach to the Future

Macon's public and private schools, and six post-secondary institutions receive positive support from the entire community to create an exciting educational environment here. Innovative programs closely bind the schools and the area's industries in a reciprocal relationship: the businesses offer insights to increasingly high-tech fields while the schools provide a well-trained workforce ready for technological challenges. Reinforcing the educational system, Macon's extensive library system features computerized services and a nationally recognized genealogy department.

The Center Stage for Fun and Adventure

As the Cherry Blossom Capital of the World, Macon's Cherry Blossom Festival attracts thousands of visitors every spring. Other top-rated festivals and a multitude of sights such as the Hay House, Ocmulgee National Monument, the Museum of Aviation, and ten historic districts draw tourists and conventions here. The Macon Coliseum, one of the largest convention centers outside of Atlanta, and part of the Macon Centreplex, also welcomes thousands of people to Macon annually. In addition, local theaters and museums continually provide forums for the fine arts.

Building on History for Progress

The romantic notions of southern living, captured in the historic homes, form a gracious foundation for Maconites' lifestyles. Strong neighborhood associations, public safety departments, churches, and volunteer organizations work to create a peaceful environment for families and businesses to grow. The hundreds of parks designed by the city planners thrive even today, welcoming afternoon strolls and family picnics. All around Macon, recreational activities beckon. The Macon Braves play in one of the nation's five oldest ball parks and nearly any sport, social club, or support organization can be found in the area.

On Target for Tomorrow

Poised and ready to bring Macon to new heights by the 21st century, the area's leaders look forward to realizing the results of years of planning. A variety of programs promise to keep Macon and its citizens at the forefront of a changing world. Seizing the opportunities of technological advancements and maximizing Macon's central location allow the city to confidently welcome the new century.

CONTENTS

PART TWO: Macon's Enterprises

NETWORKS 114—125

MANUFACTURING & DISTRIBUTION 126—145

BUSINESS & FINANCE 146—161

PROFESSIONS 162—169

BUILDING GREATER MACON
170—175

EDUCATION & QUALITY OF LIFE
176—181

HEALTH CARE   182—193

THE MARKET PLACE   194—203

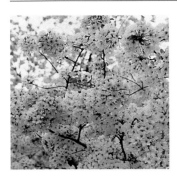

FOREWORD

This is a pivotal time for Macon, Bibb County and Central Georgia. In a very few years, we will enter the twenty-first century; the next millennium. During the past decade, we have seen this area and this country transition into the information age and from cold war with its constant nuclear threat into a true peacetime economy. We have seen major changes in the economy, from agricultural to manufacturing to service industries. Traditional lifestyles have given way to nontraditional. We have moved from isolated, protected local economies to a global economy.

Macon and Bibb County have prospered and grown and adapted to these changes. During 1996, Georgia's most significant event, the 1996 summer Olympics will take place in Atlanta. The eyes of the world will be focused on Atlanta and the rest of Georgia. We have a once-in-a-lifetime opportunity to show the world what we are and who we are.

It is altogether appropriate that we produce a work that says "Here's where we are today!" This book, *Macon, The Center of Georgia* was commissioned to do just that. We expect to have many international visitors during the year of the Olympics. We want them to be able to take home a comprehensive presentation of the area. In a larger sense, we know that this will be a very different place after the Olympics and after the year 2000. We want visitors and natives alike to have a permanent record of what Macon and Bibb County were like before the change.

The Greater Macon Chamber of Commerce

(Above left) Photography by Dorothy Hibbert Krakow.
(Above right) Photography by Ken Krakow.
(Right page) Photography by Rob Blount.

IN HONOR OF THE
GEORGIA MUSIC HALL OF FAME
OPENING IN DOWNTOWN
MACON IN MARCH '96

PREFACE

When my husband and I first moved to Macon from Minneapolis, we quickly learned what "Southern hospitality" truly means. It's more than genuinely nice people and heaping helpings of indescribably delicious food. In Macon, it's also an invitation to experience a city successfully blending a rich heritage with a progressive attitude. This book provides an introduction to Macon's fascinating people and places. I've tried to include the same things we've pointed out to our visitors: the unusual, unique, and impressive stories and facts. I'm afraid space limitations kept me from including them all, and I hope the omissions or misinterpretations will be forgiven. Again, this book is only an introduction to Macon. For Southern hospitality at its finest, please visit Macon and experience its warm welcome for yourself.

Tracy Maurer

ACKNOWLEDGMENTS

Exploring the multiple facets of Macon has been a rewarding adventure, thanks to the many residents who helped point me in the right direction: people who granted interviews, dug out old speeches and reports, or provided the latest statistics and analyses. My gratitude especially extends to everyone at the Greater Macon Chamber of Commerce, Community Communications, Marilyn Ashmore, Stevens D. Ashmore, Tami Hutchings, and Charles Richardson. To my tireless "tour guides," Tim and Sharon Vacula, David Clark, and Beverly Ashmore, and to my parents and infinitely supportive husband, Mike, a heartfelt thanks.

Tracy Maurer

12 (Above left) Photography by Ken Krakow.
(Above right) Photography by Dorothy Hibbert Krakow.
(Right page) Photography by Ken Krakow.

INTRODUCTION
& HISTORY

A Center of Attraction from the Earliest Times

Nestled beside the Ocmulgee River, Macon's lush forests and rolling hills attracted settlement long before written history. The fruitful fields and mild climate sustained some of the earliest known North American cultures and eventually piqued the interest of European explorers. After Hernando DeSoto arrived, the location grew in importance as a trading post and treaty meeting place. Macon became a thriving city; and, spared the ravages of the Civil War, created its place among Georgia's premier communities.

Because so many of Macon's older homes have been restored and several serve as museum homes, this city has become a favorite stopping point on "Georgia's Antebellum Trail." Photography by Ken Krakow.

For more than 10,000 years, the towering pine trees, fertile soil, and temperate climate of the site where Macon now stands sustained inhabitants and attracted new settlement. This pristine area along Georgia's fall-line, an imaginary line where the hilly Piedmont from the north meets the sedate Coastal Plain stretching to the Atlantic Ocean, provided an accessible meeting place and trading site. The river waters of the Ocmulgee, pronounced "oak-mull-ghee" and meaning "boiling water" in the Hitchiti Indian tongue, allowed navigation throughout the region as it joined the other rivers in the area. Macon's geographical location on both banks of the Ocmulgee River and just 18 miles northwest of the actual center of Georgia, earned it the name "The Central City of Georgia" as early as 1879.

Situated, too, at the heart of Dixie, Macon's character is undoubtedly New Southern, a fascinating blend of progressive thinking and respect for history. Maconites exude the famous Southern hospitality, embracing visitors and newcomers with a surprising warmth and graciousness. Elegant introductory remarks flow freely at business meetings, and superb impromptu speeches frequently highlight social gatherings. People here liberally extend invitations to join any of their numerous churches, community organizations, or business groups.

Macon's geographical location on both banks of the Ocmulgee River and just 18 miles northwest of the actual center of Georgia, earned it the name "The Central City of Georgia" as early as 1879. Photography by Ken Krakow.

With gentility not forgotten from the antebellum days, Macon retains its Southern flavor and blends it with the vitality of contemporary living.

One local historian and tour director, R. Martin Willett, explained that what makes Macon stand out are "the people, the place, and the pride." The diverse population here maintains the steadfast course for a strong and safe community, continually looking to improve Macon's impressive quality of life. According to the 1990 census, the city held more than 100,000 residents, and Bibb County counted over 150,000 people. The citizens represent virtually every race and religion, yet they share a common appreciation for their Macon home and the sense of community it offers.

In the years of its existence, Macon's people have repeatedly demonstrated their determination, creativity, and dedication and filled the record books with achievements of all kinds. When much of the "civilized" world questioned the propriety of educating women, Macon's Georgia Female College, now called Wesleyan College, granted them degrees. When the northern states dominated baseball, the Macon Peaches professional South Atlantic League baseball team featured such legends as Pete Rose and Tony Perez. When air travel seemed an uncertain venture, the first commercial airplane cotton crop-dusting experiments took place here and that enterprise later became Delta Airlines. When rock-and-roll music spilled across the airwaves, famous musicians like Otis Redding and "Little Richard" Penniman brought their Macon heritage to the scene. Not all attempts at fame and fortune produced success, but the city's list of "firsts" and notable citizens runs long and certainly adds to the sense of pride Maconites feel.

The place itself, now a contrasting mosaic of historic buildings

When much of the "civilized" world questioned the propriety of educating women, Macon's Georgia Female College, now called Wesleyan College, granted them degrees. Photography by Michael A. Schwarz.

A chorus of 2,000 Yoshino cherry trees burst into clouds of delicate pink blossoms to welcome everyone each spring. Photography by Dorothy Hibbert Krakow.

and modern structures, grew partially from energetic efforts at the Macon Chamber of Commerce and other business organizations and also from its convenient mid-state location. The city's economy continues to benefit from the central location as it draws new businesses and encourages expansions of existing facilities. Like the hub of a spoked wheel, Macon serves as the intersection of many highways and freeways extending outward to reach all parts of the state and beyond. It takes no more than four hours to go from here to the Gulf of Mexico, just under three hours to reach Savannah, and slightly over one hour to arrive in Atlanta.

Macon's crowning place along the fall-line also ensures a mild blend of maritime and continental climate types, with temperatures annually averaging near 65°F and sunny skies prevailing about two-thirds of the time. Such fair weather promotes agriculture in the area and encourages magnificent gardens all year long. The climate, combined with the gently rolling terrain, invites a multitude of recreational activities from camping and fishing to golf and baseball. Outdoor events, including the spring Cherry Blossom Festival and the fall Arrowhead Arts & Crafts Festival keep calendars packed full. As one resident put it, "It's not a problem to find something to do here; the problem is finding enough time to do it all!"

Macon's people and its place rightfully engenders pride among those who live here. However, do remember that as Southerners, Maconites rarely verbalize their pride (it just wouldn't be polite). They're much more likely to subtly show off their city with a dignified smile, knowing Macon easily impresses a fellow Southerner or newcomer from any region or country. Maconites seem to intuitively understand that the foundation of this thriving community rests on its expansive history, centralized location, and determined progressiveness. With these components balanced, Macon shines among Georgia's premier cities.

Prehistoric Beginnings

Millions of years ago during the Paleozoic period, sea waters gently rolled to the shores here. When they receded to the Atlantic Ocean, they left behind critical clues to Earth's ancient beginnings. Some of the world's largest kaolin deposits remained here and entombed early vegetation and life forms. Among the numerous fossils preserved, a 40-million-year-old whale skeleton was unearthed near Macon in addition to shark teeth, sand dollars, and other sea creatures. Today, the Museum of Arts & Sciences on Forsyth Road displays the reconstructed whale and many other fascinating artifacts.

According to evidence found by archaeologists, the first Indian tribes camped beside the Ocmulgee River about 10,000 years ago. These nomadic Paleo-Indians, among the earliest of human cultures, hunted the area's lush woodlands for large mammals. Modern excavations revealed that several different types of tribes eventually followed the Paleo-Indians over time to the Macon area. Around A.D. 900, one particular culture seems to have abruptly taken up residence here although little is known about their origins. Called early Mississippians for their likeness to

the cultures of the Mississippi River Valley, they formed the first known large town on the Macon Plateau. They were master farmers, growing corn, beans, squash, pumpkins, sunflowers and tobacco with wooden, bone, and stone tools. Decorative ceramic pots and rudimentary game-like equipment suggest they stored enough food to enjoy leisure time for pursuing arts and entertainment.

About 300 years later, the Macon plateau stood deserted and remained uninhabited until a late Mississippian town (referred to as Lamar by archaeologists) sprouted three miles down the Ocmulgee River. These ingenious people built two earthen mounds here, including one featuring a unique spiral ramp and the last known to exist in this country. The Ocmulgee National Monument, founded in 1936 and operated by the National Park Service, preserves these mounds and treasured relics of the past.

(Above) This 40-million-year-old whale skeleton was unearthed near Macon and is now on display at the Museum of Arts & Sciences. Photography by Ken Krakow.
(Left) The Ocmulgee National Monument, part of the National Park System since 1936, displays artifacts of the human inhabitants here 10,000 years ago. Photography provided by The Ocmulgee National Monument.

The Ocmulgee National Monument and its Indian mounds offer a tranquil setting in which to appreciate the area's long history.

A New Town from the Old

The Muscogee, Hitchiti, and Yamasee Indians belonging to the Creek Confederacy controlled most of the area now known as Georgia. When DeSoto discovered these Indians on his travels in 1540, the Creeks were flourishing amid plentiful natural resources. Hoping gold was one of those resources, DeSoto explored the area in depth. He made both friends and enemies among the Indians, but found only tiny quantities of precious metals. Notably, DeSoto recorded the New World's first Christian baptisms on the Ocmulgee riverbanks as two priests accompanying him performed the rites for two Indians.

Following DeSoto's early expeditions, Europeans steadily sought land on this new frontier and forever changed the Creek way of life. Historians estimate that the Indians lost about three-fourths of their population to foreign diseases, while many suffered from the insatiable European desire for land. President George Washington appointed Benjamin Hawkins, a distinguished American officer of the Revolutionary War, to negotiate with the Creek Indians in 1785. The state of Georgia, entered fourth to the Union in 1788, pushed for the removal of Indians westward. This effort received unprecedented popular reinforcement when Eli Whitney, then living in Georgia, invented the cotton gin in 1793. Simply, the agricultural-based economy demanded more and more land for cultivation.

Through the treaty signed in 1805 by the United States and the Creek Indians, the Ocmulgee River became the southwestern boundary of the new country. A year later, President Thomas Jefferson authorized the construction of Fort Hawkins, named to honor Benjamin Hawkins and his years of Indian negotiations. The fort's mission was to protect the new American frontier, and it served as a primary distribution point for troops fighting in the War of 1812 with Great Britain and the Creek War of 1813. Fort Hawkins continued its operations as a trading post or "factory" for a few years after the Creek War before it fell into disrepair. A replica of a portion of the fort stands at the site today on Macon's Emery Highway.

Macon Establishes Itself

By 1821, white settlers claimed much of the lands around Fort Hawkins and wagons continually arrived with newcomers, especially from North Carolina. The citizens renamed Fort Hawkins "Newtown" and quickly formed a bustling community complete with its own ferry across the Ocmulgee. When the Indian lands between the Ocmulgee and Flint Rivers became available after the 1821 treaty, state legislators created Bibb County in 1822. They named the new county for Virginia-born Dr. William Wyatt Bibb, who later became governor of the Alabama territory. The legislature also decreed that the county seat would be the city of Macon, in honor of modest North Carolina patriot and statesman Nathaniel Macon.

Five appointed commissioners began the task of laying out the town in a relatively undisturbed bend on the western bank of the Ocmulgee River. Local legend says that they were inspired

by the ancient city of Babylon and envisioned a "City in a Park" —as Macon came to be called. When designer James Webb completed his survey, he planned for unusually wide streets named "for the trees of the forest through which they were laid." Cross streets were numbered from First through Seventh. Only Cotton Avenue, already in place as the Old Federal Road, angled through town and provided cotton wagons a direct route to the river.

In 1823, Macon's 20 half-acre lots were eagerly purchased, bringing fast-paced growth and lasting change. Newtown now fell within Macon's boundaries and residents hurried to build a bridge across the Ocmulgee to connect the town's two riverbanks. Georgia's first railroad survey in 1825 paved the way for Macon to become the state's central city. Macon's citizens debated whether to spend money on building canals and deepening the riverways or to spend resources on the uncertain possibility that railroads would become a key transportation method in the South. The rail advocates won out, and soon Macon led all other Georgia cities in efforts to maximize the potential of train traffic. Even in the city's infancy, foresight and determination characterized the citizens settling here.

Healthy and Wealthy Before the War

The romantic notions of Southern antebellum life exaggerate the actual conditions here, although Macon certainly prospered from cotton trade. Its centralized location, easy river access, and blossoming rail services drew business from all around the region. Merchants set up shop, warehouses expanded, manufacturing began, and trade boomed; Macon lost its image as a frontier town. Toasted as the "Queen Inland City of the South," Macon saw its wealthy residents build gracious mansions and in-town cottages as retreats from the surrounding plantations. Many of these antebellum homes are preserved and listed on the national registry.

(Above) Sorrowfully long lines of Confederate and Union graves in Rose Hill Cemetery tell of the Civil War's cost to the area. Photography by Ken Krakow.
(Below) A replica of a portion of Fort Hawkins stands on Macon's Emery Highway at the site where the original Fort served as a distribution point in The War of 1812 and The Creek War of 1813. Photography by Ken Krakow.

Downtown is full of architectural details as seen in this recently renovated historic building. Photography by Dorothy Hibbert Krakow.

In all of the South, Macon's Hay House stands out as a remarkable example of pre-Civil War mansions. Instead of the white-columned Greek Revival style fashionable then, William Butler Johnston and his wife Anne opted for a 24-room Italian Renaissance Villa of 18,000 square feet. The innovative infrastructure included indoor plumbing with hot and cold running water, a central heating system, an elaborate ventilation system, speaking tube intercom system, and a coal lift. These innovations combined with the marvelous interior decoration made the house a modern masterpiece in the mid-nineteenth century. Not surprisingly, this "Palace of the South" listed at over $100,000 when other mansions in Macon cost about $6,000 to $12,000. Johnston bequeathed the home to his daughter and her husband, Judge William H. Felton. Later, Parks Lee Hay purchased the stunning mansion and renovated much of it. Following Mrs. Hay's death, the Hay family donated the home with some of its finest belongings intact to the Georgia Trust For Historic Preservation in 1977.

The Hay House captures the mythical glamour of the King Cotton era. However, most local residents did not live in such splendor. They were farmers who grew cotton on fields of 100 to 500 acres worked by 30 slaves or less. In town, slaves accounted for about 40 percent of Macon's population and despite their bondage, they demonstrated the same resourcefulness and determination common to all Maconites. Of Macon's 20-some free colored people, Solomon Humphries won the respect of both white and black alike as a profitable town merchant and cotton dealer. Major John Humphries freed Solomon and encouraged him to find his own fortune. "Free Sol" built one of Macon's first stores in 1824 and employed whites, even though he was required to have a guardian (Charles J. McDonald), and held no legal rights. Free Sol later purchased his father and wife, and the state legislature emancipated the two in 1834.

White or black, all who lived here in the nineteenth century enjoyed Macon's relatively healthy living conditions. Unlike other Southern cities plagued by yellow fever or cholera, Macon recorded no cases originating here. The city also maintained many parks to help ensure a healthy spirit. One of the town's early leaders, Simri Rose, passionately learned horticulture in addition to his duties as a newspaperman and government representative. His love for flowers still lives in the many parks cascading through Macon's downtown and in the tranquil "garden of graves" overlooking the Ocmulgee River, now known as Rose Hill Cemetery.

Academic, philosophical, and cultural pursuits thrived during the pre-war days, as they would again after Reconstruction. Schools and colleges granted degrees to both men and women. Spectacular churches graced the streets. Artists and performers frequented the town as the railroad and waterways kept Macon at the center of attention. Progress pulsed through the community. But the rumblings of abolitionists and states' rights supporters soon exploded into a war that would test the temerity of Maconites and all Southerners.

Macon Escapes the War's Ravages

With the onslaught of the Civil War, Maconites stood ready. They rallied behind the Confederacy, and Bibb County sent more troops into battle in proportion to its population than any other county, according to nineteenth-century historian John Campbell Butler. Thomas Hardeman led The Floyd Rifles, one of Macon's troops, and hoisted the first Confederate flag in the state. The city's foundries and factories quickly switched to producing armament and uniforms, and Macon became the center for Confederate armament operations and its depository since most of the state's rail lines met here. The central location, insulated from the major fighting, prompted the state capitol to temporarily move to Macon from Milledgeville in late 1864.

Macon survived "The War Between the States" virtually unscathed. Despite many threats, there were only a few skirmishes near the war's end and the city didn't fall to Federal

The inner hallway to the distinctive Hay House, a national historic landmark, shows the clever trompe l'oeil finishes on the walls. Photography by Ken Krakow.

occupation until 1865 after Robert E. Lee had surrendered. When Major General W.T. Sherman brought his "March to the Sea" to Middle Georgia, he chose to bypass Macon. He instructed Major General George Stoneman to attack the city instead and liberate the Union prisoners at Camp Oglethorpe. The glory-seeking Stoneman left but one mark on Macon with a cannonball lofted from the eastern bank of the Ocmulgee, probably intended for the Hay House (Unionists believed the Confederates had hidden the depository there). The ball landed unexploded in the parlor of Judge Asa Holt's home and it is on display today at the original site, now called The Cannonball House and Confederate Museum. Stoneman failed his mission and ironically found himself imprisoned at the same camp he sought to free.

Reminders of the devastating war remain visible in the city today. Several beautiful monuments stand as sentinels of the past throughout downtown. Eastward on the Dunlap Trail at the Ocmulgee National Monument, the earthen works still mark where the outnumbered Macon soldiers forced a Union surrender at the "Battle of Walnut Creek." The sorrowfully long lines of Confederate and Union graves in Rose Hill Cemetery also tell of the war's cost to the area.

An uncertain future loomed ahead of Maconites when the war ended. The prosperous days seemed a distant memory, but the citizens gathered what remained of their pride and rebounded with remarkable passion and speed. They helped to refurbish some of the 1,400 miles of tracks and rail equipment wasted in Sherman's conquest, rebuilt their farms, and restarted their industries. The freed blacks participated in this recovery as well, and while segregation would continue for almost a century, many outstanding black citizens would help pave the way for Macon's success. In all, post-war Macon embraced progress like a long lost friend, bringing the Central City of Georgia to prominence in the South again. ■

(Left) The Cannonball House and Confederate Museum. This 1854 home sustained minor damage when a Union cannonball sailed into the front parlor during the attack on Macon in 1864. Photography by Ken Krakow. (Below) The entrance to the historic Rose Hill Cemetery. Photography by Dorothy Hibbert Krakow.

THE BUSINESS CLIMATE

Growing Downtown and All Around

The determined efforts of the Greater Macon Chamber of Commerce, in cooperation with the Macon Economic Development Commission, the Downtown Council, local government, and state officials, have brought a multitude of new businesses to the area. The planned $50 million revitalization of downtown is quickly generating renewed interest in this historic part of the city. As easy distribution paths provided by Macon's central location bring more businesses here, the resulting influx of people to the area is producing a boom in home construction, service sector, and retail businesses.

Macon today resounds with the vitality of a continually growing city and the pride of a historic town. Photography by Dorothy Hibbert Krakow.

From its inception, Macon welcomed the entrepreneurs and visionaries who built a strong foundation for a booming business center here in the heart of Georgia. Even before the first city lots were auctioned, 500 bags of cotton went downstream in 1817 and a boatbuilding factory opened in 1819 to produce flat-bottomed pole boats for trading cotton and other goods with neighboring river towns. The first steamboat, the Pioneer, arrived in 1833 and joined the many barges routinely following the Ocmulgee River to Macon. This growing port city was a natural destination point, since its position along the fall-line prevented larger vessels from traveling further upstream. The railroads, heavily supported by Maconites well before the Civil War, quickly made Macon their main connection point for moving goods to and from the river.

The convergence of rail lines at Macon maintained the city's prominence as the hub for the region's business long after the Ocmulgee River was no longer practical to navigate. At one point, over 100 passenger trains a day rolled through the city's beautiful Terminal Station. This 520-foot long, classical structure still stands at the end of Cherry Street. Constructed in 1916 and renovated in the 1980s, the Terminal Station is one of many historic buildings connecting Macon's past with the present.

Macon's attention directly focused on its splendid downtown as the times progressed from dirt to paved streets, from horses to automobiles, from trolleys to buses. The streets bustled with shoppers and business people during the day, and several entertainment venues drew large crowds in the evenings. The Grand Opera House on Mulberry Street, which opened in 1884 as the Academy of Music, captivated audiences with tremendous productions upon its sprawling stage. The Douglass Theatre introduced black audiences to legendary musicians, including Bessie Smith and Macon residents "Little Richard" Penniman and Otis Redding. Cotton Avenue supported a multitude of black-owned businesses as well as Capricorn Records, once the world's largest independent recording company. Nearby, the favorite diner of the Allman Brothers Band, the H and H Restaurant, still fills plates with "soul food." Around the corner on First Street, City Hall continues to draw downtown

Terminal Station is one of the many historic buildings connecting Macon's past with the present. Photography by Ken Krakow.

activity, just as it did when it gallantly served in 1836 as a bank, later as an innovative fireproof cotton warehouse and, in 1864-65, as the temporary capitol of Georgia and host of the March term of the Supreme Court of Georgia.

The city limits expanded continually until the 1950s to encompass the land of surrounding villages. Interestingly, Payne City, a small municipality named for the mill owned in 1899 by William Sims Payne, resisted annexation. Macon dauntlessly grew around it instead. Today Payne City is said to be the only separate city operating inside another city. Despite this aberration in the Macon planners' goals, at one time or another a large portion of Macon's addresses boasted a successful shop, popular restaurant, active church, prominent bank, stately office, or well-kept home. This would change with the movement of businesses and residences outward to the "suburbs" in the 1960s and 70s.

The Business Center

Macon today resounds with the vitality of a continually growing city and the pride of an historic town. The area's healthy economy and viable business opportunities blaze like a beacon throughout downtown and the surrounding county, attracting

developers, commerce, and new residents. Sounds of hammers and saws punctuate the enthusiasm as construction projects for new homes, refurbishing, tourist attractions, and businesses spring up on every part of Macon's map.

The city and county's central location immediately gets attention among national and international business owners and developers. Literally in the middle of the state, the Macon-Bibb County area encapsulates three interstate highways and several four-lane roadways, connecting businesses and residents here to virtually every major city in Georgia. New street improvements promise even more convenient travel within the city and county. This centralized network of roadways increases the accessibility of statewide sales territories while it decreases travel time. Commuters easily drive to or from Atlanta, and Maconites can reach the Atlanta Hartsfield International Airport in slightly over one hour. For retailers, this just as easily brings people to Macon. Studies show shoppers drive from as far as 32 different counties to make purchases here.

Macon's central location similarly provides an optimal distribution point for industry. More than 30 over-the-road hauling companies operate trucks through Macon, and air service is readily available from Atlanta's Hartsfield International Airport, the Middle Georgia Regional Airport, or Herbert Smart Airport. Three railroad companies provide service in Macon; and the nearby ports of Savannah, Brunswick, Jacksonville, and Charleston offer international shipping. Attesting to its viability as an economical and efficient distribution hub, Macon serves as the headquarters for the United States Postal Service South Georgia District which processes over a million pieces of mail daily.

The Mercer University School of Engineering and Mercer Engineering Research Center instituted programs which train students for professional careers and simultaneously assist local industry with ongoing research and development projects. Photography by Ken Krakow.

Ready to Work

The central location also allows employers to hire from a 22-county area surrounding Macon. An estimated pool of 267,275 men and women comprise this highly trainable, loyal, and hard-working civilian labor force. Not surprisingly, the area's unemployment rate tends to run lower than that of Georgia or the United States.

Cooperative efforts between businesses and educators continue to advance the workforce skill level. The Mercer University School of Engineering and Mercer Engineering Research Center instituted programs which train students for professional careers and simultaneously assist local industry with ongoing research and development projects. Macon Technical Institute, Macon College, Wesleyan College and other state educational facilities also work closely with business leaders to provide students with appropriate courses for local job opportunities.

The educational and business partnership particularly works to fulfill the need for highly trained employees in the aerospace, health services and back-office fields. Dominating "Aerospace Alley," Robins Air Force Base and Air Logistics Center employs some 12,500 civilians and 4,000 military personnel within the Macon/Warner Robins Metropolitan Statistical Area (MSA). The "Big Three" aerospace firms, Boeing, McDonnell Douglas, and Northrop Grumman, operate facilities here and their combined employment accounts for about 2,300 jobs.

The Macon area also employs some 9,000 people in health service positions. A large portion of those jobs support Macon's six major hospitals. Likewise, the estimated 11,725 firms located in central Georgia need an ever-increasing number of skilled people to fill back-office positions.

The higher employment rates here, in turn, attract major retailers to Macon. Employment translates into greater amounts of dollars for shoppers to spend. Per capita income in the Macon/Warner Robins MSA has shown a significant increase since 1970, closely following the statewide growth; the median household effective buying income for Macon and Bibb County stood at $31,484 in 1993. Also, the population in Macon-Bibb County generally remains young with the early thirties as the median age for men and women—a significant market for many retail businesses.

Built Better for Business

Macon and Bibb County's sound infrastructure adds another enticement to developing industry and businesses here. Georgia Power Company supplies most of the electrical energy to the area as well as to much of the state. Using its "high reliability" distribution system, power conditioning equipment, or the uninterruptible power supplies option, commercial and industrial customers receive a continuous power flow without concern for the slight chance of equipment problems or momentary outages. EMCs also offer high-quality electrical service to the area.

Major natural gas pipelines run through Macon and Bibb County and efficiently meet even heavy industrial demands. The Colonial Pipeline Company, Georgia Natural Gas

Officers patrol the city on bicycles to protect and serve citizens. Photography by Ken Krakow

Company, and Southern Natural Gas Company work in cooperation to assure a consistent supply for the area today and in the future.

For many facilities, profitable operations also require afford-able water supplies. The Macon-Bibb County Water and Sewerage Authority's monthly charge to industrial and commercial customers averages about 20 to 25 percent less than the national average, according to a survey conducted by the engineering firm of Ernst & Young. Adequate water and sewer capacity exists to the year 2050 with the current systems. Daily, Macon distributes only 50 percent of its water capacity; another 25 million gallons could be produced. The Great Flood of 1994 stirred up heated debates over Macon's water system, but it also cemented plans for a new floodproof water treatment facility. The new system will provide 60 million gallons, with up to 90 million gallons possible—far more than most cities in the United States.

State-of-the-art telecommunication services for both commercial and residential customers are another significant component of the area's impressive infrastructure. Provided by BellSouth, more than 90,000 access lines and about 16,000 miles of optical fiber

The Greater Macon Chamber of Commerce remains committed to supporting existing industries and attracting new businesses. Photography by Ken Krakow.

currently link the Macon exchanges to the global communication network. BellSouth's advanced electronic switching system also enhances the selection of additional features available to business subscribers. Nearly instantaneous and highly dependable data transfer, information processing, and video transmission become a reality through these optional systems.

Rejuvenating the City's Center

Macon's strong business climate permeates its downtown's central business district and the areas circling it. The downtown area's resilience today traces much of its success to the retailers, business owners, and residents who remained in the city limits when so many others tested suburbia. Together, these devoted downtowners wisely began saving what already existed: valuable pieces of American history.

The Middle Georgia Historical Society established itself in 1964 and various preservation efforts soon began, such as the restoration of the Grand Opera House in 1970, the $2.5 million renovation of the copper-domed Macon City Auditorium in 1979, and the refurbishing of Luther Williams Field in 1991—built in 1929 and the nation's second oldest minor league baseball park. The Middle Georgia Historical Society and the Intown Macon Neighborhood Association formed the Macon Heritage Foundation, helping to establish the Historic Zoning Ordinance in 1976 and eventually placing ten historic districts and over 40 individual sites on the National Register of Historic Places.

Merging the old with the new, the downtown planning continues today and an exciting new role for this distinctively historic and highly progressive area is forming. Already, the Parks and Recreation Department plants thousands of flowers each season throughout much of the city's 919 acres of parks. Colorful pansies and chrysanthemums in the fall, pink tulips and daffodils for the spring's Cherry Blossom Festival, marigolds and other bright annuals in the summer all seem to herald the renewed spirit of this beautiful downtown area.

The New Old Meeting Place

The rejuvenation plan positions downtown as the central meeting place, whether for business or pleasure, where something is always happening. Consolidating similar types of businesses or attractions into adjoining districts when it's feasible is a key component in the plan. A pedestrian plaza linking several of these districts serves as a congregating point for visitors, residents, and downtown workers.

The historical aspects of the city stand as a tourism attraction in themselves, and the Georgia Music Hall of Fame and Georgia Sports Hall of Fame highlight the tourism district in the new vision. This is complemented by an entertainment district, featuring venue enhancements such as the renovation of the Douglass Theatre. It also incorporates the $15.8 million renovation and expansion project for the Macon Coliseum. The updated Coliseum, part of the Macon Centreplex, doubles the original in size and offers a premium multi-purpose convention site along I-16.

(Above top) One of the many intown neighborhood gardens found in Macon's historic districts. Photography by Ken Krakow.
(Above bottom) The copper-domed Macon City Auditorium with its stately limestone Greek Doric columns lining the wide terraces. Photography by Ken Krakow.

The integrated development strategies for downtown also propose hospitality and retail districts, commercial and industrial sections, and increased housing availability. The Mayor's Housing Challenge encourages first-time homeowners to purchase inner-city homes by offering city assistance.

City leaders continually seek new businesses and developers, and encourage existing enterprises to expand downtown. Private capital investment of about $130 million and an additional $50 million marked for downtown construction reflects the shared commitment among government and private businesses to secure the downtown's continued success.

Incentives such as grants and low-interest loans resulted in the rehabilitation of 80 buildings during the 1980s. More recent major renovation or restoration projects geared toward increasing the number of downtown employees include the Georgia Federal Building for The Medical Center of Central Georgia, the Hardeman Building for Lawrence Mayer's Florist, the Capricorn Records studio for Phoenix Sound Recording, the old Woolworth's and Galleria Buildings for the Bankruptcy Court of the U.S. Judiciary Department, the old Zayre Shopping Center for the Bibb County Board of Health, the Wachovia Building for the Bibb County Board of Education, and the old Macon Library for the Macon Heritage Foundation. In addition, construction of the Peyton Anderson Community Services Center, multiple expansion projects, and plans for a small-and minority-business incubator also help ensure a strong future for downtown.

The influx of new residents to Bibb County has kept construction workers busy building homes, schools, churches, and stores. Photography by Ken Krakow.

Busy Beyond Downtown

Sharing the excitement of a rejuvenated downtown, commercial and residential developers also look to complement those efforts in every direction outward from the city limits. "Controlled growth" are the key words as the Macon-Bibb County Planning and Zoning Commission and its Long-Range Planning Strategy Committee prepare for the area's future. From 1980 to 1990, the Macon/Warner Robins MSA experienced a 6.6 percent population spurt and projections estimate another 30,000 people will move to the MSA by 2005.

The influx of new residents to Bibb County has kept construction workers busy building homes, schools, churches, and stores. New home sales and home resales climbed above predictions, especially in 1994. The first comprehensively planned sub-community broke ground that same year at Plantation Centre in the northwest section of Bibb County. This multi-purpose development plan features housing, offices, stores, services, restaurants, entertainment, and more. The

concept focuses on cohesive construction, rather than the typical piecemeal approach, to produce an updated, orderly, and convenient mini-town.

Other new residential developments encircle Macon's downtown. Some of the single-family home subdivisions feature adjoining golf courses, such as Barrington Hall and River North. Others concentrate on the tranquillity of graceful ponds and lakes, such as Rivoli Downs or Lake Wildwood. Spacious apartment complexes, including River Place, Spring Creek, Forest Pointe, and many others, encourage a community atmosphere. With elegant names, grand entrances and carefully landscaped streets, most of these developments emerged according to planned construction sites and self-imposed covenants for protecting the quality of their neighborhoods.

Commercial developments continue to crop up near the burgeoning residential areas, making it even more convenient to grocery shop, rent movies, bank, or dine out. Adding the planned expansions of Macon Mall and Westgate Center, the Planning and Zoning Commission expects that the total retail space in Bibb County will have increased by one million square feet at the turn of the century.

Industry, too, has found the perimeter of Macon condusive to manufacturing, warehousing, and distribution. More than 350 manufacturing firms operate in the area, many of which are located in Macon's large industrial parks. Since 1990, over 30 industrial expansions, employee relocations, and new industries have brought some 9,000 jobs to the Macon area.

Strong Economic Encouragement

Just as a good gardener tends to each new seedling, Macon's leaders have carefully helped the city grow and blossom. In the 1890s, the Macon Board of Trade actively supported the area's agricultural and retail base, while the Macon Chamber of Commerce, also formed in the late 1800s, embraced similar goals of economic development for the city. Now called the Greater Macon Chamber of Commerce, this non-profit organization remains committed to supporting existing industries and attracting new businesses in conjunction with other agencies and governments at all levels, including the city, county, and state.

One local leader commented, "I think one of the unique things about Macon is how the leaders work together and how the people care about the city. We may have differences in opinion, but in the end, we're all trying to do what's best for the area."

The City of Macon and Bibb County share a positive and complementary relationship with the various organizations working toward the area's economic development. The "Macon-Bibb County" prefix in many business and organization names stands as a constant reminder of the cohesiveness and interdependence of the city proper and its surrounding area. A long list of non-governmental organizations work with the Mayor's office, City Council, County Commissioners, Middle Georgia Regional Development Center, Macon-Bibb County Planning and Zoning Commission, Macon-Bibb County Water and Sewage Authority, and other elected and appointed offices. Some of these volunteer-based groups include the Macon Economic Development Commission, Urban Development Authority, Downtown Council and their umbrella organization, the Greater Macon Chamber of Commerce. In addition, The Macon-Bibb County Convention & Visitors Bureau and the Middle Georgia Historical Society diligently pursue efforts to ensure that Macon maintains a high profile and positive image worldwide. Together, the city's leaders from all facets of the community continue to expand and support the region's economy. ■

(Left) City leaders work together to expand and help Macon grow and prosper. Photography by Ken Krakow.
(Above) Ranked as the top destination in Central Georgia, Macon Mall is the area's largest retail shopping center. Photography by Ken Krakow.
(Below) Many residential developments feature adjoining golf courses that help create a peaceful environment for families and businesses to grow. Photography by Ken Krakow.

3

INDUSTRY & MANUFACTURING

The Industrial Economy Takes Off

Five major industrial parks serve heavy to light manufacturing, high-tech operations, and warehouse/distribution facilities in the area. Some trace their history to the textile mills while others developed when Macon established military units here, especially Robins Air Force Base and Warner Robins Air Logistics Center. Employing thousands of civilian and military personnel, the base helped spur Macon's "Aerospace Alley" and a multitude of government operations. The area's leaders continue to work toward expanding the industrial economy, predicting considerable growth well into the next century.

The first Japanese firm to invest in Georgia, YKK Corporation of America rates as the world's largest zipper manufacturer. Through vertically integrated manufacturing, YKK produces its own brass with the finest copper and zinc. The metal from this brass wire plant goes into YKK sliders and zipper teeth. Photography by Ron Caudle.

When the Selig Center for Economic Growth at the University of Georgia announced that Macon's economy grew faster than any other city in Georgia except Atlanta in both 1993 and 1994, Maconites were certainly pleased—but not surprised. They knew the city's pro-business attitude and capable workforce invited serious consideration from companies looking to relocate or expand. The Macon Economic Development Commission's public and private partnership diligently courted over 300 new national and international business prospects in the decade's first three years and assisted numerous existing firms with expansions. The Macon-Bibb County Industrial Authority worked with other agencies to help secure land, mostly in the major industrial parks surrounding Macon. Various tax credits and other financial assistance further confirmed Macon's commitment to converting prospective businesses into job opportunities for the area. Also, the Greater Macon Chamber of Commerce assembled a team of business volunteers and designed company-specific employee relocation programs, sometimes traveling to the home city to introduce Macon to the newcomers, or leading community tours here. In 1993 alone, the cooperation of government and private industry brought over 200 new businesses into the area. And the effort continues.

The cohesive approach to "marketing" Macon generally targets prospective firms that can benefit most from the city's proximity to natural resources, its central location, an excellent transportation system, and impressive human resources. This combination of key assets has always existed in one form or another, attracting a diversified economic base to Macon. Similar to most other cities in the United States, Macon's emphasis shifted from agriculture to manufacturing, then to service and retail. However, remnants of the early eras remain intrinsically woven into Macon's economic tapestry.

Mills Weave the Past to the Future

After driving from Wisconsin to work at a plant in Macon, a computer system analyst seemed perplexed upon his arrival. "Where's the city?" he asked. "It's all around you," the plant engineer replied.

The visitor expected the conglomeration of factories, tall smokestacks, and dense

Some of the single-family home subdivisions feature the tranquillity of peaceful ponds and lakes. Photography by Ken Krakow.

traffic more common in the northern cities of the United States. Instead, most of Macon's modern manufacturing facilities operate in spacious pockets of industrial parks skirting the city's perimeter. Although most northern cities now have similar industrial parks in their suburbs, Macon and many other southern metropolises can trace the roots of their manufacturing districts to the heavy influence of the textile industry.

During Reconstruction and after the turn of the century, textile mills opted for locations on the city fringes for easier access to raw material and the nearby rural labor force. The fields around Macon yielded ample supplies of cotton even before the Civil War, so it simply made sense to build mills there. Macon's downtown business district also provided the textile firms with a centralized commercial trading center and convenient railroad distribution network. The city's expansion in the twentieth century eventually encircled two of these "outskirt" mill areas, and this single pair of in-town industrial zones remain as viable today as their modern counterparts.

Hillcrest Industrial Park in the northwestern section of Macon once seemed far from the hustle and bustle of the city. Originally cleared in the mid-1800s for Governor Charles McDonald's expansive summer home, the site also served as a Confederate arsenal during the Civil War. In the late 1890s, the Payne Mill began manufacturing operations and support businesses moved into the area. The Macon-Bibb County Industrial Authority, formed in 1962, set aside acreage for further industrial purposes. Macon's residential growth in the following decades helped determine Hillcrest's present size of about 60 acres. By 1989 the mill had ceased operations, but vestiges of the textile-related beginnings remain and the Hillcrest enterprises today continue to prosper, primarily focusing on light industry and business-to-business services.

The downtown industrial district, a loose grouping of businesses now bordering the southeastern edge of the city, also evolved in the late 1800s. Bibb Manufacturing Company purchased the Macon Manufacturing Company's mill on Oglethorpe Street in 1878 to complement its plant across from the Macon Coliseum. Renamed The Bibb Company in 1971, the firm's logo can be found on linens in homes and hotels across the country.

Macon's nearby railroad hub simplified transportation of raw and finished materials for the mills and other businesses in the area. The Norfolk Southern Brosnan Yard assumes a large portion

Hillcrest Industrial Park encompasses about 60 acres in the northwestern section of Macon and focuses on light industry and business-to-business services. Photography by Ken Krakow.

of today's downtown industrial district and the Norfolk Southern Corporation employs around 800 people in the area. Named for D. William Brosnan, president of the Southern Railroad Company which initiated the yard in 1965, this busy railyard vividly reminds Maconites of the significant role railroads play in the city's industrial history and current economy.

Recording all of the city's development over the years, the original business of *The Macon Telegraph* still thrives in the downtown industrial district. Dr. Myron Bartlett founded the newspaper in 1826, not long after the city's incorporation. Today, *The Macon Telegraph* claims the second largest circulation in the state, and its printing facilities, expanded by 49,000 square feet in the late 1980s, feature advanced printing machinery with exceptional color capabilities for its daily editions. Downtown industrial district businesses have access from Seventh Street to the new Fall Line Freeway, providing a vital link to the four-lane connector between Augusta and Columbus for the future.

Beyond serving as a catalyst for the early industrial districts, Macon's textile mills forged a foundation for related twentieth-century businesses. When YKK Corporation of America sought a location for its new production facility in 1973, then-Governor Jimmy Carter extended a warm reception. A combination of several favorable variables, including the area's familiarity with manufacturing and textiles, helped sway the corporate decision makers. The first Japanese firm to invest in Georgia, YKK (USA), Inc. rates as the world's largest zipper manufacturer. The company employs over 1,000 people to produce millions of zippers daily on its expansive 300-acre campus in the Ocmulgee East Industrial Park.

This newer park, located just six miles from the downtown business district, was the original site for Camp Wheeler during World War I and World War II. In the early 1940s, the barracks, firing range, and administration buildings of the 11,500-acre camp gave infantrymen their first taste of military life. Today, Ocmulgee East Industrial Park encompasses about 1,500 acres. Exceptionally clean and maintained by covenants, this industrial area attracted other textile-related firms as well, including Texprint (Ga.), Inc. and TKG International Corporation. The Bibb Company,

Bibb Yarns, Georgianna Products, Politex (U.S.), and similar textile manufacturing firms located throughout the area employ about ten percent of the present Macon MSA workforce.

Agriculture Grows Into Industry

Just as the textile industry entwines Macon's history with its current manufacturing base, agriculture, forestry, and mining also significantly contributed to the area's development over the years. Tobacco, the South's earliest cash crop, grew readily in the rich soils and gentle climate. Farmers still harvest it today within a 500-mile radius of Macon. The city's central location amid the tobacco-growing regions helped prompt Brown & Williamson Tobacco Corporation to purchase over 200 acres in the Ocmulgee East Industrial Park from the Macon-Bibb County Industrial Authority. There, Brown & Williamson built one of the world's most advanced cigarette manufacturing plants. The first carton came off the line on September 21, 1976. Since then, the company's facilities have expanded to house several million square feet and over 2,500 employees.

Georgia's claim to fame as the "Peach State" began near Macon at the city of Fort Valley. Peach blossoms flooded the fields with their delicious aroma and delicate colors as early as 1884. Historians credit Samuel Henry Rumph for planting Fort Valley's first orchard, developing a feasible refrigerated rail car, and introducing the Elberta peach to Fort Valley. Nearby, John David Duke also established an orchard he called the Diamond Fruit Farm. This became the Lane Packing Company-Southern Orchard Farms, now nationally recognized for its automated packing plant and mail-order business. Several other businesses, most family-owned, operate in the area to help rank Georgia as the country's third largest producer of peaches. Not coincidentally,

(Left) *The Macon Telegraph* newspaper claims the second largest circulation in the state. Photography by Ken Krakow.
(Above) Pictured above is the Saddle Creek Warehouse. This is just one of the many industries located in Ocmulgee East Industrial Park which encompasses about 1,500 acres and is located just six miles from the downtown business district. Photography by Ken Krakow.
(Below) The Norfolk Southern Brosnan Yard assumes a large portion of today's downtown industrial district. Photography by Ken Krakow.

(Below) Kaolin, or sometimes called china clay, is a naturally occurring mineral formed during the glacial period of America and its rich deposits in Georgia helped to make the state the leading producer of the clay. Photography by Ken Krakow.
(Right) Georgia's claim to fame as the "Peach State" began near Macon as early as 1884. Photography by Ken Krakow.

the Georgia National Fairgrounds & Agricenter opened in 1990 just south of Macon in the city of Perry to promote agriculture and agribusiness, especially among the youth. The State Farmers Market on Eisenhower Parkway in Macon overflows with bountiful—and tasty—crops from the area's growers at the height of the vegetable and fruit seasons.

Macon's early agricultural base has developed over time to employ about 15 percent of the workforce in food and related businesses. The Greater Macon Chamber of Commerce includes seven of these companies on its list of firms with over 200 employees. Cagle's, Inc., a chicken processor, employs about 1,000 people and the Keebler Company is not far behind, with 750 employees. Frito-Lay, Borden, Colonial Baking Company, Restaurant Management Services, and Timberlake Grocery Company together employ close to another 1,500.

Natural Resources Attract Business

The abundant pine forests surrounding Macon also drew industry to the area, as did another local natural resource: kaolin, sometimes called china clay. An extensive deposit of this white, crumbly material formed between 50 and 100 million years ago in a broad swath following the fall-line from Augusta through Macon and toward Columbus. Active mining takes place on about 3,700 acres and reclamation projects follow every completed mining site to restore the land for agriculture, forestry, or wildlife. Unlike coal or natural gas, kaolin must be refined in complex processes before it can be used in products such as paper, paint, medicine, plastic, toothpaste, tiles, cement, or ceramics. About 80 percent of the state's high-grade kaolin is used in the paper industry, especially for filling and coating stock. Georgia's kaolin industry developed in the 1920s and gained global recognition by the 1970s. Today, its overall economic impact on the state is estimated at $771 million, with over $36 million in Bibb County alone.

At least two of the area's larger businesses came to Macon for its trees and continued operations here for the convenient access to kaolin. Both Georgia Kraft and Armstrong World Industries opened facilities here in the late 1940s. Georgia Kraft, a joint venture between Mead Corporation and Temple-Inland Company, later became Macon Kraft. Temple-Inland maintained ownership of its corrugated box plant connected to the mill, Inland Container Corporation. Riverwood International Georgia purchased the paper mill in 1992 and now employs more than 550 people from Middle Georgia. Recent multimillion-dollar facility upgrades reduced the plant's emissions to the lowest possible levels while increasing energy efficiency. Costly major modifications converted one of the mill's linerboard machines to produce quality coated board for the beverage, carrierboard, and folding carton markets. In addition to using area fresh-wood products and 800 tons per day of post-consumer recycled corrugated containers, Riverwood consumes over 30 million pounds of kaolin annually—much of it supplied by local firms.

Like Riverwood International, Armstrong World Industries first came to Macon for the plentiful pine forests. At that time,

fresh wood was used to make commercial and residential ceilings. Now wastepaper furnishes the wood fiber in the company's raw material formula. However, the Macon area continues to provide Armstrong easy access to locally mined clay, one of the company's major raw materials in ceilings and coatings. Over 20,000 gallons of coatings are made daily and applied to the ceilings at the 35-acre facility, establishing Armstrong as one of the largest paint manufacturers. For 25 years, the Macon plant was the world's largest ceilings plant (now it shares the title with a sister plant). The total ceilings manufactured since Armstrong began production in Macon would make a path 15 feet wide from here to the moon!

Both Armstrong World Industries and Riverwood International operate their facilities in the Allied Industrial Park. This centralized area covers approximately 450 acres, with plenty of room for heavy manufacturing, warehousing and distribution, and business-to-business services. The Allied Enterprise Center within the industrial park serves as a small business incubator. Beneath the park, underground utility-line tunnels recall the safety concerns of the original plant built there. The fuse-loading assembly plant operated by The Reynolds Corporation for the Naval Ordnance program during World War II couldn't take chances with above-ground sparks! This was just one of the national defense projects in Macon in the early 1940s. Another would have an enormous and lasting impact on the region, the state, and the country.

Robins Air Force Base and Warner Robins Air Logistics Center Forms

Military preparedness topped the nation's attention in 1940 as the prospect of another world war hammered home. The area's city and county governments joined forces in cooperation with Congressman Carl Vinson, then Chairman of the House Naval Affairs Committee, to bring national defense units here. The Macon Chamber of Commerce and the City of Macon purchased 3,108 acres of land about nine miles from downtown for the government to use as a military aviation training base. It was named "Flying School Number One" to emphasize its importance and to help ensure it would become operable before similar projects across the country.

Today Robins Air Force Base (RAFB) and Warner Robins Air Logistics Center's 8,722 acres constitute the state's largest industrial complex. RAFB also maintains one of the state's largest payrolls; it's 10 times the size of the next largest area employer. Worldwide management and engineering for the F-15 Eagle, C-130 Hercules, and C-141 Starlifter, all Air Force helicopters, and all special operations aircraft take place at the base. Maintenance and training are critical components of mission readiness. RAFB has earned national recognition for its environmental quality standards and received official praise from the chairman of the Joint Chiefs of Staff for speedily refurbishing the C-141 Starlifter fleet.

Historically, Macon's existing industries have presented compelling reasons for companies to begin new operations here. This is especially true in the aerospace industry which has

established a "critical mass" in the area, often called "Aerospace Alley." In 1994 alone, RAFB awarded over $130 million in contracts to Middle Georgia businesses. This includes larger firms, such as McDonnell Douglas, Northrop Grumman Corporation, Boeing Georgia, and smaller businesses, too. The Warner Robins Air Logistics Center's Small Business Office, serving as a liaison between industry and the Air Force, awarded over $50 million to the area's small businesses in 1994. Of the 50-plus firms supporting the aerospace industry here, many are located between RAFB and Macon in the Airport Industrial Park. Zantop International Airlines is just one of the notable names at this 1,750-acre site. The park's proximity to the downtown business district and the Lewis B. Wilson Middle Georgia Regional Airport makes it a premier location for Macon's growing aerospace industry.

The highly specialized technical training required for RAFB and area aerospace jobs has also created a strong bond with local educational institutions. Five area colleges and universities developed educational centers at RAFB, offering 19 different undergraduate degree programs and 13 different graduate

(Left) The vast pine forests surrounding Macon draw industry to the area. Photography by Ken Krakow.
(Below) Centrally located with abundant natural resources and highly skilled human resources, Macon continues to invite a diversified industrial base for a strong economy well into the next century. Photography by Ken Krakow.

of the area's workforce. Macon's central location in the state and its proximity to Atlanta have brought more than 50 major state and federal offices to the area, such as the U.S. Bankruptcy Court, the U.S. District Court, and a branch of the Secret Service. Half of the state's corrections facilities operate in Middle Georgia; the state's largest prison complex in Milledgeville employs over 1,000 people. Georgia's Department of Human Resources, Forestry Commission, State Board of Pardons and Paroles District Office, Bureau of Investigation, and Middle Georgia Regional Development Center all support offices here, and the internationally-recognized Georgia Public Safety Training Center in nearby Forsyth prepares the state's police, fire, and other emergency personnel for duty.

Macon's Progress Continues

Macon's industrial base today delivers an incredible range of products: airplane coatings, egg cartons, plastic rings for soda six-packs, pizza boxes, bricks, clothing, air-conditioning equipment, furniture, and candy, to name only a few. Even the nation's largest school bus manufacturer, Blue Bird Corporation, is located in the area, with headquarters in Macon. The investments of nearly 20 international firms representing countries across the globe have also enhanced the array of products shipped from Macon's Metropolitan Statistical Area. Centrally located with abundant natural resources and highly skilled human resources, Macon continues to invite a diversified industrial base for a strong economy well into the next century. ■

programs. Georgia College worked with RAFB and the Society of Logistics Engineers to create a unique Logistics Systems degree; Macon Technical Institute established an Aircraft Structural Technology diploma program and in 1994 began construction on a 51,000-square-foot, multipurpose facility which houses an aircraft hangar to enhance aerospace training.

At the military and local leadership's request, Mercer University opened its School of Engineering in the 1980s. One component of the school, Mercer Engineering Research Center, coordinates the efforts of engineers, scientists, project managers, and technicians with the Department of Defense and national businesses to develop solutions for engineering-based challenges. Many of the center's innovations apply directly to improving efficiency and minimizing environmental impact for the aerospace industry: a robotics system to speed aircraft wing maintenance, computer-generated models to determine load capacities, an optical fiber testing method for passenger planes. In addition, RAFB and the Mercer Engineering Research Center developed a medium-pressure aircraft paint-stripping process which earned this Department of Defense installation high honors for its environmental friendliness.

Macon's involvement with military and government operations stretches back in time to at least the Civil War, when Confederate troops guarded prisoners at Andersonville and Oglethorpe camps, and Macon's own W.B. Johnston looked after the Confederate treasury. Currently, local, state, and federal government agencies, including the Department of Defense, employ about 26 percent

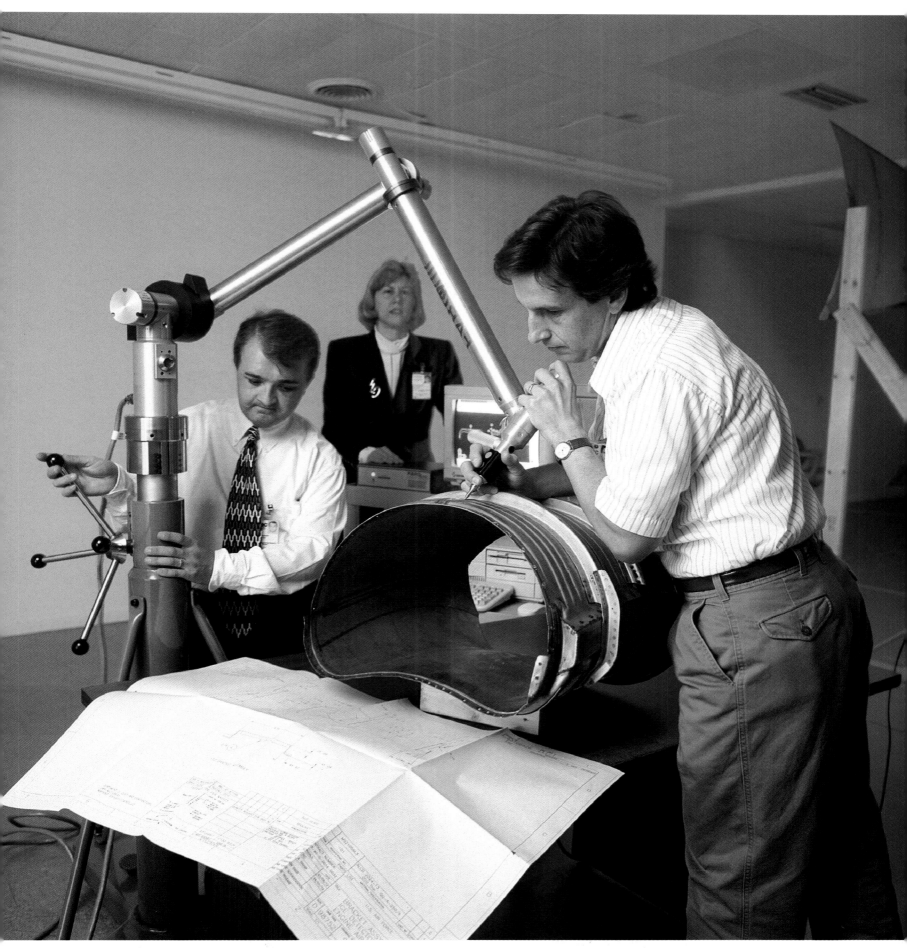

(Left) Robins Air Force Base and Warner Robins Air Logistics Center's 8,722 acres constitute the state's largest industrial complex. Photography by Ken Krakow.

(Above) The Mercer Engineering Research Center directly bridges academia with industry to creatively solve real-world challenges. Photography by Rod Riley.

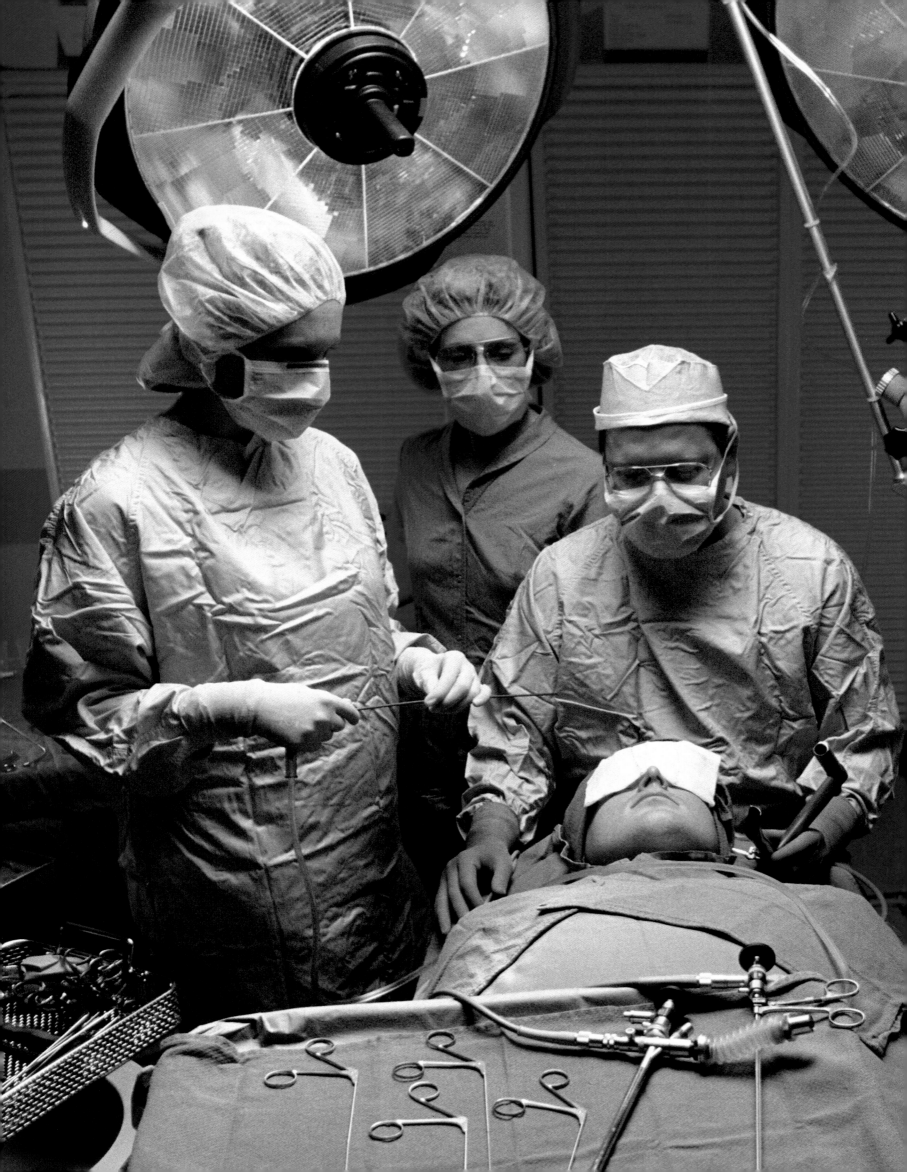

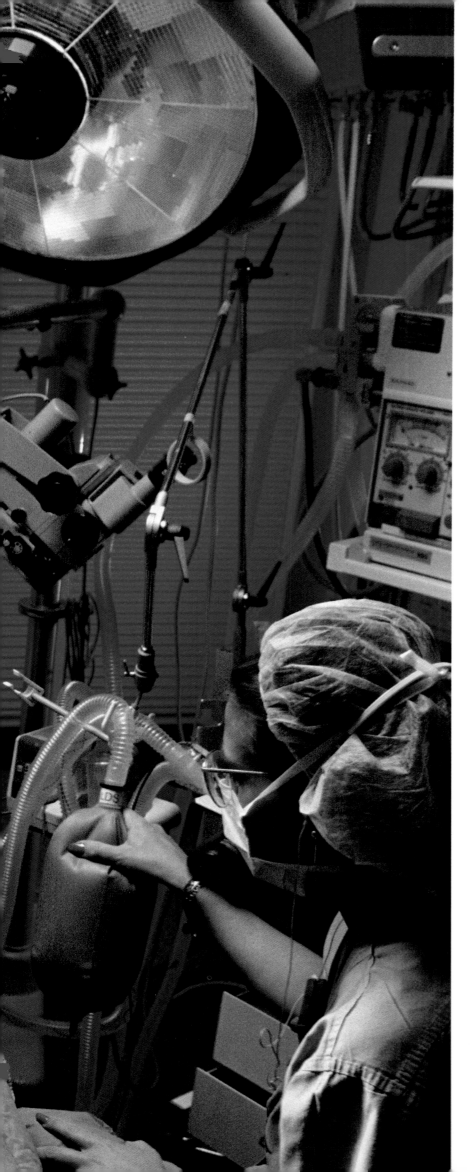

4

HEALTH CARE, SERVICE, & RETAIL BUSINESSES

A Healthy Service Center

Like most of the country, Macon's economic focus has shifted from agriculture to manufacturing to service and retail sectors. The health care industry dominates Macon's service sector, with six hospitals serving patients from across the state's mid-section. The central location makes doctor visits, consultations, and hospital stays convenient for everyone. Banking, insurance, and other "back-office" industries evolved with the health care firms and employ thousands of people here. Retail growth has also exploded throughout Macon.

Macon's climb to become one of the country's premier regional medical centers reveals the city's dedication to enhancing the well-being of its populace and its commitment to progress. Photography by Bill Lisenby.

The Medical Center of Central Georgia serves as the primary teaching hospital for Mercer University's School of Medicine students. Photography by Ken Krakow.

Wounded Civil War soldiers found their way to Macon in droves, creating an overwhelming demand for physicians, nurses, and medical supplies. Women's relief groups sewed bandages and tended to the injured in makeshift hospitals, while the apothecaries supplied prescriptions concocted from dogwood, slippery elm bark, gentian root, red-pepper pods, herbs, and other ingredients. The influx of patients during the Civil War first positioned Macon as a regional medical center.

The health services industry has grown over the years in the area to exceed the national average of hospital beds and physicians, according to a study for Robins Air Force Base. The Georgia Department of Labor reported the health services industry growth-rate in the 1990s for 11 counties around Macon is double that of the area's other industries. Almost 100 dentists and more than 500 physicians in nearly every facet of medicine, including highly specialized disciplines, treat thousands of patients here. State-of-the-art equipment and facilities allow this corps of professionals to effectively perform simple to complicated procedures. Typically, only transplant operations are referred to other locales. One former patient commented, "If a person must get sick, Macon's one of the best places to do it!"

Four general medical and two specialized hospitals form the foundation of the health care industry in Macon. This core group and other neighboring hospitals helped develop a broad support network of clinics, pharmacies, medical equipment suppliers, home health care services, and related businesses. An integrated relationship between the hospitals and the state's educational institutions produces a well-trained workforce. The Medical Center of Central Georgia serves as the primary teaching hospital for Mercer University's School of Medicine students; courses and programs offered by Wesleyan College, Macon College, Georgia College, Macon Technical Institute, and Fort Valley State College also reinforce the industry's strength in Central Georgia.

Historians note that the South generally lagged in health care providers for many years after the Civil War, partially due to the rural economy. However, recent decades have propelled southern medical institutions into the nation's sphere of health care leaders. Macon's climb to become one of the country's premier regional medical centers reveals the city's dedication to enhancing the well-being of its populace and its commitment to progress.

Early Physicians Establish Macon's Medical Community

Named after a physician, Dr. William Wyatt Bibb, the county attracted doctors to the city of Macon even in its infancy. Dr. Ambrose Baber, Macon's first practicing physician in the 1820s, also heavily influenced the city's formation until his shocking death. Historical references relate that Dr. Baber prescribed a dose of cyanide of potassium according to the instructions in Ellis' Formulary. The pharmacist who filled the order advised the patient not to take the prescription because the dosage seemed far too strong. Heeding the warning, the patient questioned Dr. Baber. The doctor confidently swallowed the prescription to prove its accuracy and he died almost immediately. Apparently, the prescription book contained a typographical error (belatedly corrected in the next edition).

Maconites mourned the passing of their civic-minded doctor, but welcomed others who followed him. Two of these early physicians were women. Testifying to Macon's prevailing progressiveness, the first female doctor offered services here in the 1880s. The second physician was a Wesleyan College graduate, Dr. Mary Eliza McKay, who returned to Macon after studying at the Women's Medical College of Baltimore.

The growing city dedicated its first permanent hospital in 1895 on Pine Street after six years of fund-raising efforts. Named the Macon Hospital Association, it housed 20 beds monitored by a single doctor and nurse team. For over 100 years, the area

Researchers play an important role in the medical community at the Mercer University School of Medicine. Photography by Ken Krakow.

(Below) In 1993 alone, some 1,400 babies came into the world via the HCA Coliseum Maternity Center. Photography by Drake White.

bordered by Pine and Hemlock Streets has hosted health care providers, although the facilities and staff sizes have markedly multiplied.

Today, The Medical Center of Central Georgia employs about 3,300 people in medical, administrative, and support functions, and ranks as one of the state's largest employers. Its direct and indirect payrolls total about $251 million and the hospital shoulders much of the county's indigent care costs. Also large in size and scope, the HCA Coliseum Medical Centers employs more than 800 people. Together, The Medical Center of Central Georgia, HCA Coliseum Medical Centers, HCA Coliseum Psychiatric Hospital, Macon Northside Hospital, Middle Georgia Hospital, and Charter Behavioral Health Systems considerably influence Macon's economic health as well as the area's physical and emotional well-being.

The Medical Center of Central Georgia Grows with Macon

Reigning over a large portion of downtown Macon, The Medical Center of Central Georgia provides a 518-bed regional referral center for most of Georgia's 159 counties. This full-service, acute-care facility addresses a wide range of health concerns through more than 20 specialized centers, services, and programs. It also serves as a teaching hospital for several universities. One Macon-Bibb County Hospital Authority board member noted, "If there's a need for a certain type of doctor or program and we don't have one, we work to find the best to bring to Macon." Confirming its leadership position, H.C.I.A., Inc. and Mercer Management Consulting, Inc., ranked the Medical Center among America's 100 top-performing hospitals.

The various Medical Center services developed over a century, most often reflecting the advancements of medical capabilities and philosophies. The hospital began treating cancer patients in the 1930s, and this grew into the well-known Cancer Life Center. The hospital's Georgia Heart Center, initiated in the 1960s, gained national recognition for its full cardiovascular services. In the next decade, the Medical Center brought the first birthing room to Central Georgia. Today, the home-like suites of the Family Birth Center allow expectant mothers to share the delivery experience with the new father, and there's even a rocking chair if grandma wants to lullaby the new baby to sleep.

Other Medical Center programs include Focal Pointe Women, a resource center exclusively dedicated to enhancing women's physical and emotional health, and Hospice of Central Georgia, a program designed to bring dignity to the lives of those with terminal illnesses. Additionally, the Medical Center operates Central Georgia's only children's hospital, the region's only sleep disorder facility, four urgent care centers, three fitness/education centers, psychiatric and addiction facilities, imaging center, diabetes treatment center, rehabilitative hospital, and occupational health center. In 1991, the Medical Center completed its largest project, the 185,000-square-foot Surgery Center for inpatient and outpatient services.

(Below) In 1993 alone, some 1,400 babies came into the world via the HCA Coliseum Maternity Center. Photography by Drake White.
(Right) The Medical Center of Central Georgia is a full-service, acute-care facility that addresses a wide range of health concerns through more than 20 specialized centers, services, and programs. Photography by Bill Lisenby.

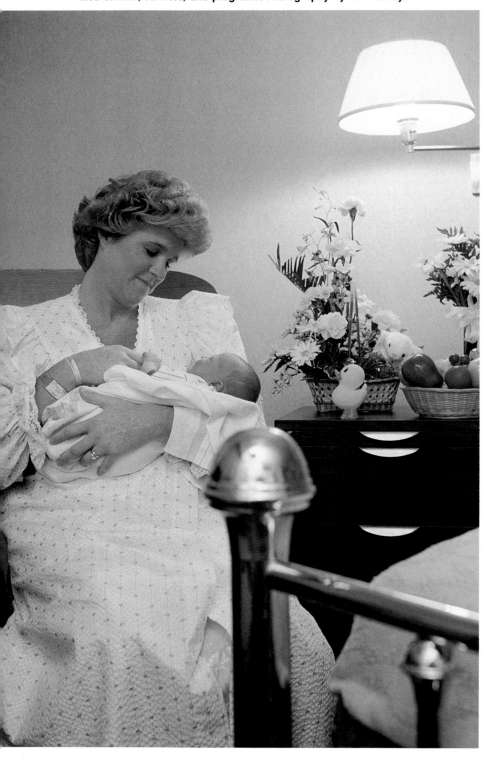

HCA Coliseum Medical Centers Enhances Downtown Health Services

As Macon's population grew, so did the need for more health services. HCA Coliseum Medical Centers located here in the 1970s just behind the Macon Coliseum. This formidable complex of buildings, including the 258-bed hospital, sprawls across the hillside above the Ocmulgee River. The Coliseum Women's Center shares a large portion of the space for its mammography, ultrasound, and densitometry services. The Women's Center houses the cozy, private rooms of Coliseum Maternity Center, plus the newborn nursery and a neonatal ICU. In 1993 alone, some 1,400 babies came into the world via the Coliseum Maternity Center.

HCA also operates the 92-bed Coliseum Psychiatric Hospital with a 24-hour telephone helpline and a specialized outpatient center for families. Through a "systems" approach, HCA Coliseum Medical Centers oversees two urgent care facilities and centers for outpatient diagnostics, rehabilitation, breast health, weight control, diabetes management, and same-day surgery. Other services include physician referral, health education programs, and support groups.

Middle Georgia Hospital and Macon Northside Hospital Add Options

Downtown Macon features a third hospital within the city limits. First opened in 1911, Middle Georgia Hospital offers general, acute, and surgical care. Its private rooms for outpatient surgery enhance the comfort of patients who travel from the entire Central Georgia area for treatment. The hospital also provides exceptional cardiology services, x-ray and laboratory diagnostics, heart catheterization, and an impotence program. Additionally, it operates the Middle Georgia Urgent Care Center on Forsyth Street where a physician is on duty around the clock. The hospital's Ask-A-Nurse℠ physician referral and health information service effectively answers many health-related questions. This service is a cooperative program with Macon Northside Hospital, the city's newest hospital.

Individual attention to each patient is very important in Macon's medical field.
Photography by Ken Krakow

Opened in 1984 on a 40-acre wooded campus, Macon Northside Hospital shares the beautifully landscaped site with an adjacent medical office building and two separate office complexes. The soothing environment outside seems to drift through the private hospital's 103 rooms and enhances recovery from general, acute, or surgical care. The hospital's full-service emergency room features an innovative Chest Pain Center to quickly determine the cause of chest discomfort and treat it appropriately. Macon Northside Hospital also operates an advanced intensive care unit, inpatient/outpatient surgical suites, state-of-the-art endoscopy lab, non-invasive echocardiography, advanced pulmonary lab with registered respiratory therapists and technicians, physical therapy department, imaging services, nuclear medicine, and a variety of support programs.

Health Care for the Times

Macon's major general hospitals evolved over time in response to the community's changes and the dynamics of the medical profession. And they continue to grow to expand their facilities and services. Similarly, Charter Medical Corporation, founded here in 1969 by William A. Fickling, Jr., shifted from its initial focus to become one of the leading companies in the psychiatric and addictive care field. The company headquartered in Macon's tallest building for about 25 years; today some 200 people still work in the corporation's satellite office here. Charter Medical currently operates over 100 hospitals in the United States and foreign countries.

One of those hospitals is Macon's Charter Behavioral Health Systems of Central Georgia in the Charter Lake Hospital Building. Set on 18 lush acres and a small lake, Charter Behavioral Health Systems confidentially helps children, adolescents, and adults deal with emotional, behavioral, substance abuse, or addictive disease problems. Its 24-hour Crisis Line receives about 600 calls a year, and every caller gets help: answers, an offer for free in-person assessment, or a referral. The stacks of thank-you notes collectively tell of the programs' successes. About 150 employees run the two outpatient centers, partial hospitalization program, and 118-bed inpatient facilities. The professionals also direct several specialized services, such as employee assistance, senior citizen, or Christian-based programs.

Another health care resource for the community can be found at the Macon-Bibb County Health Department's new headquarters on Emery Highway, and the Georgia Department of Human Resources' Family and Children Services on Oglethorpe Street. Both provide immunization and well-baby check-ups. They also offer the developmental hearing, dental, and vision screenings required for all new students in Bibb County Public Schools.

For those whose school days were many decades ago or for those with incapacitating conditions, the many high-quality home health care agencies here deliver a positive alternative to hospitalization. This vast force of traveling nurses and aides administers the care and treatment that allow sickly or handicapped individuals to live in the comfort of their own homes. And if home care is

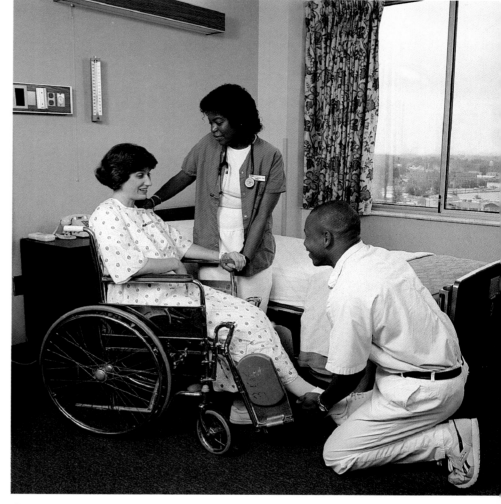

The postive care patients receive in the hospital makes for a smooth transition to home. Photography provided by Coliseum Medical Centers.

(Above) The Charter Medical Building and the modern headquarters of First Liberty Bank overlook the surrounding downtown area. Photography by Ken Krakow.
(Right) The contemporary five-storied building of the Georgia Farm Bureau Federation houses a wide range of services for its statewide membership. Photography by Ken Krakow.

no longer an option, area nursing homes tend to the convalescing and infirm.

The city's rise as a regional health care provider continues to stimulate the area's economy. When calculating the dollars a medical facility brings to an area, economists use a higher multiplier for these institutions than for most other types of businesses. The theory seems to apply to Macon. Indirect job growth generated by the health care industry, especially its hospitals, and the city's centralized location, helped to dramatically increase "back-office" industries. This includes insurance and financial industries and other companies providing non-selling services such as legal, accounting, record-keeping, and communications.

Back-Office Comes to the Front

Shadows of Macon's contemporary back-office industry peek from the city's historical photographs and documents. These early employees worked behind the scenes, counting cotton receipts, issuing railroad train notes, or running messages between offices. As the country's economy shifted in time towards a service base, Macon's did, too. Numerous financial and insurance firms established their regional, state, or national headquarters in the city, giving center-stage importance to Macon's increasing back-office workforce.

Macon hosts ten main banks with over 50 branch offices today. First Liberty Financial Corporation, the largest publicly held corporation based here, serves as the holding company for First Liberty Bank. Established in 1926, First Liberty now provides banking and financial services at more than 25 offices throughout Georgia and employs about 375 people in Macon. Its modern headquarters overlooks the surrounding downtown businesses.

Another homegrown firm, the Georgia Farm Bureau Federation, created its headquarters here in 1941. It moved several times within Bibb County to continually accommodate the expanding breadth of services and memberships. Enlarged from 1,313 members in 1941 to 234,700 in 1993, the Georgia Farm Bureau Federation now employs about 380 people. Its contemporary five-storied building on Bass Road houses an amalgam of insurance, investment, and real estate subsidiary companies, and a wide range of services for its statewide membership.

Macon's central location in the state and its healthy industries captured the attention of large national and international firms, and they, too, developed headquarters here. CIGNA Insurance Company traces its development in Macon to 1948 when the Insurance Company of North America (INA) opened an office downtown. In just six years, INA began constructing a beautiful brick facility on Coleman Hill with a commanding view of the entire city. Mercer University purchased the site in 1977 for its Walter F. George Law School and maintained much of the original architectural embellishments, particularly the stately cupola. Camera-buffs find the building irresistible and it's one of the most frequently photographed buildings in Macon—probably second only to its neighbor, the famous Hay House—and likely one of the few law schools in the country featured on post cards, calendars, and brochures!

INA later merged with Connecticut General Insurance Company to form CIGNA Insurance Company, the namesake for one of Macon's largest office buildings. This site also won architectural awards. About 450 CIGNA employees work there, handling business in 31 states across the country.

Other insurance companies found Macon conducive to their operations. The Government Employees Insurance Company (GEICO) now employs more than 1,300 people on its eight-acre campus in the Ocmulgee East Industrial Park. Since 1974, the offices have served as the headquarters for GEICO Region III, the company's largest territory. GEICO also credits the Macon facility, serving 15 states, as its most productive.

Similarly, Aetna Life & Casualty Company and GE Capital Credit Services headquartered offices in Macon, too. Together, they employ an additional 600-plus back-office workforce.

Alco Capital Resource came to Macon in the 1980s for many of the same reasons the other back-office businesses did. However, this national headquarters for office equipment leasing found an additional incentive to settle here besides the central location, growing economy, or high-caliber labor force: Macon's Acme Business Products. Alco Capital Resource cooperatively took over the leasing division of Acme in 1983 and moved from a building behind the business products dealer to its 37,000-square-foot office complex in 1994. Acme Business Products, which started on a shoestring in the early 1970s, now employs more than 650 people covering Georgia and territories across the southeast. Its headquarters for the 35 branch offices remain in Macon.

The service sector, including health care and back-office industries, accounts for more than one-third of the firms in Macon's MSA. The success of the service and manufacturing forces continues to help raise the area's overall buying power. Now ranked as the third greatest MSA buying power in the state by the University of Georgia, Macon's MSA supports some 1,700 retail trade businesses—second only to the number of service firms, and evidenced by the assortment of shopping bags passing around town.

More in Store in Macon

As long as any Maconite can recall, shoppers have flocked to the city from all around the region to find their dresses, suits, housewares, furnishings, and sundry items. Of course, precisely what they purchased over time has changed from wagon wheels to all-season tires; hand-crank phonographs to multimedia

(Left) A variety of retail shops are available along the Tom Hill, Sr. Boulevard. Photography by Ken Krakow.
(Right) Mercer University's Walter F. George Law School. While Macon's healthy manufacturing, service, and retail industries provide residents with plenty of places to make money, save money, and spend money, they also emphasize the importance of education, and improve the quality of life. Photography by Ken Krakow.

computers; parasols to beach blankets. Today's retailers in Macon provide the full array of big-city merchandise, but if an item isn't in stock, they order it with the genuine warmth of small-town service.

The downtown area, once the hub of general merchandisers, now attracts shoppers to its increasing variety of specialty stores. Many of the family-owned businesses, such as Arleene's, Bowen Brothers Clothiers, Karla's Shoe Boutique (owned by two women of the Otis Redding family), and Bert Maxwell Furniture Company, represent long-term success stories. The rebirth of the downtown area in the 1990s promises to further enhance the downtown shopping experience.

At the same time, commercial developments continue to expand in the suburban areas. Westgate Mall, opened as the state's first enclosed shopping complex in 1961, prepared for major remodeling and expansion in 1994. The new collection of outstanding anchor stores in a contemporary power-strip design prompted a proposal to change the name to Westgate Center.

Macon Mall, the area's largest retail shopping center, also announced extensive expansion plans featuring additional big-name anchors. Built in 1975, it encloses over 30 acres under its roof on an 85-acre site. A stroll through the parking lot on any day of the week reveals license plates from a 30-county radius and often from other states. Studies showed Macon Mall ranked as the top destination in Central Georgia; Westgate Center ranked as the second most heavily shopped retail complex.

As other retailers opened in the vicinity of Westgate Center and Macon Mall, they formed a prime retail corridor roughly between Eisenhower Parkway and Mercer University Boulevard and from I-475 to I-75. Some 96,000 cars pass daily through the intersection of Pio Nono Avenue and Eisenhower Parkway near the entrance to Westgate Center. With the completion of the Fall Line Freeway, the corridor can more accessibly draw traffic from east Macon and all of Central Georgia. "If we could relocate the Macon Mall," a manager commented, "we would put it right back where it is."

In every direction around the city, grocery stores, restaurants, hardware stores, automobile dealerships, and hundreds of other retailers welcome patrons. Some can be conveniently found in the many strip shopping centers or in their own buildings. It's also an easy drive to nearby outlet stores and the new Centerville Galleria Mall. While Macon's healthy manufacturing, service, and retail industries provide residents with plenty of places to make money, save money, and spend money, they also emphasize the importance of education, and improve the quality of life. ■

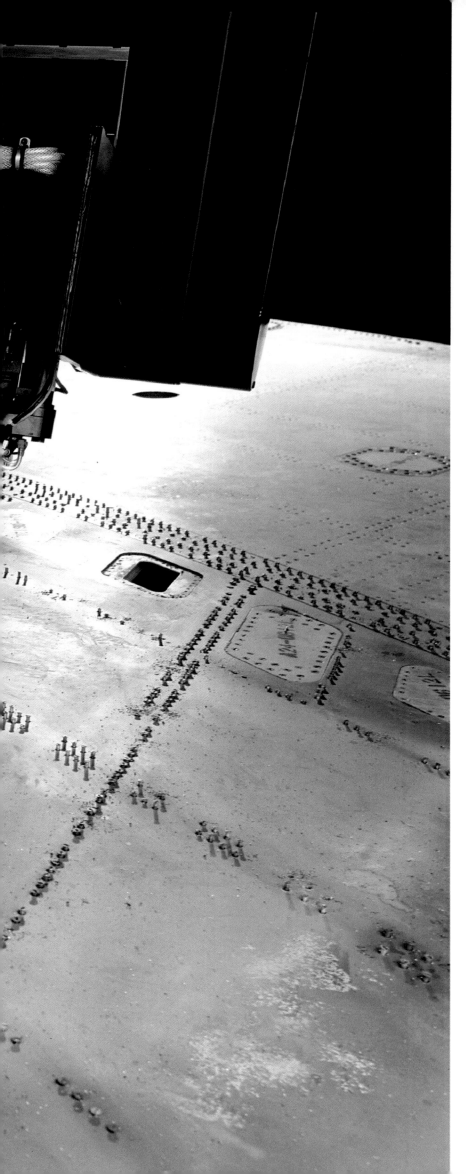

5

EDUCATION

A Smart Approach to the Future

Macon's public and private schools, and six post-secondary institutions receive positive support from the entire community to create an exciting educational environment here. Innovative programs closely bind the schools and the area's industries in a reciprocal relationship: the businesses offer insights to increasingly high-tech fields while the schools provide a well-trained workforce ready for technological challenges. Reinforcing the educational system, Macon's extensive library system features computerized services and a nationally recognized genealogy department.

The cooperative efforts of the area's post-secondary institutions help to maximize the educational opportunities at the schools and advance the area's economic development. Photography by Rob Reilly.

Macon's students today hold the promise for the next century's community and leadership. The area's educational institutions fully intend to prepare them for the technology-based world they will inherit. A sharpened focus on educational quality, generated from the grassroots level to the state's legislature, provides innovative programs, financial assistance, and more demanding standards for every instructional level. The goals of raising aspirations and expectations, and creating a culture of excellence in education, permeate every program in some way or another.

The Macon 2000 Partnership was established in 1992 to improve the quality of education in Bibb County. Macon 2000 relies heavily on community involvement to achieve its goals. Educators, parents, students, clergy, government, businesses, and social service personnel work together to put plans into action for the public school system. The organization's efforts, especially in seeking grants, have brought the schools an array of programs without imposing additional tax costs. These include tangible programs for at-risk, gifted, or challenged students. Macon 2000 Partnership successes have earned national attention, and the organization serves as a state model for other educational partnerships.

Connecting with the Working World

School administrators, from the Bibb County School System to the post-secondary institutions, forged partnerships with area businesses to further elevate students' prospects as employees. These programs introduce classrooms to realistic challenges and advanced technology, helping to ensure the readiness of tomorrow's workforce. The Greater Macon Chamber of Commerce, an active supporter of the educational community, developed a presentation illustrating the benefits of business involvement in education and encouraging participation. The Chamber of Commerce also assists with career workshops and offers "shadowing" or on-the-job mentorship opportunities for students. Over 60 businesses, agencies, churches, and civic groups have adopted Bibb County schools to provide insightful information and instructional materials beyond the curriculum.

Additionally, all of the area's post-secondary institutions, including Mercer University, Wesleyan College, Georgia College, Macon College, Fort Valley State College, and Macon Technical Institute, linked their respective educational facilities to industry through various programs. These cooperative efforts help to maximize the educational opportunities at the schools and advance the area's economic development.

State Educational Support

The Georgia Legislature heard the concerns of parents, educators, and businesses and acted to encourage post-secondary education for the state's high school graduates. Now every Georgia high school graduate pursuing a degree, diploma, or certificate at any of the state's public or private colleges, universities, or technical institutes can apply for financial aid through the state's unique HOPE (Helping Outstanding Pupils Educationally) program.

Youth Leadership Bibb County participants engage in a team-building exercise at their retreat. Photography by April Faith Copeland/Perdue Design Group.

Elementary students learn through the innovative television studio program at the Winship Geography & History Magnet School. Photography by Ken Krakow.

Students at The Clisby Fine Arts School receive hands-on experience from dedicated instructors. Photography by Ken Krakow.

Funded by the Georgia Lottery for Education and administered by the Georgia Student Finance Commission, the HOPE program also provides financial assistance for schools seeking computers and other advanced equipment.

The Georgia Legislature also allocated funds to provide training assistance for new and expanding industries planning to hire large numbers of personnel. Named Quick Start, this economic development tool minimizes start-up problems for the participating companies and creates an immediate skilled labor force; it's a win-win program for employees and employers. Schools such as Macon Technical Institute and Macon College also offer short-term programs for companies looking to train a group of employees on a particular subject.

The current strength of Macon's educational climate owes a great deal to the efforts of contemporary local, regional, and state leaders. They took their history lessons to heart and vowed to create a truly progressive educational experience for all Maconites.

Macon's Early Lessons on Education

As a frontier town in the 1820s, Macon invited adventurers and entrepreneurs, but few children. To the city's credit, the Bibb County Academy and a singing school opened in 1824. Macon became a central location for learning institutes mainly after the Civil War. Some early schools here resulted from the city's progressiveness; others formed out of necessity due to the traditional segregation of the times. A few of these institutions disappeared into the history books when the Civil Rights Movement rendered them unnecessary. Many endured the troubled eras and evolved into leading educational facilities.

One of the South's first specialized educational programs opened a new world to nine vision-impaired children in 1852. The Georgia Academy for the Blind has continuously taught since then, even during the Civil War when it moved its classes to Fort Valley for safety. The school returned to Macon and later established its Vineville Avenue campus. The nation's third-largest school for the blind now offers some 170 disabled students regular high school and special education diplomas. About 135 staff members and 50-plus volunteers help students learn marketable skills and participate in numerous community activities. The Academy also provides internships for student teachers from six post-secondary schools, including Macon College and Mercer University.

Twenty years after the Georgia Academy for the Blind broke new ground for special-needs children, other private elementary and secondary schools initiated programs here. Mount de Sales Academy began with associations to the Catholic faith in the 1870s and remains an active private school. In addition, some 15 other private institutions and over 40 private pre-school facilities now accept students in the Macon area.

Many of the other elementary and secondary schools built in Macon's early history reflected the segregationist beliefs embedded in the Southern society at the time. The Bibb County Public School and Orphanage System organized common free schools for whites in 1872. Schools for black children, such as Lewis High School, were independently created during the latter part of the nineteenth century. Central City College, later renamed Georgia Baptist College, formed in 1882 and remained the only local post-secondary institution for blacks until Maconite Minnie Smith founded the Beda-Etta College in 1921. "Miss Minnie" taught children during the day and adults in the evenings at a building she purchased with her life savings. Her dedication to education, intensely shared by so many leaders of both races, helped heal the scar left by the South's racism. By 1964, black school children sat in classrooms next to white children. Today, cultural awareness and appreciation for diversity come across clearly in the school lessons, moving the community forward in equality.

Quality Education in Bibb County Public Schools

When national consultants surveyed the Bibb County School System in the 1990s, they raved about the variety of successful new programs available to students. Certainly the Board of Education's television studio and cable broadcasts rank among the more creative efforts to involve the community in the educational process. Over 25,000 students in the Bibb County system learn through an array of innovative programs and the dedicated efforts of professional instructors. About 75 percent of the certified staff hold advanced degrees; many have earned state and national recognition, including presidential citations.

The school system features four magnet schools among its 31 elementary facilities. Alexander II Math-Science School began in 1979 and Clisby Fine Arts School, Hunt Language Arts & Spanish School, and Winship Geography & History School followed. All of these schools teach students from kindergarten through sixth grades. Seventh and eighth grade pupils attend one of the four middle schools: Appling, Ballard Hudson, McEvoy, or Miller. Each middle school receives Channel One and holds "Explorations in Technology" labs. Four high schools offer grades 9 though 12 three diploma sequences. Students may opt for the standard high school path, a vocational-technical route, or a college preparatory

Seventh and eighth grade pupils attend one of the four middle schools in the Bibb County school system. Photography by Ken Krakow.

format. Two facilities also address the needs of exceptional students.

As part of the school system's goal to prepare students for the high-tech world ahead of them, all the high schools teach an "Introduction to Technology" class to give students insights and hands-on experience with the latest advancements. Additionally, the school system equipped every classroom to download a variety of satellite cable programming. Computer labs, a two-way video and audio teleconferencing system, and other technology connect the schools—and the students—to the next century.

Post-Secondary Progressiveness

A little more than a decade in existence, Macon took its first bold step into the world's post-secondary educational arena. The novel idea of a school granting degrees to women generated considerable debate. Fortunately, the majority believed the time had come "to place the Females of our beloved State so far as science and literature are concerned, on a footing with the males, and by a practical, useful, and thoro' [sic] education, fit and prepare them for all the duties of life . . . ." as stated by the Georgia Female College's first Board of Trustees in November 1836. One month later, the charter for the world's first college for women was granted. By the 1860s, students at Georgia Female College formed the nation's first two sororities, The Adelphean Society (Alpha Delta Pi) and The Philomathean Society (Phi Mu). Renamed Wesleyan College in 1917, the school also claims the world's oldest alumnae association. Wesleyan College's alumnae currently number above 7,500 in cities spanning the globe.

About 500 young women attend Wesleyan annually from all around Georgia, different states, and foreign countries. Ranked fifth in the South among regional liberal arts colleges by *U.S. News & World Report*, Wesleyan's average student-to-faculty ratio of 10:1 ensures personalized attention. Over 20 Bachelor of Arts major degree programs, including pre-professional programs in law, medicine, veterinary medicine, dentistry, and health sciences, provide a strong foundation for a lifetime of learning. The school maintains its affiliation with the United Methodist Church and retains its progressive approach to education. Modern communication equipment connects the entire campus. Each Freshman student receives a computer to plug into the college network. The system provides access to InterNet and assignments can be "handed-in" online.

The 200-acre campus of Georgian-style buildings and cascading lawns, established in 1928, beautifully enhances the suburban area of Macon. It isn't the only landmark Wesleyan College bestowed on the community. The school's first location on College Street gracefully overlooked Washington Park until it burned in 1963. Now the Federal Building housing the United States Post Office stands in its place, constructed to remarkably resemble the school's original building.

Computer labs at Southeast High School connect the school and the students to the next century. Photography by Ken Krakow

The Walter F. George Law School of Mercer University is one of the oldest law schools in the South. Photography by Ken Krakow.

Mercer University Expands Macon's Educational Horizons

Just as Wesleyan College grew from Macon's early history, another post-secondary school located here in the nineteenth century and earned national and international acclaim. Georgia Baptist leader Jesse Mercer founded Mercer University in 1833 at Penfield, Georgia, and relocated the institution to Macon in 1871. That year, the school officials hired Chicago architect G.P. Randall to construct Mercer University's central administration building. During the Great Chicago Fire (the infamous conflagration kicked off by Mrs. O'Leary's cow), all of Randall's drawings for the building burned. He reportedly built the entire structure as planned from memory, completing it in 1874. Restored in 1980 and listed on the National Register of Historic Places, the central administration building still houses the university's main offices.

Even before finishing the original administration facility construction, Mercer University established its Walter F. George Law School in 1873. One of the oldest law schools in the South, it came four years after the school's cornerstone academic program, the College of Liberal Arts. The Law School moved to the Coleman Hill site in the 1970s, but the College of Liberal Arts remains on the 130-acre central campus. Now drenched in ivy garlands and shaded under a canopy of magnolia and pine, the main campus also encompasses the School of Engineering, School of Medicine, Eugene W. Stetson School of Business and Economics, and University College. The Southern School of Pharmacy occupies Mercer University's Cecil B. Day Campus in Atlanta.

Today, Mercer University's combination of programs in liberal arts, business, engineering, medicine, pharmacy, and law issue some 20 undergraduate and professional degrees. No other independent university of Mercer's size in the country offers such an impressive range of programs. The school ranks among the top ten colleges and universities in the South and extends the best value among southern regional universities, according to *U.S. News & World Report*. The school's 6,700-plus students also position Mercer as the nation's largest (and the world's second largest) Baptist-affiliated institution.

The school's administrators shared the city's concerns about economic development and actively responded. A lack of family practitioners, especially in the rural areas, prompted the creation of Mercer's School of Medicine in 1982. The American Academy of Family Physicians presented the school with a Gold Achievement Award, noting that among all medical schools in the country, Mercer produced the highest percentages of graduates pursuing family practice residencies.

In 1985, Mercer University established the state's second engineering school to fulfill the demand for qualified aerospace employees. The Mercer Engineering Research Center, initiated two years later at Warner Robins, directly bridges academia with industry to creatively solve real-world challenges. Allied with this center, the Mercer University Research Office focuses on faculty and staff projects, and assists them in seeking funds. The Research

Office opened in 1994 and quickly took a leadership role in developing new medical treatments, devising better testing methodologies, creating useful theoretical equations, and many other accomplishments that may hold keys to greater health and scientific understanding in the future.

The Atlanta-based Center for Business Research and Development, part of the School of Business and Economics, invites Georgia municipalities and businesses to use the facility for market research, seminars, and workshops. Professional continuing education programs offered by the University College at Macon and five other locations further reinforce the link to the business community. This fast-growing school for non-traditional students, including business people, gifted children, and senior citizens, reflects Mercer's ability to readily adapt to changing educational needs. With highly automated libraries, computerized campus facilities, active student organizations, and one of the country's largest academic book presses, Mercer University promises to remain one of Macon's proactive educational institutions.

The University System of Georgia's Area Colleges Open Opportunities

Three more educational institutions followed Wesleyan College and Mercer University to the area, greatly contributing to the growing regional education center here. All part of the University System of Georgia, Fort Valley State College and Georgia College began instruction in the late 1880s; Macon College opened its doors almost 80 years later, answering the call for a two-year facility conveniently located in Central Georgia.

Georgia College, established in 1889 with its main campus at nearby Milledgeville, now offers an easily accessible branch facility in Macon's CIGNA Building. The school's ten undergraduate degree programs at Macon include business, education, legal assistance studies, criminal justice, nursing, and general studies. The Georgia College graduate programs also reflect some of the city's primary growth industries: business, nursing, education, and public administration. Continuing education classes similarly support the local workforce. Besides the modern classroom facilities, Georgia College in Macon houses a comprehensive computer lab, full library/media center, bookstore, and accessible faculty offices for a complete college experience within a professional setting.

Fort Valley State College began as Fort Valley Normal and Industrial School in 1895. A merger with the Forsyth State Teachers and Agricultural College in 1939 prompted the change to its current name. Located on a handsomely landscaped 650-acre tract in Fort Valley, the main campus hosts the School of Agriculture, Home Economics and Allied Programs; the School

Fort Valley State College offers several graduate programs, concentrating on education and counseling fields. Photography provided by Fort Valley State College.

of Arts and Sciences; and the School of Education, Graduate, and Special Academic Programs. The University System of Georgia's newest 55,000-square-foot meeting facility, the C.W. Pettigrew Farm and Community Life Center, accommodates up to 600 guests for conferences, conventions, or arts performances. About 300 of Fort Valley State College's 2,700 students attend classes in Macon, also at the CIGNA office complex. The Macon branch offers several graduate programs, concentrating on education and counseling fields. Undergraduate degree programs at Macon include business, education, and criminal justice disciplines. Macon's central location and the school's flexible scheduling draw students from all around the area.

On the opposite side of the city, Macon College welcomed the state's largest post-secondary charter class ever when 1,110 students began studying there in 1968. The Greater Macon Chamber of Commerce, the Bibb County Board of Commissioners, and other regional leaders had campaigned for a public institution of higher education, understanding the need for a centralized school to serve the growing community. Instead of a four-year school, they worked toward creating a two-year institution—a progressive concept at the time. By the 1990s, the school enrolled about 5,000 students from a broad radius of counties surrounding Macon.

The main campus stands on a wooded, 167-acre site partially hidden from Eisenhower Parkway and I-475. The tranquil setting even invites Canadian geese to pause there every spring to visit Lake Kneedeep. The campus started with seven buildings. Student population growth and expanded missions brought four more structures, including a library in 1994 and a classroom/auditorium building in 1995. To maximize its accessibility, Macon College also operates branch facilities in the downtown historic Capital Theatre building, at Robins Air Force Base, and in the Middle Georgia Technology Development Center at Warner Robins.

Macon College's programs closely relate to the area's industries, including health services and aerospace. Students choose from over 38 two-year transfer programs; some 15 two-year career programs; and a variety of two-year cooperative or one-year certificate programs. In addition, Macon College expanded its continuing education courses in conjunction with the Central Georgia Small Business Development Center, and created its Center for Educational and Economic Development to present applicable professional educational opportunities and serve as a liaison between the public school system and area industries. Macon College also cooperates extensively with the Macon 2000 Partnership to encourage students to raise their aspirations and reach their goals.

A brilliant gingko tree heralds the beginning of fall classes at Georgia College in nearby Milledgeville. Georgia College also offers degree programs at its Macon campus and sponsors an Educational Technology Center in Macon to support the infusion of technology as an instructional method in K-12 schools. Photography by Timothy Vacula.

Macon Technical Institute Fulfills a 1917 Objective

Less than 50 years since the Civil War had abruptly halted many classrooms, Georgia earned the country's respect for its forward-thinking leaders. Dudley Mays Hughes reigned among them as a State Senator and U.S. Congressman. A native of nearby Twiggs County, Hughes led much of the early efforts to establish public vocational-based educational institutions for the benefit of the nation's youth and the country's businesses. The history books most frequently mention this tireless visionary for the 1917 Smith-Hughes Vocational Education Act. Hughes' innovative measure defined a new type of school curriculum and authorized federal money to advance vocational education for the first time. The same year, Hughes helped form the Georgia State Board of Vocational Education—a predecessor to the Georgia Department

A part of The University System of Georgia, Macon College offers students a variety of traditional collegiate programs with a special emphasis on majors related to health and technology. Photography provided by Macon College.

of Technical and Adult Education. This department oversees Macon Technical Institute (MTI) today.

The current MTI programs embody much of the concepts first introduced by Hughes. Established in 1962, the school moved to its spacious campus off Eisenhower Parkway in 1978 and created a satellite campus in Milledgeville 12 years later. MTI teaches technical studies covering about 74 areas, concentrating on high-demand fields, such as accounting, practical nursing, medical lab technology, or computer programming. Its Aircraft Structural Technology diploma program produces highly skilled graduates for the region's aerospace industry; the program's success warranted construction of a new airplane hanger at the school for hands-on training. The advanced facilities and superb placement rates attract students from 35 counties seeking technical certificates, diplomas, associate degrees, or continuing education courses. Cognizant of its critical ties to area employers, MTI's Business and Industry Services department promotes economic development and works with area firms to create specialized training courses for employees. The school honors the Department of Technical and Adult Education's Technical Education Guarantee, ensuring competent and appropriately trained workers.

Macon Technical Institute teaches technical studies covering about 74 areas. Photography by Macon Technical Institute.

Educational Support for All Ages

The educational opportunities seem boundless in Macon. The Middle Georgia Regional Library system particularly encourages lifelong learning. Incorporating three branch locations in Macon and the main collection at the Washington Memorial Library, the system serves all of Bibb County and beyond. Constructed in the 1920s, Washington Memorial Library now holds some 415,000 books for adults and children, *The Macon Telegraph* issues from 1823 to the present, an African-American collection, the local-history archives, CD-ROM and other computer-based catalogs, and many other resources. The library also houses an extensive collection for the blind and the world-renown Genealogical & Historical Room. About 15,000 national and international researchers annually peruse through the 16,000 volumes and 6,000-plus microfilm reels for information on early pioneers, the 13 colonies, and the Revolutionary War.

Besides the fine public schools and private institutions, commercial vocational schools and multitudes of organizations also offer specialized training. If a person wants to learn about something—anything—there's a resource in Macon. ■

TOURISM, EVENTS, & THE ARTS

The Center Stage for Fun and Adventure

As the Cherry Blossom Capital of the World, Macon's Cherry Blossom Festival attracts thousands of visitors every spring. Other top-rated festivals and a multitude of sights such as the Hay House, Ocmulgee National Monument, the Museum of Aviation, and ten historic districts draw tourists and conventions here. The Macon Coliseum, one of the largest convention centers outside of Atlanta, and part of the Macon Centreplex, also welcomes thousands of people to Macon annually. In addition, local theaters and museums continually provide forums for the fine arts.

Hot air balloons fill the sky at the annual spring Cherry Blossom Festival. Photography by Ken Krakow.

At the supermarket or the coffee shop, or just about anywhere else in Macon, it's common to hear someone whistling a tune, singing a song—not just humming, but really singing!—or sharing a piece of poetry. The rich cultural heritage here softly seeps into daily life, continuing to change and grow over time as new performers and artists add their personalities. Macon especially celebrates its musical heritage, which extends from the early plantation days, but it also honors its writers, actors, painters, and sculptors. A formidable list of Maconites who achieved fame outside musical circles includes author Harry Stillwell Edwards, best known for his short book, *Eneas Africanus*; Charles Coburn, who

Macon's Southern Jubilee, held each fall, pays tribute to the city's phenomenal musical heritage. Photography by Ken Krakow.

thrilled stage, screen, and radio audiences; Col. Robert L. Scott, author of the book, *God Is My Co-Pilot*, that later became a Warner Brothers movie; Susan Myrick, technical advisor for the film *Gone With The Wind*; and Miss America 1953, Neva Jane Langley (Mrs. William A. Fickling, Jr.). Macon itself became part of Tennessee Williams' *Cat On A Hot Tin Roof*, which he wrote here with roles based on local characters.

The artistry of Maconites in any form adds vitality to the city's atmosphere and provides an appealing contrast to the steadfast historic neighborhoods. Instead of glitzy theme parks or fabricated *Gone With The Wind* settings, the creative, forward-thinking individuals, amid a historical treasure-trove, introduce visitors to an authentic whole-city attraction. Tourists can still feel the nostalgia and the essence of the Old South, but they only see the genuine relics. They can share the excitement of a New South here as well. Called "cultural tourism," it's a careful balance of visionaries and preservationists wrought by the leaders of the artistic communities, heritage organizations, and tourism agencies. Working in partnership, these groups help ensure progress without sacrificing the past. They focus on educational programs, community awareness, and worldwide publicity. Through their efforts, Macon has become the state's top tourist destination outside of Atlanta. According to the Georgia Department of Industry, Trade, and Tourism (GDITT), Macon-Bibb County showed a 9.9 percent increase in tourist expenditures from 1992 to 1993, a percentage greater than the entire state's.

Over a million visitors discover Macon's wonders every year. Many of them stop at the I-75 Welcome Center first, one of the busiest in the southeast, where the well-trained staff piques curiosity with brochures and enthusiasm. Similarly, the Macon Downtown Welcome Center in the Terminal Station answers questions and directs visitors to the city's historic, entertainment, and cultural attractions. Both Welcome Center staffs can arrange reservations in seconds for any of the area's 3,500 hotel and motel rooms, 200 restaurants, various entertainment venues, and tours. The Macon-Bibb County Convention & Visitors Bureau, also housed in the Terminal Station, books group tours, conventions, and meetings too. In 1994, the agency booked more than 600 groups and arranged 250 conventions with 152,660 delegates attending. Macon's central location

Most of Macon's historic homes have been renovated for business or remain private residences. Photography Dorothy Hibbert Krakow.

helps tremendously, making it easy for delegates from across the state to arrive within hours, and increasing the number of attendees for meeting planners. The GDITT statistics for 1994 show the economic impact of delegates and groups exceeded 254 million dollars. City leaders expect the numbers to continue to climb. Georgia's largest convention center outside of Atlanta, the Macon Coliseum is a superb site for everything from big-name entertainment to colossal trade-shows.

Four Seasons of Festivals

"A City For All Seasons," the Macon travel brochures proclaim, and with good reason. Throughout the year, the city hosts several festivals sparkling with music and dance, crafts, fine art, food, and more food. Perhaps the most recognized of the city's events, the annual spring Cherry Blossom Festival spans two weeks in March with fun and excitement. The first celebration was held in 1983 with about 40 events and has grown to encompass more than 400 activities, such as a televised parade, spectacular hot air balloon lift-off, exhibits, shopping, and a gigantic street party with fireworks. Named a Top 100 Event in North America and a Top 20 Event in the southeast by the Southeastern Tourism Society, the Cherry Blossom Festival attracts more than 400,000 people annually, including those who arrive on 250 motor coaches from all over the United States. A chorus of 200,000 Yoshino cherry trees burst into clouds of delicate pink blossoms to welcome everyone. Mr. William A. Fickling, Sr., a respected Macon businessman, discovered these Japanese fruitless beauties in the 1950s and shared them with the community. Now Macon boasts more Yoshino cherry trees than any other city and appropriately earned the title of "Cherry Blossom Capital of the World."

In late spring and early summer, the city's attention turns to the arts in earnest. "On My Own Time," a judged exhibition in May sponsored by the Macon Arts Alliance and local corporations, displays the creative talents of area employees. The Macon Arts Alliance, a nonprofit organization, supports Middle Georgia arts groups and promotes the community's cultural growth through education, funding, and coordination. It also operates ARTSLINE, a hotline to the area's calendar of entertainment and cultural activities. Topping the calendar in June and July is the MidSummer Macon Arts Festival coordinated through The Wesleyan College Center for the Arts. This three-week celebration emphasizes educational activities for all ages and culminates in a variety of exhibitions and performances.

With September's cooler weather comes another Top 20 Event in the southeast, Macon's Southern Jubilee. This two-week extravaganza pays tribute to the city's phenomenal musical heritage and encourages community pride. Like the Cherry Blossom Festival, Southern Jubilee's list of activities includes a humongous street party where local and national musicians on several different stages play everything from jazz, blues, rap, and Southern rock.

Special tours during the festival trace the evolution or, perhaps, the revolution, of music here. Although not all sites are open to the public, it's possible to see the birthplace of Maconite Sidney Clopton Lanier, a 19th century flutist who played among the world's finest symphonies and reportedly couldn't read music. Stroll Cotton Avenue, where a blind street singer named Rev. Pearly Brown sang for some 40 years. Brown mastered the guitar at Macon's Academy for the Blind, going on to play Carnegie Hall; he also became the Grand Ole Opry's first black performer. Drive over the Otis Redding Memorial Bridge and see the late star's country estate, or discover the childhood home of "Little Richard" Penniman in the Historic Pleasant Hill District. With the restoration of the Douglass Theatre, visitors can witness performances again on the same stage that introduced James Brown, Little Richard, Otis Redding, Lena Horne, and other local musicians to black audiences. Built in 1911 by entrepreneur Charles Henry Douglass, the theatre's other performers included Cab Callaway, Ma Rainey, and Count Basie during the 60 years it was open. Not far away, the Phoenix Sound Recording Studio now operates in the historic Capricorn Records Studio building. The Capricorn label's famed astrological symbol above the door is still visible from the street. The Allman Brothers Band, which gave rise to Southern rock-and-roll, recorded here at the Capricorn studio, and the "Big House" on Vineville Avenue where most of the band members lived can be seen by appointment. The final resting places of band members Duane Allman and Berry Oakley in Rose Hill Cemetery bring fans from all over the globe to Macon.

The Southern Jubilee isn't the only autumn event to bring visitors to Macon. In October, the Arrowhead Arts & Crafts Festival launches a two-day spectacular under the shady trees at Lake Tobesofkee. More than 100 fine artists and crafters set up booths displaying items available for purchase. Shoppers and participants rest on hay bales as home cooking fills the fall air with warm aromas, and entertainers generate a spirit of camaraderie. The annual fair comes to Central City Park at about this time, too, with a splendid collection of garden harvests, exciting rides and exhibits, and more delicious foods.

Soon after the fall festivities, the holidays arrive with another Top 20 Event in the southeast: White Columns & Holly—an Old

(Left) Maconites enjoy a picnic in Third Street Park at the Cherry Blossom Festival. Photography by Ken Krakow.
(Above) The Macon Symphony Orchestra rehearses for many events held throughout the city. Photography by Ken Krakow.

Kwanzaa, a celebration of African heritage, takes place in Macon each December. Photography by Ken Krakow.

South Christmas in Macon. Decorated homes and businesses light up the night as beautifully as the giant Christmas tree brightens downtown with the season's spirit. A parade also shares the holiday magic with Maconites and visitors. Various organizations hold teas and socials, some to raise money to help others enjoy the holidays. Kwanzaa, a nonreligious and nonheroic week-long celebration of African heritage, takes place this time of year, too. The finale of December's activity is First Night Macon, sponsored by the Macon Arts Alliance. This nonalcoholic New Year's Eve party for the city celebrates the performing and visual arts. Venues throughout downtown host musical and dramatic performances or fine art exhibits. An explosion of fireworks at midnight welcomes the new year. On New Year's Eve, thousands of Maconites enjoy over 50 performances and First Night Macon's popularity continues to grow.

Sites and Sights to See

Macon's mild climate and central location invite tourists all year long, and residents, too, can enjoy playing tourist in their own town. The Macon-Bibb County Convention and Visitors Bureau (MBCCVB) keeps plenty of brochures available that suggest different self-guided walking tours. A collaboration of Macon agencies created the nation's first African American Tour here. Winding through historic neighborhoods and downtown, this tour insightfully highlights the black leaders and achievers from Macon. Other walking tours focus on specific types of architecture, historic structures in downtown or "Rose Hill Rambles" through the terraced hillsides of Macon's 19th century cemetery park. In addition, two regularly scheduled riding tours through Macon point out the city's history and progress.

Travelers on I-16 or I-75 already have discovered the convenience of staying in Macon and taking day trips to visit nearby attractions. Within easy driving distance, they can reach the 1847 Jarrell Plantation, the Whistle Stop Cafe and the set of the movie "Fried Green Tomatoes," Callaway Gardens, Franklin Roosevelt's Little White House, Stone Mountain Park, Six Flags Over Georgia, Hawkinsville Harness Horse Racing, Andersonville National Historic Site, the city of Plains and the church where former President Jimmy Carter still teaches Sunday School.

Two self-guided driving tours loop through the city on a path that covers the Historic Heartland of Georgia. "Georgia's Antebellum Trail" meanders through several towns, passing by mansions and cottages of note. Because so many of Macon's older homes have been restored and several serve as museum homes, this city has become a favorite stopping point. The distinctive Hay House, a national historic landmark, commands immediate attention for those following the Antebellum Trail. Its well-trained docents share the home's secrets with guests, explaining the clever trompe l'oeil finishes and the other capricious touches in the home. The Old Cannonball House and Confederate Museum also attracts many of those traveling the Antebellum Trail. This 1854 home sustained minor damage when a Union cannonball sailed into the front parlor during the attack on Macon in 1864.

The Christmas tree at the Hay House is authentically decorated each year by area volunteers. Photography by Ken Krakow.

The Warner Robins Museum of Aviation houses over 100,000 square feet of displays. Photography by Ken Krakow.

Today, the Sidney Lanier Chapter, United Daughters of the Confederacy own the home and its museum, and they use this site for their headquarters. The Middle Georgia Historical Society similarly uses the Sidney Lanier Cottage, a restored 1840 Victorian cottage, as their headquarters. A few of Macon's homes may be seen by appointment, such as the Woodruff House. This Greek Revival plantation-type mansion, now owned by Mercer University, gazes down over the city from the top of Coleman Hill. The Federated Garden Clubs of Macon accept appointments to tour The Garden Center, an early 1900s brick home designed by Neel Reid. Most of the other historical homes have been renovated for businesses or remain private residences, and open their doors to curious guests only for special occasions.

The plethora of historical homes, not surprisingly, has inspired a large antique market here and Macon sits prominently along Georgia's Antiques Trail. It winds through the state's heartland to reach Macon, where the city rewards antique hunters with almost 100 dealers and 25 antique shops and malls.

Some valuable antique and modern artwork in Macon can be seen along the city's streets and in the parks. Macon's monuments and public art date from the 19th century to the present. The carved Italian marble Confederate Monument, dedicated in 1879, now stands at Cotton Avenue and Second Street. Other war memorials include the World War I Monument placed at Coleman Hill in 1922, the Middle Georgia Veterans Memorial set outside the Macon Coliseum in 1988, and the Sgt. Rodney M. Davis Monument at Cotton Avenue and Poplar Street, honoring Macon's only Medal of Honor recipient; he died when he fell on a grenade, protecting his platoon in Vietnam.

Public art inspired by peace and friendship can be seen throughout the city, too. The hand-carved, three-ton granite Japanese lantern, or ishidoro, now in Third Street Park came from Macon's sister city, Kurobe, Japan, in 1983. YKK Corporation of America, Texprint (Ga.) Inc., and TKG International Inc., three of the city's Japanese-owned companies, donated the structure. The late Tadao Yoshida, founder of YKK, bestowed the city with the "Heart of Friendship" abstract now displayed in the courtyard next to the Greater Macon Chamber of Commerce. Texprint (Ga.) Inc. gave the kinetic sculpture outside the Museum of Arts & Sciences on Forsyth Road. Made of stainless steel, this piece stands 13 feet tall and silently moves with even the slightest breeze.

Museums and More to Explore

A trip to the museum, whatever museum it may be, opens windows to the world for all ages. By touring the area facilities, it's possible to cover 10,000 years of North American history and experience a wide swath of artistic and scientific accomplishments, too. The Ocmulgee National Monument, part of the National Park System since 1936, displays artifacts of the human inhabitants here 10,000 years ago. A self-guided tour brochure explains the supposed purposes of a large ceremonial earthlodge and the park allows visitors to step inside. Several platform mounds are visible, too. The museum at the center highlights the history of the Indian mounds here and a short film brings it all to life.

The newest exhibit at the Museum of Aviation also focuses on the early Native Americans in the area. Over 13,000 artifacts, recovered from 36 archaeological sites on the Robins Air Force Base property, reveal much about the people who inhabited the land long before airplanes ever flew. The Museum of Aviation and Georgia Aviation Hall of Fame covers 43 acres and exhibits more than 85 historical aircraft from World War I and World War II. Over 100,000 square feet of displays, including an authentic F-15, excite flying enthusiasts. The 250-seat VistaScope Theater films also dazzle audiences with realistic, first-person imagery.

The Museum of Arts & Sciences similarly gives visitors an exciting audiovisual experience in the skies and beyond to distant planets, stars, and galaxies. The Mark Smith Planetarium, one of the country's most sophisticated multimedia theaters, intrigues audiences with the possibilities of space. An observatory and other participatory exhibits at the center let visitors see it all for themselves. The Museum of Arts & Sciences also maintains permanent fine art exhibits and invites traveling shows. The 14 wooded acres surrounding the center offer two peaceful nature trails and provides seclusion for Macon author Harry Stillwell Edwards' Kingfisher Cabin—his writing retreat.

The hands-on approach at the Museum of Arts & Sciences is not unlike the style adopted by the Tubman African American Museum. Founded in 1981 with a mission to educate through history, art, and culture, the Tubman African American Museum focuses more on the achievements than the struggles of blacks and delves deeply into African American modes of expression. About 50,000 visitors from all 50 states and foreign countries tour the facility each year, shaking the drums, feeling the reproduction Kente cloth, admiring the works of art. "From Africa to America," a 63-foot-long mural by local artist Wilfred Stroud, takes up more than one wall, and a quilt, created by internationally acclaimed artist Wini McQueen, honors African American women of Central Georgia on another wall. The Local History Gallery features an extensive display on Ellen Craft, a Macon slave who escaped with her husband, William, in 1848. The two became respected abolitionists, writers, and educators; they eventually returned to Georgia in 1868. The Gallery also highlights Maconite Jefferson Long, the first African-American Congressman from Georgia, and the accomplishments of the Michael and Mary Healy family.

(Above) Sidney Lanier's portrait and wife's wedding dress are on display at the restored 1840 Victorian Sidney Lanier Cottage. Photography by Ken Krakow.
(Right top) The Nutcracker of Middle Georgia presents the ballet each year at The Grand Opera House. Photography by Ken Krakow.
(Right bottom) A street artist at one of the many outdoor festivals in Macon displays his creative talents. Photography by Ken Krakow.

The first-born son, James Healy, became the first black Catholic bishop in the United States; his younger brother, Patrick, also a priest, became president of Georgetown University, making him one of the earliest blacks to assume a college presidency. Additionally, portraits in the Local History Gallery painted by Wilfred Stroud honor many of Macon's black leaders.

Several other facilities in the area display an exceptional breadth of fine art. The Mercer University Hardeman Art Gallery, Macon College Library Exhibits, Wesleyan College Cowles Myles Collier East Gallery in the Porter Fine Arts Building, and other area academic centers open their collections for public viewing. The Middle Georgia Art Association, a non-profit organization, spotlights local artists in the historic Kirkland House Gallery on Spring Street.

Macon's newest museums, the Georgia Sports Hall of Fame and the Georgia Music Hall of Fame, feature interactive displays and authentic articles. City leaders expect these museums to draw thousands of tourists to the downtown area annually. Interestingly, Maconites Little Richard, James Brown, Otis Redding, and The Allman Brothers Band have been inducted into both the Georgia Music Hall of Fame and the national Rock & Roll Hall of Fame. The legacy these people created here continues to inspire local musicians and others like them across the country.

Performance Arts Showcase

The performing arts lack neither talent nor venues in Macon, and audiences frequently fill the houses to capacity. Historically, Maconites have shared a deep appreciation for theatrical and musical performances. The Grand Opera House opened initially as the Academy of Music in 1884. Designed with exceptional acoustics, especially for that time period, the theater's immense stage rivals some of the largest in the nation, and its stage height soars almost seven stories. Nearly one-fifth of Macon's population—about 2,418 people—could be seated when it became the Grand Opera House in 1905. Audiences witnessed unforgettable and thrilling performances: circuses, John Philip Sousa and his Concert Band, the "Divine" Sarah Bernhardt, Charlie Chaplin, and a production of "Ben Hur" with live horses running on a treadmill that turned the scenery behind them. Vaudeville acts always drew large crowds with names like Will Rogers, George Burns, and Gracie Allen topping the handbills. Harry Houdini cut two trapdoors in the stage floor to make an escape during a performance here, and one of them is still used as the Rat King's entrance in "The Nutcracker" production. The Nutcracker of Middle Georgia, a unique production company in the nation, presents the ballet each year.

A remodeling in 1936 changed the Grand Opera House to a movie theater and films were shown there until 1961. Then the elegant building slipped into disrepair. Threatened by bulldozers and the prospect of becoming a parking lot, the Grand Opera House was saved by the Macon Arts Council. This organization raised the funds to restore and operate it as a live performance theater once again. The Grand Opera House no longer uses the narrow slat benches of the steeply ascending Peanut Gallery, but comfortably seats 1,057 on the main floor and gilded balcony. Photos in the Encore Room, a refreshment area, recall the top performers of the last 20 years, such as Bob Hope, Vincent Price, Ray Charles, Woody Herman, and George Winston. The theater also produces its own Broadway shows, often calling on the talents of local actors.

Another striking historic venue, the Macon City Auditorium, also testifies to Maconites' appreciation for the arts. According to *Macon Magazine*, the structure was "hailed as the world's largest unsupported copper dome" and its architects derived inspiration for the design from the Mormon Tabernacle in Salt Lake City. Multimillion-dollar renovations in the late 1970s maintained the exterior's structural integrity. It looks much the same today as it did in 1925 with stately limestone Greek Doric columns lining the wide terraces. Inside, the Macon Symphony Orchestra takes the stage with up to 100 players for annual concerts, and the auditorium also hosts other musical performances, graduation and memorial ceremonies, fund-raisers, and sporting events. The venue seats more than 2,500 and its busy calendar draws large audiences throughout the year.

The Macon Little Theater and Theatre Macon accommodate smaller audiences in a more intimate setting, and they too enjoy loyal patronage. The Macon Little Theater, located next to the Museum of Arts & Sciences on Forsyth Road, tends to present popular plays and traditional musicals. Theatre Macon, however, leans more toward the avant-garde and its seasonal offerings often include productions created by local or regional playwrights. In 1995, Theatre Macon moved to the renovated Ritz movie house and now seats about 250. Both Theatre Macon and Macon Little Theater invite area actors to audition for shows, and these stagehouses also bring in nationally acclaimed thespians for special roles.

Theater and musical productions at the public and private schools, colleges and universities, and churches also feature local artists. Within the area, other communities offer stage and musical performances, too, and it's common for Maconites to travel to Atlanta for an evening of entertainment. Amateur poetry readings and acoustic performances gathered a dedicated following in the coffee shops here in the early 1990s, allowing budding artists to share their work. In addition, the local bars and restaurants continue to book local and national bands.

For Maconites of all ages with artistic interests, the area's colleges and universities, the Piano Improv Center, and the YWCA also offer group and private musical lessons and classes on creative writing, acting, and the visual arts. The community actively supports a variety of organizations that encourage individuals to pursue their talents. These symphonies, concert bands, repertoire-specific singing or dancing groups, and many others, help Macon's cultural heritage continue to grow and expand. ∎

Children especially enjoy the many festivals held throughout the year.
Photography by Ken Krakow.

The Macon City Auditorium, part of the Macon Centreplex, draws large audiences throughout the year. Photography by Ken Krakow.

QUALITY OF LIFE

Building on History for Progress

The romantic notions of southern living, captured in the historic homes, form a gracious foundation for Maconites' lifestyles. Strong neighborhood associations, public safety departments, churches, and volunteer organizations work to create a peaceful environment for families and businesses to grow. The hundreds of parks designed by the city planners thrive even today, welcoming afternoon strolls and family picnics. All around Macon, recreational activities beckon. The Macon Braves play in one of the nation's five oldest ball parks and nearly any sport, social club, or support organization can be found in the area.

A greater appreciation for the city's historic architecture in recent decades helped place 10 districts on the National Register of Historic Places. Photography by Dorothy Hibbert Krakow.

Locals say the Indians who lived in this area long ago believed that once someone drinks the water here, no matter how far away that person travels, he or she will return to Macon. Although the legend's authenticity drifted into unwritten obscurity, its prophetic notion bears some credence. It's quite possible to find the same surnames noted in the city's history books also listed in today's Macon telephone books. Generations and generations of families have lived here, sometimes passing their homesteads down through time. The residents who move away during their young adult years, traveling to other cities, states, and countries, often return to settle in Macon. Employees transferred to the city frequently choose to stay in the area when they retire.

"The biggest small-town city," as one long-time resident called Macon, offers all the amenities of a major metropolitan area without the traffic, pollution, or costs. Instead of rush-hour car horns, Macon's church bells chime out the time of day in downtown. Rather than smog, the city's wisteria, roses, or freshly cut lawns fill the air with sweet scents; its air purity effectively meets all national quality standards. Additionally, while some metropolitan areas implement even minute methods to raise revenue, Macon seeks to maintain its low cost of living. The city removed its parking meters in the 1980s, a welcome oddity when other locales now require quarters-only in their meters and charge hefty parking violation fines. City and county taxes remain modest and Georgia's income tax ranks 28th in the nation. Macon's full range of affordable housing, from decorative historic apartment buildings to well-kept suburban developments, stands out as well. According to the 1990 census for MSAs, Macon's $59,300 median value for housing compared favorably to the national average of $79,100. The median gross rent here of $364 also measured less than the national average.

Beyond the city's quantifiable attributes, Macon's remarkable sense of community seems to be one of the most prevailing reasons residents stay here. It crosses economic lines, interlocks diverse cultural groups, and strengthens neighborhoods. It's as simple as two friends waving hello at the grocery store and as complex as rebuilding flood-damaged areas in 1994. This personal sense of belonging to the city—and the city belonging to residents—forms a patchwork of smaller micro-communities quilted into the warmth of one large, dynamic community. The Indians may have believed the water bound people to this area, but more likely it's Macon's inviting quality of life that makes so many people call the city "home."

Homes, Sweet Homes

The architectural potpourri in Macon enhances the city's picturesque appeal and offers a style to suit nearly every home-buyer's preference, from antebellum to contemporary. Often, the most ardent modernists fall under the spell of Macon's captivating historical structures. Styles such as Federal, Gothic Revival, Romanesque Neo-Gothic, French Second Empire, Italian Renaissance Revival, Tuscan-Victorian, Queen Ann Victorian, and High Victorian Gothic trace the influences prominent during the city's first 100 years. Early Macon architects, such as Elam Alexander and, later, Neel Reid, gained considerable recognition for their work. Several of Reid's beautiful, moderately sized, Victorian-era homes continue to serve as breathtaking private residences as do many of the city's stately mansions.

Awe-inspiring carved Georgia marble, intricate ironworks, dazzling stained-glass windows, and magnificent brick masonry almost seem commonplace along Macon's streets. Recently, the Macon Heritage Foundation began compiling information about the black artisans and craftsmen who deserve credit for much of the city's architectural legacy. The Foundation's research discovered that the American Institute of Architects' first black member, Richard Walker, came from Macon. Although the

(Left) "Porch parties," hosted on the front verandas of the antiquated homes, have become a favorite reincarnation of an old-fashioned pastime. Photography by Ken Krakow.
(Above) The city's wisteria, roses, or freshly cut lawns fill the air with sweet scents. Photography by Ken Krakow.

city's early black tradesmen were well known within construction circles for their fine work, the history books of the segregation days failed to properly record their accomplishments.

A greater appreciation for the city's historic architecture in recent decades helped place ten districts on the National Register of Historic Places. Two of these districts, Shirley Hills and Pleasant Hill, were built almost entirely by the hands of the city's talented black tradesmen. All ten historic areas together cover about 2,000 acres—a total among the largest in the country. Many families choose to settle in these charming older areas, accepting the challenges of restoration and renovation while enjoying the quaint brick sidewalks, authentic gas streetlights, and mature shade trees that sprang from the city's youth. The historical districts' neighborhood associations actively promote restoration and preservation, in addition to social affairs. "Porch parties," hosted on the front verandas of the antiquated homes, have become a favorite reincarnation of an old-fashioned pastime.

Neighborhoods Find Strength in Numbers

The Macon Telegraph lists homes for sale by 13 residential areas, but many of these further divide into smaller community clusters. Like the historic districts, the more modern areas often support strong neighborhood associations. Most of the newer subdivisions even require a residential organization in the covenants. For families moving from another state or just across town, active neighborhood groups encourage new friendships and build a more immediate sense of belonging. The community organizations also help maintain the beauty of their areas and they frequently create a protective safety network. Either through informal positive relations with the police department or by implementing a formal Neighborhood Watch, residents work together to ensure the peacefulness of their communities.

Toward the same goal, officers patrol the city on bicycles, on foot, or in high-tech vehicles. A mounted patrol attends many public events, such as parades and street parties. Between the Macon Police Department and the Bibb County Sheriff's Department, about 500 officers protect and serve citizens. The Macon-Bibb County Fire Department also operates 18 stations strategically located throughout the county. Supporting these departments, the Emergency Management Agency provides enhanced 911 service to identify the name, address, and phone number of a caller for superior emergency personnel response. Macon is the only municipality in the United States to combine a police department accredited by the Commission on Accreditation for Law Enforcement Agencies and a fire department with an Insurance Service Office Class 1 rating.

"I've lived in quite a few places," commented a successful realtor, "but we came here to raise our family. People know each other—they watch out for each other. To me, it's home."

Many of the single-family home subdivisions feature adjoining golf courses while others concentrate on the tranquillity of graceful ponds and lakes such as Rivoli Downs shown below. Photography by Ken Krakow.

The Religious Community Reaches Out

The earliest congregations met in Macon just as the city was establishing itself in the 1820s. Before paved streets, construction began on many of the area's landmark churches. The Christ Episcopal members gathered to worship in 1825 and built their church in 1852. The First Presbyterian congregation formed in 1826 and moved into their church on Mulberry Street in 1858; in 1838 its black members created the Washington Avenue Presbyterian Church, the oldest black Presbyterian church in the state. Similarly, the First Baptist Church, organized in 1826 and settled in its impressive structure by 1887 on the corner of Poplar Street and High Place, spurred several other major Baptist congregations in the area. One of these, the First Baptist Church on New Street, was formed by black worshippers 25 years before emancipation. Another of the historic churches, St. Joseph's Catholic Church, began in 1841, but the dedication of the brick twin-spired church near the crest of Poplar Street waited until 1903.

Today, Macon houses approximately 260 places of worship, including churches, synagogues, and mosques in more than 40 denominations. Of these, nearly 20 also offer pre-school, elementary, or secondary schools. Some of the denominations

Washington Park is one of the hundreds of parks designed by the city planners that thrive even today, welcoming afternoon strolls and family picnics. Photography by Ken Krakow.

are also associated with residential facilities for foster children or disadvantaged youth, such as The Methodist Home for Children and Youth, on Pierce Avenue. This facility has operated for over 120 years in Macon. It was also a Methodist minister, Rev. W.E. Mumford, who founded the Georgia Industrial Children's Home on 200 acres here in 1899; it still welcomes youngsters today. A school teacher, Bettie Tyler, formed the Hephzibah Children's Home in 1900 and it moved to Macon in 1912, where it continues to offer its residents on-campus instruction. The only private children's home, the Masonic Home of Georgia, covers about 650 acres and operates under the ownership and funding of the Masons of Georgia.

Places of worship also serve most every community as a forum for social gatherings, and this is especially true here. Frequently, newcomers from other regions are taken aback when Maconites ask, "Would you like to attend our church?" It's a compliment to be invited, tantamount to a personal welcome to the community. Historians point out that in other parts of the country where legions of immigrants created religious tensions, the South remained relatively homogenous and considered its places of worship also as community centers. So great is the participation in church-related activities here, that many civic organizations forego Wednesday-night meetings because that's when most choirs rehearse!

As civil rights issues gained momentum in the 1940s, churches also became catalysts for involvement, while they reinforced the call for nonviolent methods. Dr. Martin Luther King, Jr., spoke at Steward Chapel African Methodist Episcopal Church in 1957. Four years after his visit, about 15 black Macon youths refused to sit at the back of a public bus; their actions led to a bus boycott, and sit-ins and picketing followed. One group of black men wore white hats to symbolize their belief in nonviolence, helping Macon avoid the riots and tragedies other cities experienced.

Sometimes the activists went elsewhere to work toward civil rights. In 1965, numerous young black Maconites participated in "Bloody Sunday" at Selma, Alabama, while marching the 54 miles from Selma to Montgomery for the subsequent rally. Many of those who marched with Dr. King or led the early campaigns for

Macon has approximately 260 places of worship including churches, synagogues, and mosques in more than 40 denominations.
Photography by Ken Krakow.

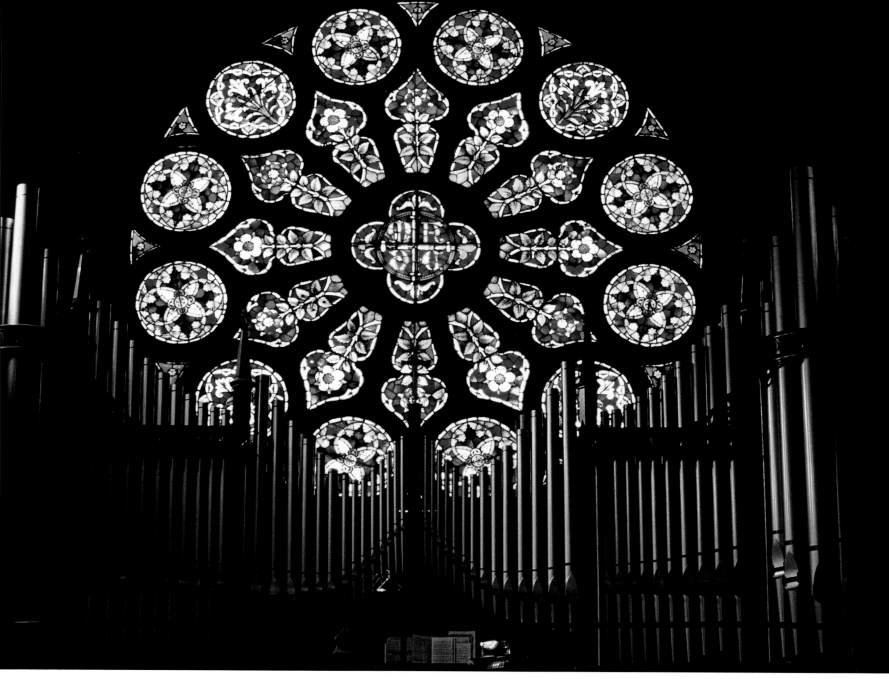

St. Joseph's Catholic Church is one of Macon's many historic churches.
Photography by Ken Krakow.

civil rights retained respected leadership positions in the following
decades. In 1995, Macon lost one of the foremost of these leaders,
William P. Randall, the first black director of the Greater Macon
Chamber of Commerce and a former president of the city's
NAACP branch. The necessary changes and the end to segregation were admittedly somewhat slow in Macon, but through the
efforts of color-blind leadership, a progressive attitude toward race
relations prevails today.

Volunteers and Organizations Working Together

A positive approach to solving community problems, a spirit
of cooperation, and a simple desire to help has created more than
200 organizations and support groups in the area. Almost all of
the places of worship operate some type of outreach program;
businesses, too, actively donate time and money to help those in
need. They bring meals to the housebound. They give toys, clothing, and school supplies to children. They visit nursing homes.
They touch lives. Local organizations and many branches affiliated
with national social agencies bring hope to the underprivileged
and disadvantaged. National health-related groups also operate

St. Joseph's Catholic Church is one of Macon's many historic churches.
Photography by Ken Krakow.

offices here. Peyton Tooke Anderson, Jr., one of Macon's prominent leaders until his death in 1988, stipulated in his will that the
majority of his estate be used for charitable purposes. Today the
Peyton Anderson Foundation supports an assortment of volunteer
organizations' efforts. So many groups, religious or secular, voluntarily help the community that a central organization, Volunteer
Macon, Inc., formed as a United Way agency in the 1970s to
match those willing to work with the tasks at hand. In the last
two decades, over 19,000 people have donated about 452,000
hours to help the 125 agencies connected to Volunteer Macon.
The plaza at the Walnut Street entrance to Central City Park honors one of Macon's most outstanding volunteers, Benny A. Scott.
Besides dedicating his life to helping others, this humanitarian is
credited as one of the first black railroad engineers in the South.

A corps of volunteers also plays a vital role in raising the quality of life here by supporting the city's many community centers
and youth groups. The Ruth Hartley Mosely Memorial Women's
Center, named for one of the first licensed female morticians in
the United States, is located on Spring Street in Mosely's historic
home and serves as a vocational resource for young women. The
Booker T. Washington Community Center, founded in 1939 in the
Pleasant Hill Historic District, offers a wide range of educational,
cultural, and social programs for 3-year-old children to senior citizens. The Center for Children and Youth opened in 1992 with an
emphasis on the arts, and the Macon Bibb County Parks and
Recreation Department's seven recreation centers present families
with an assortment of exciting and helpful activities, workshops,
and classes. These centers also provide opportunities for senior
citizens and physically or mentally disabled residents to enjoy
recreational activities. In addition, various youth organizations,
such as Big Brothers, Big Sisters, Girl Scouts of America, Boy
Scouts of America, 4-H, Boys & Girls Club, and many others,
bring together the talents and dedication of adult volunteers
to provide role models for Macon's future leaders.

Making a Difference

Thousands of Maconites volunteer their time to enhance the
city. Often just picking up litter and recycling does a tremendous
service to the community. The Keep Macon-Bibb Beautiful
Commission coordinates several of the larger environmental
projects. Macon served as one of three test sites for the very first
Keep America Beautiful Clean Community system over 20 years
ago and became one of the national models for the program. The
city's Clean Community system has won numerous prestigious
awards, including the only Keep America Beautiful international
award. The Macon Clean Community system is also the only one
of 450 to operate in its own headquarters. Today, Keep Macon-
Bibb Beautiful coordinates over 100 organizations, businesses,
families, and individuals who have "adopted" highways, streets,
parks, or spots anywhere in Bibb County. The organization also
oversees community-based energy conservation and recycling
efforts, and it serves as the parent organization to Macon's internationally known Cherry Blossom Festival. The Keep Macon-Bibb

Beautiful workshops, educational programs, and community involvement projects have made a difference in changing attitudes about recycling, dumping, solid-waste management, and pollution.

The colorful gardens adorning homes and parks in the area require quite a bit of attention and effort, and Macon is fortunate to count many green-thumbs among its dedicated residents. Often, these horticulturists join the many garden and flower clubs in the area. The Federated Garden Clubs of Macon, located in a Neel Reid home built in 1910, first organized in 1934 and now counts over 600 members from 22 clubs. The American Camellia Society, founded at the Dempsey Hotel in Macon in 1945, is headquartered at Massee Lane Camellia Gardens in nearby Fort Valley. The Society names and registers new camellia varieties and shares information with its 4,000 members. The popularity of camellias attracts visitors every spring to Massee Lane when its 2,000 plants become a living bouquet of vibrant pink, white, and red blossoms.

Social, fraternal, and civic clubs of all types invite membership around the Macon area. Homemakers, quilters, needlepointers, musicians, computer users, clowns, bridge players,

(Left) Youth groups are involved with The Booker T. Washington Community Center's annual Jazz, Arts Festival which has been staged in Macon for over 30 years. Photography provided by The Booker T. Washington Community Center.
(Above) The Macon Clean Community system has won numerous prestigious awards, including the only Keep America Beautiful international award. Photography by Dorothy Hibbert Krakow.

retirees—virtually everybody with a hobby or special interest can easily find an active group to join. In addition, multiple business organizations, from Rotary to Toastmasters, offer opportunities to "network" and contribute to the community. Most formed as branches of national associations. A notable converse exception is Pilot International, which began here in 1921 and grew to serve business and communities all over the world. On a local level, the Greater Macon Chamber of Commerce brings business owners, managers, and local leaders together to voluntarily help fulfill its mission: "To advance the economic, civic, and cultural growth of Middle Georgia, to enhance the quality of life in the community, and to foster continuous improvement of the greater Macon area as a place in which to live and conduct business." For newcomers and for residents, participating in any of these organizations

The colorful gardens adorning homes and parks in the city complement the area's natural beauty. Photography by Ken Krakow.

promises introductions to new friends and a casual education on the fascinating history and contemporary progressiveness of Macon.

A Team Spirit

Macon's four seasons encourage a tremendous variety of sports activities. The mild winters preclude hockey and downhill skiing or any other winter sport requiring snow or ice, but residents can participate in virtually all other popular pastimes. Most of the public and private schools sponsor football, basketball, baseball, and other athletic programs for boys and girls. Reportedly, the very first football game played in Georgia took place at Porter Stadium in 1925 when the University of Georgia team trounced the Mercer University players, 50 to 0.

For children and adults, the opportunities to join teams or fine-tune individual physical abilities are boundless. The YWCA welcomes new membership, offering a swimming pool and gymnasium, and a wealth of classes for all ages. Other health clubs or wellness facilities promote physical fitness and healthful living, too. Under the direction of the Macon-Bibb County Parks and Recreation Department, programs for swimming, tennis, soccer, basketball, and softball attract kids and adults. Through this department, citizens also enjoy access to an 18-hole municipal golf course and 36 lighted tennis courts in two tennis centers. The John Drew Smith Tennis Center, with 24 courts, has been recognized as one of the top 25 public tennis facilities in the United States and often hosts tournaments. Annually, the Macon-Bibb County Parks and Recreation Department coordinates The Flag City Shoot-Out, the world's largest softball tournament. About 700 teams bring 20,000 people here for the event held in Central City Park. Additionally, private clubs offer members tennis, golf, swimming, and other amenities. Excellent golf courses, some privately owned but open to the public, surround the city and it's an easy drive to the golfer's paradise in Augusta.

Throughout Macon, the clubs or league teams for boxing, bowling, darts, billiards, archery, and too many more to name, encourage novice and experienced enthusiasts to join. Several Maconites have earned recognition for their abilities in these types of sports over the years. In 1931, the world heard a lot about Macon when its famed fighter, W.L. "Young" Stribling, Jr., battled Max Schmeling for the heavyweight championship. Although

Stribling lost, proud Maconites named the Spring Street bridge in his honor.

For those who walk or jog, or simply take pleasure from strolling, Macon boasts 1,296 acres of parks in both the city and county. A favorite destination is Lake Tobesofkee, which stretches along 35 miles of shoreline. The center attraction of an 1,800-acre, year-round recreation area, Lake Tobesofkee's clean waters invite swimming, fishing, boating, water skiing, and sailing activities. Visitors and residents alike picnic or camp beside the white sand beaches of the lake's three parks. Macon's central location makes it convenient for residents to regularly fish or camp at nearby Lake Juliette, High Falls State Park, Lake Sinclair, or Lake Oconee as well. The more adventurous folks travel the hinterlands of the 5,000-acre Bond Swamp National Wildlife Refuge southeast of Macon. With the Atlantic Ocean less than three hours away, many Macon residents head to the coast for sporting and sunbathing. Also, hunters and other sportsmen, upon obtaining their permits, can easily drive to any of the state's legal hunting grounds from here.

The nearby racing venues, Twiggs County Raceway, Atlanta Motor Speedway, and Warner Robins Dragway, deliver fast-paced, hard-driving action for spectators. Racing enthusiasts aren't always spectators, however. Men and women in the Macon area regularly drive in races on the amateur level. "Did you see the finish?" often hails as the dominating Monday-morning, back-to-work question—often confusing other sports fans who think of "the finish" as the last seconds in the weekend's big basketball or football game.

Among the spectator sports played here, baseball gets top billing. The Macon Braves, a Single A affiliate of the Atlanta Braves, play at the historic Luther Williams Field in Central City

Most of the public and private schools sponsor football, basketball, baseball, soccer, and other athletic programs for boys and girls. Photography by Ray Vane.

The Macon Braves, a Single A affiliate of the Atlanta Braves, play at the historic Luther Williams Field in Central City Park. Photography by Ken Krakow.

Park. This stadium once saw Babe Ruth, Lou Gehrig, Hank Aaron, Jackie Robinson, and Pete Rose, among other greats, run the diamond. Today's team still shows a game played with heart and soul. The seats lean in close enough for fans to hear the umpire make the call before it's announced over the PA system. It's pure baseball fun, and it's affordable and with plenty of free parking. Of course, Maconites can easily drive to see the Atlanta Braves. Other professional teams in Atlanta draw fans from this area, too: the Hawks basketball team, the Falcons football team, and the Knights hockey team.

In Macon, the list of things to do or things to watch seems endless. All of the varied experiences this city offers and the positive environment in which it offers them—that's what raises the quality of life beyond any statistics. That's what makes Macon a good place to live and a place to live well. ■

For children and adults, the opportunities to join teams or fine-tune individual physical abilities are boundless. Photography by Ken Krakow.

An 1,800-acre year-round recreation area, Lake Tobesofkee's clean waters invite swimming, fishing, boating, water skiing, and sailing activities. Photography by Ken Krakow.

THE FUTURE

On Target for Tomorrow

Poised and ready to bring Macon to new heights by the 21st century, the area's leaders look forward to realizing the results of years of planning. A variety of programs promise to keep Macon and its citizens at the forefront of a changing world. Seizing the opportunities of technological advancements and maximizing Macon's central location allow the city to confidently welcome the new century.

Macon's central location, literally in the middle of the state, encapsulates three interstate highways and several four-lane roadways connecting businesses and residents here to virtually every major city in Georgia. Photography by Ken Krakow.

A city of history and a city of progress, Macon's future promises a continued course of success. The leadership today remains committed to an ever-higher standard of living through efficient government, a diversified economy, strong educational systems, enhanced arts awareness, and community pride. Like a jigsaw puzzle, these pieces fit together to reveal a picture of immense potential for the city.

In 1994, a special local committee formed to assess the efficiency of the city and county governments. The results of their studies pointed out strengths and weaknesses, and served as a catalyst for discussion and planning. Macon's small-town atmosphere, preserved despite the city's growth, encourages residents to talk with their representatives and share ideas.

The Greater Macon Chamber of Commerce specifically works with local governments and state officials toward enhancing the quality of life here and improving the business environment. A legislative committee comprised of volunteers addresses the most pressing concerns and also looks ahead to the long-term effects of pending government decisions. In the 1990s, Chamber members worked effectively with Warner Robins and other surrounding towns when the federal government considered a list of military base closings.

As the focal point of Central Georgia, Macon benefits when it works toward the good of the region. That's why many organizations and agencies envision "Macon" as the entire MSA and not just the area within the city limits. When the Macon Economic Development Commission (MEDC) recruits new businesses, it highlights the advantages of the whole MSA. "Red Carpet" or "Silver Carpet" tours for prospective companies generally encompass Macon, Bibb County, Houston County, and beyond, pointing out the benefits of the vertically integrated aerospace industry, solid infrastructure, or convenient multi-modal transportation here. The MEDC joins a host of other area agencies at the Greater Macon Chamber of Commerce's annual "Taste of Macon" in Atlanta, too. This event promotes the region to state legislators and agencies in a casual environment.

The Roads to Economic Success

Macon's leaders continue to deliver positive economic development results through constant efforts. More and more plans for new business projects and existing industry expansions get approved and put into action with surprising speed. Maconites deserve credit for much of the city's success. It was the voting public who decided to move ahead in 1994 with significant highway, street, and sidewalk improvements. New traffic signals, safer intersections, more convenient sidestreets, and other upgrades prepare the city for some of the transportation demands of the 21st century. The city recently named a section of I-75, The Reginald Trice Parkway, in honor of the man who was instrumental in bringing the freeway and its economic benefits through Macon. This freeway breezes with a steady flow of traffic spread across three lanes in each direction. Interstate 75 delivers many of

(Left) One of Macon's many new industries, GE Capital Credit Servies is one of the largest credit card providers in the nation and produces more than 200 million cards a year. Photography by Ken Krakow.

(Above) The Greater Macon Chamber of Commerce regularly hosts its informal "Business After Hours" for its members. Photography by Ken Krakow.

Macon's tourists as they travel north to Atlanta or south into Florida. Intersecting with I-475 and I-16, the I-75 freeway also reinforces Macon's over-the-road distribution capabilities. The Fall Line Freeway, another major road improvement project, further emphasizes Macon's central location as it reaches across the state's midsection and through the city.

The Macon-Bibb County Convention & Visitor's Bureau expects these smooth freeways to help boost tourism's impact on the economy here. The revitalization of downtown will increase the numbers of visitors, too. The Georgia Sports Hall of Fame and the Georgia Music Hall of Fame welcome tourists, and the Macon Centreplex is hosting bigger conventions, events and trade shows than ever before. With all the attractions, Macon still has room to grow. The Ocmulgee River has yet to be developed as a recreational or tourism asset, and possibilities such as a bike path and habitat preserve may be considered in the future. Activities and events which increase awareness and appreciation of Macon's vast artistic talents should generate even more support of the arts community, in turn drawing more favorable attention to the city. Another possible attraction under evaluation by the neighborhood associations in the historic districts would feature nighttime tours. Carefully placed outdoor lights, according to this proposal, would highlight architecturally significant portions of selected historic homes. Just how everyone gets around on these tours, or how they travel about town in general, is also a subject of serious consideration. Speculation about public transportation improvements occasionally make the headlines of *The Macon Telegraph*, as the tourism agencies, city and county governments, and other organizations work together to find a positive solution. Changes for the better sometimes take longer than expected, but Macon is definitely working toward positive changes with an admirable intensity and dedication.

Focused on Education

Macon's future greatly depends on the children educated here today. They hold the key to sustained growth and success. The city shares the nation's concern for building stronger school systems, reducing juvenile delinquency problems, decreasing teenage

pregnancies, and increasing academic standards. The leadership here has renewed its dedication to creating a superior environment in which students can learn. The Bibb County public school system developed and implemented a variety of new programs in the 1990s designed to challenge gifted children, re-motivate potential dropouts and disruptive students, increase students' familiarity with computers, and directly involve businesses in their prospective workforce. The efforts of the Macon 2000 Partnership paved the way for many of these innovative programs by seeking and securing funding from sources other than tax revenues. Some pilot programs may be implemented system-wide, while others may evolve into entirely different avenues for reaching students. From unconventional methods to the tried-and-true strategies, the school system is using what works best toward benefiting today's students for a better future.

The powerful momentum shows no sign of slacking as the new century peeks over the horizon. The strong partnership between corporations and universities here promises discoveries which could lead to entirely new industries. A Mercer University professor and his assistants unearthed a deposit of thallium near Macon, an element never before found in Georgia. Many analysts expect demand for this material to grow as its use in high-tech applications increases, but no reserves have been recorded in the United States. Even if the University's work shows that the thallium deposit here is too small to have any economic impact, the discovery does offer an opportunity for further study on this rather elusive element.

The area's strength in health care and engineering also makes it possible that the biomedical field may grow significantly in the future. Macon's leaders are also positioning the area to become a new senior market: the mild climate, low cost of living, superb health care, and the central location could bring an ever-increasing number of residents 55 and older to live in the community. Then, too, as more businesses locate here and more people choose to move here, Macon will likely see more retail establishments, restaurants, and services. It's an upward spiral—planned and welcomed—which in total, helps to raise the standard of living for everyone. It's progress, tempered by a city that graciously cherishes its past. ∎

(Left page) The plans for the Georgia Sports Hall of Fame, one of Macon's newest museums, feature interactive displays and authentic articles. Photography by Ken Krakow.
(Right page) A city of history and a city of progress, Macon's future promises a continued course of success. Photography by Ken Krakow.

(Above) Participants in Youth Leadership Bibb County listen to health care issues from Don Faulk, CEO of the Medical Center. Youth Leadership Bibb County is a cooperative effort of the Macon 2000 Partnership, the County Extension Office, the University of Georgia Fanning Leadership Center, and alumni of Leadership Georgia. Student participants represent the public and private schools of central Georgia. Photography by H. Lee Perdue/Perdue Design Group.

(Right) Maconites Little Richard, James Brown, Otis Redding, and The Allman Brothers Band have been inducted into the Georgia Music Hall of Fame, shown here under construction in downtown Macon. Photography by Ken Krakow.

WILLIAM M. WADLEY

MACON'S ENTERPRISES

Photography on this page by Ken Krakow.

NETWORKS

Photography by Ken Krakow.

MACON WATER AUTHORITY

With 50,000 customers on tap, the task for the Macon Water Authority seems simple: Keep the water pumping to homes and businesses in Macon and Bibb County . . . as much as 51 million gallons per day.

In fact, the actual process of drawing water from the Ocmulgee River and delivering it clean to customers is a multi-step undertaking that involves about 225 employees, miles of underground distribution lines, and a great deal of planning by the Authority's governing board.

Throw in the additional operation of two large wastewater treatment plants—the Rocky Creek plant serving West Bibb County and the Poplar Street plant serving East Bibb County—and the Authority's vast responsibility becomes clear: provide two essential public services at a reasonable cost for people in the Bibb County service area.

The Authority's current members are Frank C. Amerson, Jr., Chairman; Herbert L. Dennard, Vice Chairman; Albert Billingslea; Robert J. Campen, Sr.; Ed DeFore; Barbara Knight; and Javors J. Lucas. Billingslea and DeFore represent the County and City respectively.

Gene Holcomb, the Executive Director of the Macon Water Authority, is employed by the board, a quasi-governmental entity that meets on the first Thursday of each month. The Authority meetings, including monthly committee meetings that cover the areas of personnel, finance, engineering, and pension, are open to the public.

Holcomb, hired as Executive Director in March of 1988, is responsible for four divisions: Business Operations, Finance, Field Operations, and Plant Operations. In short, Holcomb's duties include overseeing the operations of the water treatment plant and the distribution system within the service area. Although the system has about 50,000 customers in Macon and Bibb County, the Authority may serve anywhere in Bibb County.

In addition to the water treatment plant, the system's two large wastewater treatment plants boast a combined constructed capacity of 41 million gallons per day, with 21 million at the Rocky Creek plant and 20 million at the Poplar Street plant. A small, 1-million-gallon plant at the Macon Municipal Airport serves the airport industrial area.

Disposing of biosolids in the wastewater treatment plants is a continual issue for the Authority. Currently, the Authority has a contract that permits land application of biosolids from the wastewater treatment plants at sites in Bibb, Houston, Peach, Macon, and Dooly Counties. In the process, the biosolids are dewatered, then picked up by a contractor who applies the solids to the land and performs all monitoring for the system.

The Rocky Creek Water Pollution Control Plant manages 21 million gallons per day.

Officially established in 1974, the current Authority was created by a merger of the Macon Water Board with the Bibb County Water and Sewerage Authority. Managed by a seven-member board, the Authority is comprised of five elected district members, with one appointed member each serving from Macon City Council and the Bibb County Board of Commissioners. The chairman is elected county-wide.

Currently headquartered at 780 Third Street, the busy Authority office will soon move into a new building at 790 Second Street. The Authority is building a new support services facility for water distribution and sewerage collection crews in conjunction with a central laboratory at Martin Luther King Boulevard and Oglethorpe Street.

The Riverside Water Treatment Plant manages 40 million gallons per day.

The move to larger quarters cannot come too soon for the employees at the main office downtown. On one recent day, a steady stream of water customers kept workers occupied inside and put parking at a premium on the street. Shifting its office operations to more spacious quarters is not the only move afoot for the Macon Water Authority. Plans are under way for moving the Authority's water plant away from the banks of the Ocmulgee River, a safeguard prompted by the infamous flood of 1994.

In July 1994, Tropical Storm Alberto dumped more than 18 inches of rain over Macon and Middle Georgia, pushing the Ocmulgee over its banks and leaving a path of destruction in its wake. One of its victims was Macon's 104-year-old water treatment plant, built in 1891 on North Pierce Avenue. Four years earlier, after the then record flood of 1990, the Authority had already decided to move the plant to higher ground, on a site adjacent to the current plant, but the 1994 flood caused the Authority to cancel those plans and propose a plan to relocate an expanded treatment plant in Jones County at the site of its 625-acre Town Creek Reservoir, which was completed in 1994.

The new plant will feature a 60-million-gallon-per-day capacity, expandable to 90 million gallons. This state-of-the-art treatment plant will

The Poplar Street Water Pollution Control Plant manages 20 million gallons per day.

pump water out of the Ocmulgee River into the Town Creek Reservoir. The reservoir will allow solids to settle, and provide a constant quality of water going into the plant.

The quality of water at the reservoir will be protected by an additional 3,000 acres which is owned and controlled by the Authority. The Authority has developed a monitoring system for the Ocmulgee River and tributaries to the Town Creek Reservoir to ensure that the water quality remains high. Opportunities for fishing will be offered after the reservoir is filled.

The new plant will feature computer operation, yet will have local manual controls. Slated to be operational by late 1998, the plant carries a $125 million price tag.

Jones County, often plagued by its own water woes, will be able to buy water from the Authority. The Town Creek Reservoir is a good example of what can be accomplished when two entities work together. The Macon Water Authority purchased the land with the assistance of Jones County, and Jones Countians will benefit from an additional water supply. ■

PILOT INTERNATIONAL

Pilot International is among the world's most established civic service organizations in existence today. Founded in 1921 in Macon, Georgia, Pilot is made up of executive, business, and professional leaders working together to improve the quality of life in communities throughout the world. The name Pilot, meaning leader and guide, and the riverboat wheel emblem, which symbolizes a steady course, are befitting symbols of the organization's purpose.

Members combine their diverse talents and resources to further medical research, education, and caregiving programs in the vast area of brain-related disorders. Pilot International's service focus involves promoting an awareness of brain disorders, which fall into six general categories: traumatic brain injuries (TBI), developmentally disabled, chemical dependency, dementia, mental and emotional disorders, and brain disorders caused by tumors, neuromuscular diseases, strokes and overmedication. Pilot's goal is to help those affected by brain-related disorders through voluntarism, education, and financial support.

Pilot members do not fly planes; however, they soar with the eagles when it comes to helping those in need. Currently, Pilot International has 17,000 members worldwide, and recently chartered a new club in Singapore. Pilot members can also be found internationally in countries such as Australia, the Bahamas, Bangladesh, Bermuda, England, France, Philippines, South Africa, Canada, and the United States. Japan is one of the largest and fastest growing of the 22 Pilot districts and clubs outside of established districts.

In 1975, Pilot International chose to maximize its charitable activities by establishing a Foundation. Today, Pilot International Foundation carries out the organization's humanitarian efforts through grants and scholarships. Grants are awarded to educational institutions, research facilities and hospitals, health and social service agencies, nonprofit organizations, and clubs to support various worthwhile projects. The Foundation's four scholarships provide financial assistance to students preparing for careers working with people who have brain- related disorders or disabilities. International students and adults preparing for second careers are also eligible to apply for Foundation scholarship funds.

Another important part of Pilot International is its youth program. In 1952, Anchor Club was established as a volunteer service organization for young people. Pilot sponsors Anchor Clubs in schools and as independent organizations. Membership consists of high achievers who value serving the community and helping others. There are 10,000 Anchor members who, like their sponsoring Pilot Clubs, volunteer many hours to projects that improve the community and help people in need.

Pilot is committed to helping those with brain-related disorders, and works closely with national and international organizations that support this focus. Through these efforts, both Pilot and Anchor Clubs have opportunities to participate in numerous projects that help people with such devastating disorders. For three years, Pilot International Foundation has been a national sponsor of the Alzheimer's Association Memory Walks. By participating in

this event, Pilot and Anchor members have helped raise more than 6 million dollars to combat Alzheimer's disease. Clubs have also taken part in the "Calling on America Campaign" with the National Organization on Disability. This campaign involves a presentation of the *Harris Survey of Americans with Disabilities* to city and county officials. The event's purpose is to increase awareness of the needs of 49 million Americans with disabilities. Pilot also

Pilot International Foundation awards scholarships to students preparing for or working in careers that help people with brain-related disorders and disabilities. International students and adults preparing for second careers are also eligible; however, all applicants must be sponsored by a Pilot Club.

sponsors projects associated with the National Mental Health Association, such as the National Depression Screening Day and Physicians' Education Program.

Pilot International Foundation and the Brain Injury Association joined forces in July 1995 in a cooperative effort to heighten awareness of traumatic brain injury. This fund-raising project, called "Brown Bag It," benefits education and prevention programs for children. Another outstanding fund-raising program, also announced in 1995, is the "Pitch in with Billy Casper and

Save Our Kids from TBI" campaign. Golfers at more than 1,000 ranges throughout the United States had an opportunity to partici-pate. This annual cam-paign helps increase public awareness of our focus, and generates funds for the traumatic brain injury programs. Pilot's commit-ment to its service focus received international recognition at the First World Congress on Brain Injury in 1995. As a pre-senter and exhibiter at this momentous event, Pilot had the rare opportunity to network with some of the most prestigious scientists, medical professionals, and rehabilitation specialists in the world.

Besides the service focus on brain-related disorders, Pilot is also making a positive differ-ence in the areas of safety and security. As a member of the National Safety Council, Pilot International encourages Pilot and Anchor Clubs to sponsor projects that promote safe and secure communities. As the needs concerning these issues vary from one community to the next, so do the projects that serve them. Any club that sponsors a project associated with safety and security may enter Pilot's awards competition, funded by a grant from the Allstate Foundation.

Besides awards programs, Pilot International offers a variety of resources to the membership. Annual conventions are held on the district and international levels where members have an opportu-nity to participate in leadership training and workshops, and ex-change ideas for projects and fund raisers. Each member also receives a bimonthly publication, *The Pilot Log*, which provides up-to-date information about the organization, its focus, and club projects. Pilot International also publishes manuals, brochures, and recruiting guides that members may purchase through the catalog sales department.

October 1996 marks the 75th Anniversary of Pilot International. The celebration begins with special activities at the 1996 Annual Meeting and Convention in Nashville, Tennessee, June 29 through July 3, and continues in the city where it all began—Macon, Georgia. A "day of festivities" is planned for October 21, 1996 in Macon.

Through the years, Pilot members have given countless hours to helping others, a tradition that has continued for more than

seven decades. The organization has many accomplishments of which to be proud, including the realization of "full citizenship

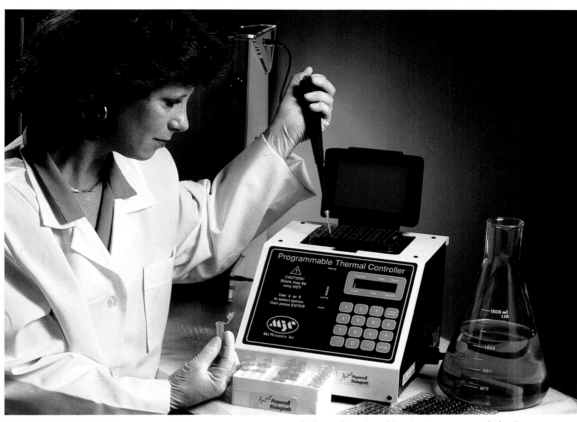

Grants are awarded to educational institutions, research facili-ties, hospitals, clubs, and other non-profit organizations to fur-ther projects that assist people with brain- related disorders and disabilities.

for people with disabilities." Pilot now champions an extension of this endeavor—helping people with brain-related disorders, a focus that enables the organization to expand its service pro-jects, and assist more people than ever before. After all, Pilot International is a dynamic civic service organization of volunteers, whose ultimate goal is improving the quality of life in our world.

For more information, call (912) 743-7403 or write: Pilot International Headquarters, P.O. Box 4844, Macon, Georgia, 31213-0599. ■

GEORGIA POWER COMPANY

Georgia Power's vision for the future is rooted in the proud traditions of its past. The Georgia Power story began more than a century ago on December 3, 1883, when Georgia Electric Light Company of Atlanta received a franchise to provide "electric lights for stores, dwellings, machine shops, depots . . . or to introduce said lights wherever desired." The company purchased its first electric light plant in 1884.

Power opened the Electric Vehicle Research Center to collect performance data on electric vehicles, batteries, charging stations, and other components.

Georgia Power is also concerned with the health and economic vitality of Georgia and its communities. Drawing on more than 60 years' experience of matching the location needs of thousands of companies with resources of Georgia communities, the company's internationally acclaimed economic development group offers unparalleled expertise and world-class technical resources. Business people looking to relocate or expand their companies can utilize the department's project management expertise and the Georgia Resource Center to efficiently identify the best place in Georgia to locate, saving considerable time, money, and effort.

Georgia Power played a supporting role in helping to secure the 1996 Olympics for Atlanta, and the company will continue the support by providing in-kind services and employee volunteers. With the eyes of the world focused on Atlanta as it plays international host to the Centennial Games, this company will be doing everything possible to help present Georgia in the best light.

True to their motto, "A Citizen Wherever We Serve," Georgia Power is a powerhouse of involvement, a positive force from one end of the state to the other. ■

By providing reasonably priced, readily available electricity, the company has helped fuel the state's economic growth and prosperity while offering sound energy solutions to Georgia's businesses. Photo by William Zachary.

Today, the company's assets include 19 hydroelectric generating plants, 12 fossil fuel plants, 2 nuclear plants, and 12 gas and oil combustion turbine plants. Serving both retail and wholesale customers, Georgia Power provides electric energy to more than 1,600 communities and more than 80 percent of the state's business.

By providing reasonably priced, readily available electricity, the company has helped fuel the state's economic growth and prosperity while offering sound energy solutions to Georgia's businesses.

In January 1991, it became the first electric utility to institute a customer service guarantee policy. The policy sharpens the company's focus on high-quality customer service and enables employees to respond quickly to meet customer needs.

Georgia Power offers customers a wide range of energy-efficiency programs that will help reduce the need to build new capacity for peak energy needs of its service area.

Electric transportation promises tremendous efficiency and environmental benefits by offering the potential to reduce major pollutant emissions up to 97 percent. In October 1993, Georgia

Georgia Power Company's Region Management offices are located at Terminal Station in Macon. Photo by William Zachary.

COX COMMUNICATIONS

For Cox Communications, a cruise down the information superhighway will mean even higher-quality customer service and future high-tech entertainment and business options for its 70,000 customers in the midstate area.

Already committed to customer service, education, and community involvement, Cox's addition of more fiber-optic cable lines will initially spell better picture quality and fewer outages in its 11-franchise local market.

In the future, such technological advances could open a new avenue of communications service, including a high-speed network capable of delivering voice, video, and data to homes throughout Middle Georgia. Most of the elements are already in place, or are being built, to put distance learning, banking, education, telephone, and health services as close to viewers as the television screen.

For now, Cox customers in the 4-county Middle Georgia area enjoy a viewing choice of more than 58 channels, including Pay Per View and premium services such as HBO, Cinemax, Showtime, and the Movie Channel. With office locations in Macon, Warner Robins, and a new facility at 6601 Hawkinsville Road in south Bibb County, the company serves franchises in Houston, Bibb, Jones, and Peach counties; and Robins Air Force Base.

All together, the company boasts 1,600 miles of cable and fiber optic lines in the Middle Georgia area. This is equivalent to the distance between Macon and Omaha, Nebraska.

Cable television first came to Middle Georgia in 1963, with 5 channels selling for $4.50 per month. Cox Communications, Inc., a multi-faceted, Atlanta-based communications company, delved into cable television in 1962, and now operates cable systems nationwide with ownership interests in international operations as well. The parent company, Cox Enterprises, also owns newspapers, radio and television stations, including WSB-TV and WSB Radio in Atlanta, and is diversified in other markets.

For Cox, quality starts with customer service, beginning with a focus on hiring the best people and training them well. In 1989, Cox established its own customer service standards, and was instrumental in persuading the rest of the cable industry to adopt nationwide standards. In 1991, Cox was the first cable company to have all of its systems in compliance with standards set by the National Cable Television Association. In 1994, for the fourth year in a row, Cox Communications in Middle Georgia earned the NCTA Seal of Good Customer Service for exceeding customer service standards.

Cox ensures its quality customer service through employee training, including the Focus on Added Value Program, which empowers employees to make on-the-spot decisions that benefit customers. Additionally, the Total Quality Program focuses on one central, market-driven concept: finding out what customers want and determining how they will get it. Quality service training also applies to the company's management team.

Financially, Cox's high level of community involvement in Middle Georgia translated into $1.4 million in charitable contributions and in-kind public service announcements and projects in 1994; not to mention countless hours of volunteer service by Cox employees. At $6 million, the company has a significant payroll impact in the community.

In 1994, for the fourth year in a row, Cox Communications earned the NCTA Seal of Good Customer Service for exceeding customer service standards.

Cox's community involvement also includes a firm commitment to improving educational opportunities in its franchise areas. Through the cable industry's Cable in the Classroom Program, the company offers commercial-free educational programming at no charge to 90 schools within its franchise area. Cable connections are free to participating schools, and Cox also holds workshops and technical training for teachers and media specialists who use the program. Cox also provides Bibb and Houston county schools with an educational channel. ■

ELECTRIC MEMBERSHIP CORPORATIONS OF MIDDLE GEORGIA

For more than 58 years, EMCs have been enhancing the quality of life in Georgia. What is an EMC? EMC stands for Electric Membership Corporation, and that means electricity and much more to over 3 million Georgians in 73 percent of the state's land area. From new business and economic development to commuity and civic activities, Georgians have always been able to count on their EMCs.

EMCs differ from other electric utilities. There are three different types of electric suppliers in Georgia: cooperatives (EMCs), investor-owned utilities (IOUs), and municipals. Cooperatives have been unique since their beginnings in the middle 1930s.

Electric service had been available commercially for 50 years by 1935, but only 10 percent of Americans had power and these 10 percent were city dwellers. IOUs and municipals were not interested in running lines into rural areas because it would not have been profitable for stockholders.

Then, when President Franklin D. Roosevelt signed the Rural Electrification Administration (REA) into law, rural Americans created not-for-profit, consumer-owned cooperatives. These cooperatives qualified for REA loans to build electric distribution systems.

There are today more than 1,000 electric cooperatives nationwide with 42 serving Georgians. Thirty-nine of these EMCs purchase power from their wholesale supplier, Oglethorpe Power Corporation, which is the largest generation and transmission cooperative in the United States.

EMCs provide electricity efficiently and they have always done more with less. While serving fewer customers per mile of line and generating less revenue per mile of line than IOUs and municipals, they have invested more in serving each customer. While REA loan programs have allowed EMCs to serve customers more cost-efficiently, they are not alone in receiving government assistance. The government actually provides more assistance per customer to IOUs and municipals through federal tax benefits.

EMCs are an important part of the future. The REA, now known as Rural Utility Services (RUS), with its network of electric membership cooperatives, is one of the most successful and admired government programs in America's history. They have spurred economic growth and development in the nation's rural areas and helped raise the U.S. standard of living above most other countries.

Electric membership cooperatives, like the ones that serve the area around metropolitan Macon—Central Georgia, Flint, Lamar, Oconee, and Tri-County—have provided an invaluable service for over 50 years. EMCs have set the standards and are living proof of the power of individuals who band together to accomplish a common goal.

Although Georgia's EMCs vary greatly in size, together they own more than 125,000 miles of line comprising the largest distribution network in the state. They bring power to 1,012,390 members and serve over 2.7 million people. They employ 4,000 workers.

Though not-for-profit, electric membership corporations such as Flint Electric Membership Corporation, Tri-County Electric Membership Corporation, Oconee Electric Membership Corporation, Lamar Electric Membership Corporation, and Central Georgia Electric Membership Corporation pay their fair share of property taxes throughout Georgia. In 1994, the electric membership cooperatives, along with Oglethorpe Power, paid more than $149 million into state, federal, and local tax coffers.

In Georgia, on loads of 900 KW or greater, the customer can choose his power provider from the cooperatives, the municipal

Complete transformer overhaul can be accomplished at the Flint Service Center in Houston County. Transformers can be repaired, rebuilt, repainted, and have the oil changed or cleaned.

power systems, or the investor-owned utilities. For the last several years, the majority of customers with large loads have chosen the EMCs. The EMCs serving Bibb County and Middle Georgia are prepared to serve any electric load. ■

Macon-Bibb County Convention & Visitors Bureau

MACON-BIBB COUNTY CONVENTION AND VISITORS BUREAU SELLS AMERICA'S DREAMTOWN

With the economic impact of tourism exceeding $250 million a year, you can be sure that the Macon-Bibb County Convention and Visitors Bureau is hard at work keeping visitors to America's Dreamtown happy and satisfied with their stay.

Janice Marshall, CVB Executive Director, has seen Macon's tourism industry skyrocket since she started work there in 1983. Marshall predicts that "tourism will be the next big industry in downtown Macon," and it looks as though she is right. Over 600 tour buses visit the city each year and the I-75 Welcome Center, 10 miles north of town, sees over 1,300,000 tourists annually.

Funded by local hotel and motel sales taxes, the staff of 13 aggressively goes after 3 primary markets: the convention and meeting market, the traveling public market, and the tour bus market. In 1985, they joined forces with the Tourism Development Committee, whose 20 members represent the historical district, the arts, transportation, and elected officials, in order to showcase and promote Macon's wide variety of offerings.

Using a sophisticated marketing effort, the group not only reaches but successfully brings in visitors from all over the world year-round, celebrating Macon's many festivals and true southern hospitality. In addition to promoting existing events and attractions, the bureau entices visitors with a number of fascinating tours including Sidney's Tours of Historic Macon which allows visitors to leisurely stroll through majestic homes in historic downtown and visit antebellum and modern landmarks. The African-American Experience, a self guided tour, stops at 21 spots around Macon which highlight the city's impressive black heritage. Soon, the bureau will be able to boast of yet another way to see their fair city by way of a moonlight tour called Intown Illuminations, which showcases the city's magnificent architecture using dramatic lighting techniques.

Networking with other Georgia communities has also proven successful for Macon's Convention and Visitors bureau. The Antebellum Trail winds its way from Athens to Macon showcasing the beauty and grandeur of the Old South that is still evident today, and Georgia's Antiques Trail loops out of Atlanta to Macon and 7 other communities offering 100 antique dealers and attractions.

Visitors to Macon's downtown Welcome Center in the Terminal Station enjoy Sidney's Tours of Historic Macon.

With the opening of the Georgia Music Hall of Fame, the Georgia Sports Hall of Fame, the restored Douglass Theater, and the newly expanded and renovated Macon Centerplex, Macon will be host to more and more visitors each year. You can bet that the award-winning team at the Macon-Bibb County Convention and Visitors Bureau will be inviting and welcoming them with tours, events, and attractions to keep America's Dreamtown, Macon, Georgia, on their minds. ∎

Cherry blossoms create the perfect backdrop for welcoming springtime visitors to beautiful Macon.

BellSouth

The definition of a leader in our fast-paced world of telecommunications translates to a company that is competitive, on the cutting edge of technology, committed to customer first and accepts only a high-performance team.

BellSouth Georgia Pioneers paint a map for an educational project at a local elementary school.

As a major employer in the Central Georgia area, BellSouth plays an important role not only in telecommunications, but also in the community. With over 600 employees in the area, BellSouth provides state-of-the-art telecommunications to thousands of customers, as well as volunteers to numerous organizations. The employees are active in scouting, United Way of Central Georgia, chambers of commerce, civic and cultural activities, and many other volunteer efforts.

Among the most visible of volunteer groups in our area is the BellSouth Georgia Pioneers, a group of active and retired employees of the telecommunications industry. These individuals are dedicated to projects such as: Make-A-Wish, Mapping a Playground (MAP), Smart Bears, Adopt-A-School, Habitat for Humanity, Keep Georgia Peachy Clean; Prevention of Child Abuse, a partnering effort with the Georgia Council for Prevention of Child Abuse; and Life Enrichment, a project to build five fishing docks for the physically challenged.

BellSouth believes that the way to a skilled work force is through high-quality education. The company sponsors or participates in many educational programs, including: the Teacher Mini Grant Program which provides teachers with a way of implementing innovative teaching ideas in the classroom, Georgia Teacher of the Year conferences; the Georgia Industrial Fellowship for Teachers (GIFT) Program, a partnership with local business, community and educational leaders; Adopt-A-School Programs, the Georgia Youth Science & Technology Center of The Robins Air Force Museum of Aviation, and the Partnership for Excellence in Education.

BellSouth's presence in Central Georgia includes a Small Business Telecommunications Center, Consumer Services Center, Customer Payment Center, Residence Repair Center, Directory Assistance Center, BellSouth Business Systems Marketing Center, and several Network centers. Many of these operations are open twenty-four hours a day, seven days a week, working together to make BellSouth a telecommunications leader.

BellSouth has introduced services designed to improve the quality of life in the communities where we live and work. One example is the Georgia Statewide Academic and Medical System (GSAMS) network. GSAMS is the world's largest and most comprehensive distance learning and health care telecommunications network. It represents a public-private partnership between the State of Georgia and a host of partner corporations including BellSouth. Today the GSAMS network has over 200 distance learning sites with plans to expand to over 400. Every university unit in Georgia, as well as all technical and adult education schools are connected to GSAMS. Hospitals and physicians benefit by having access to the most modern advancements in medicine through telecommunications. Another example of service deployment is Integrated Services Digital Network (ISDN), providing end-to-end digital connectivity for voice, data, image, or video; separately or simultaneously over a single line. Telemedicine, distance learning, and ISDN are only a few examples of services being deployed.

Changes in state and national telecommunications laws will see the increase of competition for local and long distance telephone service and cable television. Customers will have more choices in deciding who will provide them with their local, long distance, and cable television service. BellSouth will continue its strong presence in the Central Georgia area by providing high-quality services at competitive prices.

BellSouth Telecommunications, Inc., headquartered in Atlanta, provides telecommunications services in the nine-state BellSouth region, which encompasses Alabama, Florida, Georgia, Kentucky, Louisiana, Mississippi, North Carolina, South Carolina, and Tennessee. The company serves over 17.5 million local telephone lines and provides local exchange and intraLATA long distance service over one of the most modern telecommunications networks in the world. ■

BellSouth employees place fiber optic cable for a new shopping center and subdivision. Photo courtesy of Robert Seay/The Macon Telegraph.

Photography by Ken Krakow.

10

MANUFACTURING & DISTRIBUTION

Photography by Dorothy Hibbert Krakow.

BROWN & WILLIAMSON TOBACCO CORPORATION

In the blink of an eye, hundreds of green-and-white KOOL cigarette packages zip by on a conveyor belt, never slowing until they reach a machine that places them in cartons at the end of the line.

Moving too quickly for the human eye to examine, the individual cigarette packs are visually scanned by a series of inspection cameras, that instantly identifies any product with substandard wrappings and then culls it from the ranks of finished goods.

In the blink of an eye, hundreds of green-and-white KOOL cigarette packages zip by on a conveyor belt. Photography by Ken Krakow.

Such high-tech attention to quality and detail enables Brown & Williamson Tobacco Corporation (B&W) to produce and ship more than 1,000 individual high-quality tobacco products at its plant in Macon—at a rate of up to 500 million cigarettes per day.

Located on 200 acres in an industrial park on Weaver Road, the Brown & Williamson plant officially opened in Macon on September 24, 1977.

Beginning with a capacity of 34 million cigarettes per day, the company's aggressive approach to production advances keeps the company on the cutting edge of cigarette manufacturing, affording them high yields while remaining low-cost producers.

This is now the world's largest and most technologically advanced cigarette manufacturing facility. Operating capacity is growing to some 150 billion cigarettes per year.

About Brown & Williamson

The third-largest cigarette manufacturer and marketer in the country, Brown & Williamson's roots date back to

Individual cigarette packs are visually scanned by a series of inspection cameras. Photography by Ken Krakow.

1894 when Robert Williamson and George Brown formed a partnership in Winston-Salem, North Carolina. Since 1927, B&W has been a subsidiary of London-based B.A.T Industries.

B.A.T is the world's foremost international cigarette manufacturer and a leading provider of personal finance and insurance services in the United Kingdom and North America. The B.A.T Group employs nearly 175,000 people in 80 countries around the world.

Brown & Williamson Tobacco Corporation houses its corporate headquarters in Louisville, Kentucky. The company also operates the industry's largest leaf tobacco processing facility, located in Wilson, North Carolina.

B&W's specialty tobacco products such as SIR WALTER RALEIGH pipe tobacco, BUGLER and KITE roll-your-own cigarette products, plug chewing tobaccos, and snuff are produced in Winston-Salem.

The company also operates smaller manufacturing facilities in Lancaster, Pennsylvania, and outside Richmond, Virginia. Here, sheet tobaccos are produced for use in cigarette manufacturing.

In late 1994, B.A.T Industries completed the most recent addition to its U.S. business with the purchase of The American Tobacco Company for $1 billion. The acquisition of American Tobacco, once the number one cigarette manufacturer in the U.S., boosted Brown & Williamson's domestic volume and market share by some 60 percent.

B.A.T shares an ironic link with American Tobacco. British-American Tobacco was first established in 1902 as the international trading company of James Duke's American Tobacco Company in the U.S and the Imperial Tobacco Company of Great Britain and Ireland.

In 1911, the U.S. Supreme Court ruled the structure that created B.A.T was illegal, and it became an independent company. Then, more than 90 years after being created, B.A.T bought American Tobacco, in effect purchasing its former parent company.

Top-selling cigarette brands acquired through the purchase of American Tobacco include MISTY, CARLTON, LUCKY STRIKE, PRIVATE STOCK, and PALL MALL.

They were combined with Brown & Williamson's existing brands of KOOL, GPC, CAPRI, BARCLAY, BELAIR, RALEIGH, and VICEROY to offer a broader domestic brand portfolio.

Brown & Williamson Tobacco Corporation is the world's largest and most technologically advanced cigarette manufacturing facility. Photography by Ken Krakow.

it contains its own power plant, waste-water treatment facility, leaf storage, and finished goods cold storage.

Among the local employees are 125 technical experts and scientists from 20 different countries, now housed in the corporation's new 90,000-square-foot Research & Development building adjacent to the main manufacturing facility.

The Research & Development department is responsible for the ongoing quality analysis and development of product improvements and innovations for Brown & Williamson.

Leading international brands include LUCKY STRIKE, KENT, BARCLAY, CAPRI, KOOL, VICEROY, and PALL MALL.

With these well-recognized brands, Brown & Wiliamson holds nearly 20 percent of the domestic cigarette market and more than one-fifth of the U.S. export business.

The Engineering department is housed in another adjoining building and provides corporate-wide engineering services. With a staff of more than 60 experts, department responsibilities include facility design & construction, technology selection and application, process improvements, and management information services.

A new main entrance and a massive, plant-filled atrium were completed in 1994, linking Research & Development, Engineering, Manufacturing, the cafeteria, and library with the general administrative offices.

The main building houses a new 110-seat conference theater designed for presentations and training programs.

Macon Based Operations

In Macon, Brown & Williamson employs more than 2,500 people. Local operations include cigarette manufacturing as well as several corporate functions.

Cigarette manufacturing is managed by several departments including Primary, Fabrication, and Shipping.

Purchasing, Distribution, Engineering, and Research & Development

Elsewhere, the decorative details are historically poignant. At various points in the building, including the front lobby and administrative areas, artwork and old-fashioned cigar store Indians reflect the company's strong heritage and a bygone era.

Manufacturing Innovation and Technology

Continuing technological advances have moved Brown & Williamson's Macon manufacturing plant beyond state-of-the-art.

Indeed, the Primary, Fabrication, and Shipping departments are reminiscent of a space-age movie set, as large orange robotic arms palletize cases of LUCKY STRIKE, walking traffic makes way for motorized vehicles, pneumatic tubes feed finished tobacco blends from an automated storage and retrieval system to various manufacturing points in the factory, and computers help plan and track production and quality

Pneumatic tubes feed finished tobacco blends from an automated storage and retrieval system to various manufacturing points in the factory. Photography by Ken Krakow.

have been located in Macon to provide increased interaction between production and key related departments.

The Macon complex is tremendous. With 54 acres under roof,

at individual Fabrication modules.

Each of these operating departments has undergone expansion and equipment upgrades over the past several years. New processing equipment and techniques are employed in Primary where one million pounds of tobacco can be processed in one day.

Here, the finest burley, flue-cured, oriental and sheet tobaccos come together. They are moisturized, blended, and then combined with sugar, cocoa, and other flavorings to be used in the final production of cigarettes.

In Fabrication, prepared tobacco blends are combined with paper, filters, and packaging materials by a series of automated, high-speed machines.

While manufacturing speeds of 10,000 to 12,000 cigarettes per minute on each machine are commonplace, the company is now obtaining equipment which will produce 16,000 high-quality cigarettes per minute.

Volume and speed count in production, but not at the expense of quality. From the raw leaf to shipping of final products world wide, Brown & Williamson's materials and cigarettes pass through 28 stages where quality is checked and rechecked at various points during manufacture.

Shipping provides the gateway to the world as finished products are sent to customers located as close as Middle Georgia to as distant as the Far East. More than 25 truckloads—about 8,000 cases—of finished products leave Brown & Williamson each day.

The company's Development Center was relocated from Louisville to Macon in 1995. Working closely with Marketing and Research & Development, the Development Center produces small quantities of finished cigarettes useful in testing product improvements and new product designs.

Among the many innovations pioneered by Brown & Williamson, the company was the first to nationally market a filter cigarette

Materials and cigarettes pass through 28 stages where quality is checked and rechecked at various points during manufacturing. **Photography by Ken Krakow.**

(VICEROY) and a menthol product (KOOL). That same approach to product development led to recent innovative products such as BARCLAY and super-slim CAPRI.

Quality People Make It Work

Technological innovations would be worthless without highly trained employees to make the operations run efficiently. Recruitment activities, coupled with extensive, ongoing training programs, ensure that B&W employees remain at the top of their field.

Each year an array of scientists, technicians, and engineers are recruited from the best universities in the country. After recruitment, new graduates are placed in an extensive two-year training program.

The company also recruits experienced managers with specialized skills as well as craftsmen, electronic technicians, and production employees.

Training is a major activity at Brown & Williamson and the skills of employees are constantly enhanced. The company places an emphasis on team-building and problem-solving for all employees and offers comprehensive and competitive compensation and benefits programs to attract and retain quality workers.

Brown & Williamson works closely with the leading educational institutions throughout the region. The Macon Technical Institute provides many of the ongoing training programs.

Employees are encouraged to be active participants in the future of the business by continuously looking at their jobs and suggesting improvements. The company's team philosophy ensures that all employees are working toward the same goal.

A dynamic environment and growth opportunities challenge employees to develop beyond the parameters of their immediate job. The average length of employee tenure, more than 15 years, reflects that Brown & Williamson is a good company to work for.

Management employees are brought in from around the world to participate in training programs and serve stints in Macon. Local employees are also offered opportunities to work in sister companies around the world. Such an exchange enhances the environment by opening communications between B.A.T employees worldwide.

Brown & Williamson enjoys a good working relationship with its two unions, the Bakery, Confectionery & Tobacco

In Fabrication, prepared tobacco blends are combined with paper, filters, and packaging materials by a series of automated, high-speed machines. **Photography by Ken Krakow.**

International Union and the International Association of Machinists and Aerospace Workers.

In a relationship characterized by a problem-solving approach, the unions and management operate under long-term agreements. This provides security for employees and the company alike.

The main building houses a new 110-seat conference theater designed for presentations and training programs. Photography by Ken Krakow.

As additional countries in Eastern Europe, China, and Mexico open for trade, Brown & Williamson sees literally a new world of opportunities.

The domestic tobacco business, meanwhile, continues to offer tremendous opportunity for a company ready to compete with quality products.

With a major expansion project first announced in 1993 and the transfer of former American Tobacco products, the Macon facility is completing the largest investment ever made within Brown & Williamson.

Process redesign and new equipment allows Primary to produce enough finished tobacco to meet production volumes well into the future.

The latest high-speed equipment and technology in Fabrication and Shipping readies the facility to become the world's premier cigarette manufacturer through the year 2000 and beyond.

Brown & Williamson is indeed a company with a rich history. Through product innovations and a consumer-driven approach to business, it is on a course which should provide its greatest achievements during its second hundred years. ∎

Staying on the leading edge of technology and hiring the highest caliber people allows Brown & Williamson to remain competitive in the marketplace. Making sound financial decisions, setting good objectives, and knowing the customers' needs also help to drive the business.

From top executives to production workers, the company embraces a commitment to making every dollar count. Long-term success means having the ability to market the highest quality products while being the low-cost producer.

In order to better satisfy its consumers, Brown & Williamson was the first cigarette manufacturer to offer a toll-free 800 number on its products. Company representatives talk directly with nearly 100,000 consumers each year. This is invaluable in identifying consumer preferences and managing manufacturing quality.

Through an annual economic impact of about $500 million, Brown & Williamson contributes heavily to Georgia's financial stability.

With business success also comes a responsibilty to the people of the community. Company employees take pride in personal volunteer efforts and charitable programs that contribute to the local economy and quality of life. Through United Way and other local charities, Brown & Williamson and its employees provide assistance to those in need.

The Future

The lifting of export trade barriers and the opening of new markets in the late 1980s now allows B&W to compete in established Far East cigarette markets such as Japan, Taiwan, and Korea.

Japan has since become the company's largest international market, with B&W holding about 5 percent of the total cigarette business in that country.

New processing equipment and techniques are employed in Primary where one million pounds of tobacco can be processed in one day. Photography by Ken Krakow.

TEXPRINT (GA), INC.

Walk through a major department store and chances are the women's clothing on display features fabrics printed by Texprint (GA), Inc., a Japanese-owned textile commission printer located on 30 acres in the Ocmulgee East Industrial Park. Beginning 20 years ago with about 60 employees, Texprint now boasts an approximately 246,000-square-foot facility that employs up to 250 people and produces more than 3 million fabric yards per month. Texprint's sole owner is Tokai Senko Co., Ltd., of Japan, a leading printer and dyer of high quality textiles that was established in 1941.

Rather than marketing a specific product, what Texprint sells is time on its printing machines and expertise in analyzing and committing a customer's design to fabric. With a sales office in New York and the production facility in Bibb County at 2730 Weaver Road, Texprint works on a commission basis. Taking a customer's design pattern, Texprint analyzes the different colors and designs,

benefits from such automated equipment as a color dispensing and mixing machine.

Once complete, the design is printed on fabric supplied by the customer. The multi-step printing process also includes preparing cloth for printing, printing on rotary print machines, and drying and finishing the cloth in various different finishes. Typically, the fabrics printed at Texprint include cotton, rayon, knit, and polyester. A 1994 expansion of facilities will enable Texprint to expand upon the types of fabrics used in its printing. The latest expansion is one of several that has increased productivity and diversity at the printing facility.

After a sample run is approved by the direct customer, referred to in the industry as a converter, the fabric is bulk printed and then shipped directly to the manufacturer. Most of Texprint's direct customers are located in New York's famed Garment District, with 90 percent of Texprint's finished products made

then works with its sister company, TKG International in Macon, to make the metallic screens that are used to deposit the design on the cloth. The crucial process of applying color is highly technical, with each color used requiring a separate screen. Texprint makes up all of the colors used in the printing process, and

Texprint's production facility is located in Bibb County at 2730 Weaver Road. Photography by Ken Krakow.

into women's apparel, and 10 percent into home furnishings such as upholstery and drapery fabric.

In one room at the Texprint plant, several racks of brightly colored fabric samples display some of Texprint's finished products. From greige, a raw woven cloth that is treated to remove sizing, comes spectacular prints that adorn women's clothing such as those sold at Macy's, Rich's, or JC Penney. Other, heavier fabrics may be used to fashion exquisite floral draperies or to cover upholstered furnishings such as sofas and chairs.

Although Texprint works from customer specifications and creates no original designs, the company prints more than 100 new patterns a month, according to company literature. Previously able only to print fabric, the 1994 equipment and facility expansion—which increased the facility by 32,000 feet—will enable Texprint to dye fabrics in solid colors. When the company opened in 1975, Texprint produced more than 50,000 yards of fabric a month; monthly production now is counted in the millions.

Texprint was incorporated in October 1973; the facility was completed and production began in July 1975. According to company officials, Tokai Senko provides technical support for the plant from Japan, with Japanese technicians and their families voluntarily relocating to Middle Georgia to work at the Macon facility. Texprint officials contend that Macon's reputation as an enjoyable place to live and work ensures that Japanese natives will be willing to spend time in the midstate area before returning to Japan. Families with elementary-age children have been particularly impressed with the efforts of local schools to make their children feel welcome, despite an initial language barrier. Middle Georgia's moderate climate also makes living and working in Macon an enjoyable experience for Japanese natives.

Typically, Japanese workers spend about 4 years at Texprint before returning to Japan. Currently working at Texprint are about 20 Japanese natives, including technicians and officers in Macon, and sales personnel headquartered in the New York office, plus their families.

Technological advances and innovations make Texprint a leader in the field of fabric printing. Mercerization equipment has expanded the plant's ability to prepare and print many kinds of fabrics, and a $13 million waste treatment facility underscores Texprint's commitment to environmental concerns.

When Texprint's Japanese officials visit the plant, they are charmed by the Macon area's southern hospitality, an initial drawing card in deciding to build their physical plant in the Middle Georgia area. Representatives of Tokai Senko, initially

one of three companies that established Texprint as a joint venture, were impressed with the willingness of local government officials to help make Texprint (GA), Inc. a reality, company officials said.

The three-company venture included Tokai Senko of Japan; the Hawaii Corporation of Honolulu, Hawaii; and the Chori

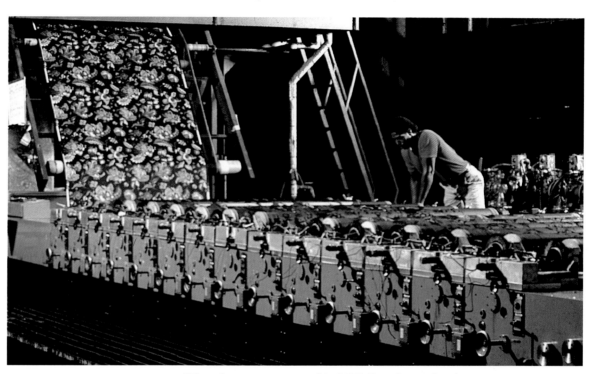

When the company opened in 1975, Texprint produced more than 50,000 yards of fabric a month; monthly production now is counted in the millions. Photography by Ken Krakow.

Company, also of Japan. Tokai Senko became the sole owner by the early 1980s. A reorganization in 1981 introduced Inabata & Company of Japan as a minority shareholder, but Tokai Senko remained responsible for management of the printing plant.

Kazuhiko Yashiro is Chairman of Texprint (GA), Inc., which has enjoyed an ongoing, cooperative relationship between international and local officials over the past 20 years. An enthusiastic supporter of Macon's Cherry Blossom Festival, Texprint has often sponsored entertainment for the annual March event, and has printed 2,000 special Cherry Blossom flags which still fly over Middle Georgia each spring.

Although not officially in the flag-printing business, Texprint has also printed flags for the 1984 summer Olympic Games in Los Angeles, California. ■

BEARINGS AND DRIVES, INC.

Bearings and Drives, Inc., began in Griffin, GA in April 1947. John Nations, one of the original founders, moved the business to Macon in 1950. Through the efforts of many local employees, the firm has grown into a multi-state concern featuring 30 locations in Georgia, North Carolina, South Carolina, Tennessee, and Florida.

With corporate headquarters in Macon at 607 Lower Poplar Street, Bearings And Drives is the largest independently owned distributor in sales and service of industrial bearings and power transmission

Andy Nations took over as president in 1983; John Nations now serves as chairman of the board, with other company officers including Edgar F. Baxter, executive vice-president; Charles Nicholson, William Chapman, and Cliff Davis, vice-presidents; and Michael Nations, secretary/treasurer.

According to published accounts, John Nations grew up working in his father's sawmill business then moved with his family to a farm in Senoia during the depression. His first full-time job was with Pye Barker Supply in Atlanta. He opened Bearings and Drives after purchasing a small Griffin business for $9,000.

Andy joined Bearings and Drives in 1965, learning the business from the ground up by working during summer vacations and after school. He began working full- time at Bearings and Drives in 1971, after graduating from the University of Georgia with a degree in finance, first in the sales division. Later, he became involved in computers and company finance.

Original founder of Bearings and Drives, Inc., John Nations, and the 1956 location at 607 Lower Poplar Street.

equipment in the Southeast. The company consistently ranks among the 50 largest industrial distributors in the United States. Through its 19 locations in Georgia, and 250 employees in the 5- state region, Bearings and Drives also sells electrical drives and controls, fluid power equipment, and materials handling systems.

Scale Systems, Inc., a subsidiary of Bearings and Drives that sells and services industrial scales, includes four locations in Georgia, with one office in Macon. A distributor of Mettler-Toledo, Inc., industrial scales, Scale Systems also sells Intermec bar-code equipment and P.C.-controlled inventory controls and production systems.

In the beginning, the company started small with only John Nations and three other employees. The first branch outside of Macon was opened in Atlanta in 1956. According to published reports, sales within the first year after opening the branch grew from $625,000 to $875,000. By 1959, sales surpassed $1 million with three branches.

During his 12-year tenure, the younger Nations has steered the business through some rough economic times. Part of the company's strength lies in its location in the Southeast, which, compared to other parts of the country, has grown rapidly over the past 30 years. Maintaining an emphasis on satisfying the customers' needs, coupled with attracting and keeping high-quality employees, also has helped the business grow.

The nature of the industrial distribution business is fiercely competitive. Considered a mid-size distributor, Bearings and Drives often competes with seven or eight competitors in an area. The company has about 3,000 customers, including such local businesses as Armstrong World Industries, Engelhard Corporation, and Dry Branch Kaolin.

A charter member of the Bearings Specialists Association, Bearings and Drives has been active in the group's leadership for a quarter century. The company also participates in the Power Transmission

In-house training sessions are scheduled several times each year at the corporate training center in Macon.

Distributors Association and the Fluid Power Distributors Association.

Nations contends that the company's strength lies in its high-quality employees and their depth of product knowledge. Through a company subsidiary, B&D Technical Services, Inc., branch employees are schooled in both product knowledge and taking care of customers' needs. In-house training sessions are scheduled several times each year at the corporate training center in Macon, with an emphasis placed on product knowledge, sales promotion, and management training. Training also is available for employees at manufacturers' facilities. Making an investment in training is the only way to stay ahead, Andy Nations maintains.

In addition to training, B&D Technical Services, Inc., is responsible for designing systems featuring products of manufacturers that Bearings and Drives represents.

What sets them apart, Nations contends, is that the company is spread out over many states and locations. The average location employees 6 or 7 people, with all 30 company branches linked by computer to the 25,000 square-foot distribution center in Macon. Also, all branch offices are networked by computer and backed by a full time data processing staff.

In addition to Macon and Atlanta, other Bearings and Drives offices in Georgia are located in Albany, Athens, Augusta, Dublin, Gainesville, Hapeville, Kennesaw, McIntyre, Newnan, Norcross, Perry, Rome, Sandersville, Savannah, Thomasville, Tifton, and Valdosta. Out of state, there are offices located in Chattanooga and Cleveland, Tennessee; Gainesville and Ocala, Florida; Simpsonville and Spartanburg, South Carolina; and in Asheville, North Carolina.

Having grown up with the company, Andy Nations said Bearings and Drives still employees personnel who were with the business when he started. "Watching their growth and progress has been rewarding," he said. "It's been exciting to see it, and be a part of the growth."

Recent promotional materials include a 10-minute videotape featuring Andy Nations, other company officers, and employees highlighting the company's goods and services. Included in the videotape are testimonials from manufacturers and customers lauding the company's high-caliber employees, its willingness to provide prompt assistance, and its 24-hour, 7-day-a-week availability.

A testimonial from T. B. Woods attributes its growth with Bearings and Drives over the past decade to the quality relationship between the company and its employees. Customers applaud their policy of customer service.

In the videotape, Andy Nations sums up the company's philosophy by stating a Golden Rule of successful business: Treat the customer the way you want to be treated. Their formula has paid off; the company's commitment to excellence was recognized in 1986, when Bearings and Drives was chosen Distributor of the Century by Industrial Distribution Magazine.

Future plans call for continued growth in both existing and new locations. ■

The Bearings and Drives, Inc. company logo and its mission statement.

YKK CORPORATION OF AMERICA

A simple, quality-minded business philosophy and a strict adherence to the company founder's vision of corporate citizenship has propelled YKK into the top ranks of world manufacturers.

From its founding as a small company that began manufacturing zippers in 1934, YKK is now a major player in two manufactured product categories: fasteners for sewn products and aluminum building products.

At YKK's birth in the depths of a worldwide economic depression, its founder, Tadao Yoshida, created a simple yet powerful philosophy called the "Cycle of Goodness." Simply put this philosophy holds that no one prospers unless he renders benefit to others. This principle is rooted deeply within the corporate culture of YKK, extending beyond policy to strengthen the resolve of employees as they pursue products and corporate/community relationships of only the highest quality.

In the spirit of its founder, the business success of YKK fuels the growth of investment and quality of life in the communities around the world in which the company has a presence. The shared prosperity of a growing, thriving manufacturing company is a boon to the many communities in which YKK has facilities.

Careful consideration is given to the location of every YKK plant or office. History and company policy show that the company's commitment to a community is for the long term. Beyond profits, an important aspect of YKK's corporate goals is to bring jobs, economic growth, environmental well-being, and corporate involvement to communities that are home to a YKK facility—whether they are located in North America, South America, the Caribbean, or another hemisphere entirely. YKK plays its role as a good corporate citizen to the highest degree of commitment and foresight.

Within the YKK America Group, prosperity begins in laboratories and research and development facilities. Corporate philosophy dictates

YKK "cut zippers" coming off the line undergo quality inspection. Photography by Rod Caudle.

a heavy investment in R & D. From product and process improvement to market research and environmental impact studies, the employees of YKK are consistently engaged in the search for a better way, or a new, improved product. As a result of this single-minded devotion to continuous improvement, more than 18,500 items have been the object

Vislon® plastic zipper for outerwear market in production. Photography by Rod Caudle.

of patent applications and utility models under the YKK name. Whether in the product categories of closures for sewn goods, or aluminum building products, the goals of the research and development arms of YKK have always been growth, evolution, and discovery.

This penchant for the discovery of new ideas and processes extends beyond the lab into the production facilities and procedures in YKK plants worldwide. An example: YKK's Vertically Integrated Production System, a policy that mandates that whenever feasible YKK manufactures everything—from raw materials to finished product to the processing equipment itself—utilizing the purest materials and the company's own facilities and expertise. For its 2.6 million square-foot National Manufacturing Center in Macon, YKK manufactures its own brass in order to produce a metal that is as close to perfect as possible. Here in Macon, that means 99.98 percent pure brass.

More than 40 years ago, in an effort to competitively secure the highest possible quality metal for zippers, YKK became involved in producing aluminum. What has resulted from this search for quality? An international aluminum building products business that now represents approximately two-thirds of the company's global sales. The people who turn blueprints into buildings have learned to rely on YKK AP (Architectural Products) not only for superior materials but also as a worldwide industry leader and stable source of supply. YKK's sprawling architectural aluminum plant in Dublin, Georgia, is the only operation of its kind in the United States where every single manufacturing

At its National Manufacturing Center in Macon, YKK utilizes tightly controlled tolerances to achieve exactness with 401 standard zipper colors and thousands more special made-to-order colors. Photography by Rod Caudle.

step, including die production, takes place under one huge roof.

Here in Macon, the company's innovations and manufacturing breakthroughs are just as impressive. Modern artisans have turned the basic zipper into a product carried in more than 1,500 styles in 401 standard colors. The YKK USA line includes many unique, value-added zippers such as the concealed Illusion®, a zipper whose teardrop pull-tab has become the much sought-after symbol of excellence in designer dresses and skirts. Luggage and sporting goods manufacturers count on YKK zippers to meet the tortuous demands of today's hurried, harried travelers. Jeans and workwear manufacturers save small fortunes in returns and claims by using YKK zippers with the company's ratcheting sliders, which slip down under pressure rather than breaking.

Whether the application is medical, automotive, high fashion, sports, marine, or heavy industrial, innovative products from YKK—zippers, hook & loop, plastic notions, and webbings—are engineered to enhance product performance. YKK has become the industry leader, the one-source resource for a dizzying array of closure combinations and variations. Why, YKK even makes closure products for fastening together artificial turf football fields such as the one at the Georgia Dome.

Vislon® is an injection-molded zipper with memory that is at once fashionable and durable in extremes of temperature. YKK's brand of woven hook and loop fastening tape is SmartTouch™, a product that features an army of tiny nylon hooks designed to grab loops faster and hold tighter than any other woven hook and loop. It is also available in a wide variety of styles and colors. The Cosmolon PowerHook™ brand of molded hook comes in four styles—nylon, polyester, polypropylene, or PBT. FastenMates® is an innovative line of plastic

buckles and notions. YKK Webbing is produced in 14 standard polypropylene colors. A Jacquard loom can even weave distinctive designs right into the fabric.

An integral part of the YKK America family of companies is Universal Fasteners Inc. (UFI), the nation's largest sales and service organization producing metal closures and machinery. UFI manufactures buttons, burrs, rivets, along with a whole range of metal and nylon closure products including snaps, Snapets®, and hooks and eyes—plus the automated equipment to attach them. UFI's two manufacturing locations in Kentucky and Tennessee produce millions of closure components every day.

In its global operations, YKK has a presence in 47 countries—bringing with it the company's time-honored commitment to manufacturing excellence. As the new century approaches, YKK sees sweeping changes, exciting product breakthroughs, major expansion opportunities, and continued development of cutting-edge equipment to automate manufacturing systems.

Still, the things that matter most will stay firmly rooted and immutable: a firm commitment to quality and service and the hard-earned trust of many satisfied customers. The "Cycle of Goodness," a neverending spiral generating progressively better things for people, enterprise, and the world, remains the cornerstone of YKK's mission. ∎

YKK also manufacturers polyester and polypropylene webbing for the luggage, medical and many other markets. Photography by Rod Caudle.

McDonnell Douglas Aerospace

Many companies tout their presence in the communities in which they operate. They foster long association with a town's people, herald their ties, support, and contributions to the community. In this tradition, the McDonnell Douglas Corporation has a long-standing relationship with the Southeast.

The Macon plant of McDonnell Douglas is one of two exclusive builders of major sub-assemblies for the C-17 aircraft. Photography by Horace Holmes Photography Studio.

But no other company can lay claim to the very special relationship—and certainly not the longevity of that relationship—that exists between the people of McDonnell Douglas, the Southeast, and Macon.

William Archie McDonnell of St. Louis, Missouri, brother of the founder of the McDonnell Douglas Corporation, feels a genuine closeness to the Southeast. His grandfather, Archibald McDonnell, born in 1768 in North Ireland, immigrated to the United States in the early 1800s, settling in the Southeast. In 1815, his son (also named Archibald) was born in Huntsville and became one of the early graduates of the University of Alabama in Tuscaloosa. He returned to Huntsville to marry Mary Sophia Jones in 1846. The couple had 12 children.

One of his children, James Smith McDonnell, Sr., born in Huntsville in 1859, also attended his father's alma mater, earning both a bachelor's and a master's degree at the University of Alabama in Tuscaloosa. He would eventually marry and move west to Arkansas to operate a general merchandise store. In 1899, his wife gave birth to a son, James Smith McDonnell, Jr. Forty years later, that son would found McDonnell Aircraft, forerunner of the McDonnell Douglas Corporation. The company began operations in St. Louis, Missouri, in 1939. Over the next 40 years, plants were opened

The highly motivated, well-trained workforce operate in an environment of continuous improvement. Photography by Horace Holmes Photography Studio.

in Melbourne, Arkansas; Huntsville, Alabama; Titusville, Florida, and other areas in the Southeast.

The U.S. Air Force, in early 1981, announced that the McDonnell Douglas Corporation won the contract to build the C-17 airlifter, the most versatile large transport in the world. The C-17 is the first military transport to enter the U.S. Air Force service in more than two decades. The C-17 significantly modernizes the U.S. airlift force and provides new capabilities for direct delivery of cargo to forward airfields. The C-17 is the right aircraft at the right time, with all the capabilities needed in our changing world. Its size, cargo compartment volume, speed, range, short field performance, reliability, and low operating cost make it the platform of choice for a wide range of miliary applications, as well as an ideal candidate as a commercial freighter.

To support this effort, McDonnell Douglas Corporation expanded its operations to Macon in June 1988. Initially, the work at the Macon plant was 60 percent commercial (MD80) and 40 percent military (C-17 for the USAF). In 1992, the company realigned into two self autonomous groups—commercial and government—and at the same time divested itself of excess capacity. As a result, the MD80 commercial work was moved to the Salt Lake City, Utah facility. Additional C-17 work was transferred to Macon to optimize the capacity of the plant. Since its opening, employment at the facility has grown tenfold from 53 to 560, and has earned the reputation of being one of the premier performers within the corporation.

Subsequently, a second building was opened in late 1994 to accommodate the administration, procurement, and inventory stores activity. Today, the Macon plant is one of two exclusive builders of major subassemblies for the C-17 aircraft.

To ensure the maintenance of high standards and continuous improvement, regular training programs are conducted for all teammates. Photography by Horace Holmes Photography Studio.

The 560 McDonnell Douglas teammates in Macon work in the forefront of aircraft technology to support the United States' defense goals. Additionally, they work and contribute to support the community in which they live, giving countless hours and untold monetary support to many local civic, cultural, educational, and health/wellness organizations.

A cornerstone of the McDonnell Douglas philosophy is taking an active part in public welfare activities through employee participation in community service and by corporate philanthropy. In addition to individual and corporate support, both the Employee Community Fund and the McDonnell Douglas Foundation are major contributors to the community. Recipients of their efforts include students of Weir Elementary School, where 30 teammates are involved in encouraging students to remain in school and to concentrate on math and science; the annual Macon Cherry Blossom Festival, Macon Mayor's Council for Disability Issues, American Red Cross Board of Directors, Governor's Council on Science and Technology, Georgia Partnership for Excellence in Education, Georgia Youth Science and Technology Center at the Warner Robins Air Force Museum of Aviation, Middle Georgia Youth Aerospace Apprenticeship Program, Space Museum, Special Olympics, Georgia Industrial Children's Home, Macon Sickle Cell Society, Georgia Hall of Fame for Aviation, Better Business Bureau, Macon Chamber of Commerce, Georgia Chamber of Commerce, United Way, March of Dimes, Junior League of Macon, Macon Arts Alliance, and many others.

The key to the outstanding performance of the Macon facility is the highly motivated, well-trained, self-directed workforce operating in an environment of continuous improvement, constant two-way communication between management and the workforce, and a unique management philosophy that emphasizes innovative teams with a sense of individual responsibility for quality work.

Individual and group two-way communications between management and shop floor teammates is stressed and meticulously maintained. Roundtable meetings with teammates and management are held so that concerns can be surfaced for resolution. Plant-wide meetings are also held monthly to make sure teammates are fully informed of circumstances that affect the company in general and their jobs specifically. Weekly meetings involving representation of all teammates are held on safety, quality, and performance.

To ensure the maintenance of high standards and continuous improvement, regular training programs are conducted for all teammates. To deal with the unique challenges of self-managed teams, managers and team leaders go through intensive skills courses. The highly trained workforce is the result of a public-private industry partnership with the Georgia Department of Technical and Adult Education. A standardized aerospace curriculum has been adopted at technical schools statewide, including instruction in total quality management and in reading the drawings and processes used by the aerospace industry. With this widespread educational effort, the Macon facility has been able to raise its technical recruitment and application standards to accept only those who have completed a 12-month technical school diploma course. This means the workforce is trained before coming on the job. To keep skills at a high level, quality is monitored at the teammate level.

The objective at McDonnell Douglas-Macon is to be the preferred producer of assemblies ahead of schedule, with superior quality and cost performance, within an empowered total quality management environment, and committed to the achievement of total customer satisfaction.

Today, nearly 200 years after Archibald McDonnell crossed the ocean to settle in the Southeast, the aerospace operation his descendants founded is an important part of the Middle Georgia community and plays a vital role in the nation's defense programs. ∎

Communications between management and shop floor teammates is stressed and maintained. Photography by Horace Holmes Photography Studio.

BLUE BIRD CORPORATION

Blue Bird Corporation is the largest manufacturer of school buses in the world and currently supplies about 45 percent of all new school buses sold in North America. It also has the largest combined school and commercial bus building capacity in North America, with nearly 2 million square feet of capacity.

Paul Glaske, Chairman of the Board, President, and CEO of Blue Bird Corporation.

Corporate headquarters for the Blue Bird Corporation are located in Macon. Its major manufacturing facilities for school buses, commercial buses, and motor homes are in Fort Valley, Georgia. Blue Bird also has other school bus facilities in LaFayette, Georgia; Mount Pleasant, Iowa; and Brantford, Ontario, Canada. A new plant is under development near Monterrey, Mexico.

Formally founded in 1932, it is the only company to manufacture school and commercial buses and recreational vehicles. The United States Government is one of their major customers, and they're also a major force in the international marketplace.

Blue Bird vehicles have achieved widespread publicity because they are designed, engineered, and manufactured to meet the unique requirements of specific bus markets. They incorporate features that directly contribute to increased reliability, easier maintenance, and improved customer convenience, and they identify the particular needs of potential customers. The company's ability to provide cost-efficient, dependable vehicles without sacrificing quality or styling has much to do with their leadership role in the school transportation and RV markets and the success of their product offerings in the commercial bus field.

In 1927, the first Blue Bird bus was built. In 1948, the world's first transit-style school bus, the heavy-duty all-American, was

built. In 1987, the TC/2000 became the country's first medium-duty transit-style bus. In 1992, the first Blue Bird NGVs were delivered. As a result of such innovations, Blue Bird is a world leader in the production of school buses, with a combined total of over 2,000,000 square feet of manufacturing space in 4 modern plants.

Due to their experience and expertise in other bus applications, Blue Bird is in a unique position to take advantage of the rapidly developing commercial bus market. The flagship of their commercial line is the Q-bus, which has both the style and strength common to all Blue Bird buses. A versatile vehicle, it can be specifically configured to satisfy individual customer demands in the transit, commuter, shuttle, and tour/charter markets.

The CS Series, Blue Bird's other commercial line, further expands their ability to meet the diverse requirements of the commercial bus market. It has a hard-working, practical, and affordable design that represents impressive overall value.

For those who want to see the country in style, the Wonderlodge and the BMC are two of the most luxurious choices. Their well-appointed features are the result of more than 30 years spent continually perfecting and updating style, interior design, and overall comfort.

Early in 1992, Blue Bird's president, Paul Glaske, orchestrated a leveraged buyout of the company. Under the terms of the buyout, Merrill-Lynch Capital Partners became the majority owner, key company managers assumed minority equity positions, and Glaske was appointed Chairman of the Board, President, and CEO.

Mr. Glaske serves on the Board of Trustees of Trust Company Bank of Middle Georgia; Borg Warner Automotive, Inc., and the Georgia Industry Association; and is a trustee of the Georgia Foundation for Independent Colleges. ■

Blue Bird is a world leader in the production of school buses, with a combined total of over 2,000,000 square feet of manufacturing space in 4 modern plants.

BURGESS PIGMENT COMPANY

The Burgess family knows kaolin.

In 1880, John W. Burgess owned a clay mine in Hockessin, Delaware. In 1917, John Burgess III co-owned a kaolin company in Dry Branch, Georgia. As a youth, Malcolm Burgess, Sr.'s first job was carrying 10-gallon buckets of water to kaolin miners in Dry Branch. He continued to work there on and off over the next few years while finishing high school and attending Brewton Parker College, and in 1930 at 23 years of age, he was put in charge as plant superintendent.

furnaces, which run continuously 24 hours a day, 7 days a week. With 155 full-time employees working 4 shifts, the kaolin is treated using a highly technical process that requires constant monitoring. With the help of computer technology, it is classified by particle size. A typical fine particle of kaolin is less than 2 microns thick or 40 times smaller than the eye can see. The kaolin, in dry form, is then ready to be delivered to the customer. Thousands of tons of kaolin are processed through Burgess Pigment each year.

With the production end of the business located in the heart of Washington County and the executive officers located on Pierce Avenue in Macon, Burgess Pigment Company doesn't stop there. They proudly ship their product to major corporations around the world. Their product can be found in a variety of forms used in the manufacturing of paint, wire and cable, rubber, plastics, adhesives, ceiling tile, floor moldings, and make-up.

Burgess Pigment has gone from processing a few hundred tons of kaolin in 1948 to producing many thousand tons of clay today without ever leaving behind the family values that it was founded on. From Malcolm, Sr.'s original vision for the future and Malcolm, Jr.'s leadership ability and expertise in kaolin, Burgess Pigment Company will continue to provide their customers with a high-quality product for generations to come. ■

Burgess Pigment Company is one of the leaders of their field in producing calcined clay.

In 1945 Malcolm's wife Nell encouraged him to start his own company. Taking that advice, he founded Burgess-Washington Clays. Three years later in September of 1948, he founded Burgess Pigment Company, and over four decades later Burgess Pigment Company is one of the leaders of their field in producing calcined clay.

Malcolm Burgess, Jr. followed in his family footsteps and in 1961 he began spending his summer breaks from school at his father's business. In 1971, returning to Georgia after three years in the army, he began working at Burgess Pigment Company full-time. Since his father's retirement in March of 1991, Malcolm, Jr. has taken over as president and chief executive officer of the corporation and has continued to lead the company from its humble beginnings in 1948 to where it is today—a multimillion-dollar business.

Kaolin is a naturally occurring mineral formed during the glacial period of America and its rich deposits in Georgia helped to make the state the leading producer of the clay.

Burgess Pigment Company processes hydrous kaolin by removing the water from the mineral using high temperature

Thousands of tons of kaolin are processed through Burgess Pigment each year.

VOLUMATIC, INC.

Volumatic, Inc. was incorporated in November of 1969 in Long Island, New York, and was organized by Robert W. Schmucker, the current president. The company was formed to supply custom machined parts and assemblies to the commercial, electronic, and aircraft/aerospace industries, primarily in the Northeast.

In 1979, Volumatic purchased its first computerized numerical control (CNC) machine. CNCs have internal computers which control the machine movement and direction. This, in turn, allows the precise machining to a customers' exacting standards. At present, there are 12 CNC machines with a capacity of 68 inches by 144 inches, which include 5 axis.

In 1989, the company relocated to Macon, Georgia. Their move to the Southeast coincided with several customers' migration from the Northeast, in addition to the severe reduction of manufacturing in that area. The tremendous support from the

every year since the move. Square footage has been increased by 65 percent during the past year and certified welding has been added to the company's capabilities. Also added is a large Coordinate Measuring Machine, which allows greater flexibility and accuracy in recording very precise inspection of close tolerance parts.

In 1990, Volumatic was awarded the United States Small Business Administration "Administrators Award for Excellence." From 1990-1995, the company has been a "Blue Ribbon Vendor" for the Warner Robins Air Logistics Center. This requires a 99 percent on-time delivery record and a 99 percent quality acceptance of parts. In 1993, Mr. Schmucker was a Greater Macon Chamber of Commerce Small Business Owner of the Year finalist.

Macon was chosen by Volumatic, Inc. due to its location in the center of what is called Aerospace Alley. This terminology refers to the large and diverse aerospace representation in Georgia and to its steady growth. In addition, Macon offered a quality of life which includes affordable housing, a lower tax structure, and a labor force which is not only trainable, but has a remarkably strong work ethic.

The benefits brought to the Macon area by Volumatic are reflected in jobs and taxes. They have grown from 2 people in 1989 to 16 today. This trend is expected to continue and perhaps accelerate. Volumatic has supported the Georgia State Chamber of Commerce, the Greater Macon Chamber of Commerce, and the Warner Robins Chamber of Commerce. There are many charitable organizations which are supported by Volumatic. They are committed to the Middle Georgia community, believing that to be a good community partner, involvement is the answer, and they look forward to continuing to doing their part. They support the Macon chamber's efforts to encourage new industry location to Macon and consider themselves the head of the class when expounding

Volumatic purchased its first computerized numerical control (CNC) machine in 1979. CNCs have internal computers which control the machine movement and direction.

Macon-Bibb County Industrial Authority was a determining factor for relocation. With their help, a smooth transition became reality. Along the way, many friendships have grown and continue to grow. The organization is dedicated to expanding community involvement.

Volumatic's sales in Georgia have grown at a very healthy pace by comparison to the Northeast and the volume of sales has increased

the many merits of this fine community.

Georgia has shown tremendous growth in the manufacturing sector and Volumatic believes that growth will continue—they expect to be a leader in the field by maintaining the most sophisticated manufacturing facilities. They chose Macon as home and believe the choice has proved to be an excellent one. ■

J.M. Huber Corporation

The J.M. Huber Corporation has been active in the kaolin clay industry in Middle Georgia since the 1930s.

Huber has put its emphasis on the people of Middle Georgia. The company and its people have continued to grow, not only through expansion, but also in its commitment to serve the various industries throughout the country.

The company's concern and involvement with the community is evidenced in their support and involvement in Macon's annual Cherry Blossom Festival, their participation in American Red Cross blood drives, and in their preparation of recreational areas for local residents. In their effort to be a good neighbor to the people in the community, J.M. Huber was one of the largest suppliers of emergency drinking water to the Macon area during the flood of 1994, enabling many sister industries to continue their activities.

J.M. Huber is also very involved in education in the community. In an effort to show support of local schools, they have participated in career outreach programs and various science projects. They have also established a letter jacket program for those students exhibiting academic excellence. Other activities which foster Huber's community partnership include "Coop" student participation, "Partners in Education," service on local college advisory boards, and chairmanships of science and engineering. The company also has a long-term commitment to educating their employees on the job, including teaching both job and communication skills.

As a result of J.M. Huber's determination to be a major industry in the community on a long-term basis, the company is continually modernizing operations in order to be better positioned for the future. The company believes that working together with suppliers and customers is a very important part of the Huber Corporation's role in the Middle Georgia community.

During the 1940s and 1950s, J.M. Huber's clay operations expanded, and technical advances significantly altered the company's various methods of production. An event of major consequence occurred in 1965 when the company opened up its first kaolin operation in East Georgia near the town of Wrens.

Huber produces hydrous and calcined clays, as well as other specialty clays unique within the industry.

J.M. Huber's processing facilities and administrative systems have continued to gain recognition for their excellence. Photography by Horace Holmes Photography Studio.

Evidence of the company's long-standing tradition of concern for the environment is also seen in its very active land reclamation program. Abandoned mines have been turned into fields, woodlands, and ponds. J.M. Huber's processing facilities and administrative systems have continued to gain recognition for their excellence. The headquarters in Huber, Georgia, has earned the ISO 9002 worldwide quality certification.

During the first part of 1995, three of Huber's mineral additive divisions combined and consolidated to form a new business sector, Huber Engineered Minerals. This consolidation was done to help customers find solutions to problems before they appear and to provide superior product and performance advancement.

The local J.M. Huber plant south of Macon serves the paper, paint, rubber, ceramics, and ink industries. It produces hydrous and calcined clays, as well as other specialty clays unique within the industry. The raw materials (kaolin clay out of the ground) are brought from the mines to the plant through a modern 22-mile long pipeline. This plant owns the world's largest industrial cryogenic magnet, which is used to raise the brightness of the clays that are produced, a process that was pioneered and patented by the corporation in the late 1960s.

Headquartered in Atlanta, Georgia, the new Engineered Minerals Division has facilities in several states, as well as in the Netherlands. The J.M. Huber Corporation is located on Huber Road just a few miles from downtown Macon. ∎

THE TRANE COMPANY

Over the past six years, Richard Beltz has accomplished what few other employees of The Trane Company could. A production worker at the manufacturing company's Macon business unit, Beltz hasn't missed a day on the job since he was hired in 1989. While several workers have amassed perfect attendance records for shorter periods, only one other employee comes close to matching Beltz's record, having missed the six-year mark by half a day.

In 1984, The Trane Company became a division of American Standard, Inc., an international leader in plumbing, air-conditioning, and automotive products.

Such employee devotion proves that this company's unique team approach to manufacturing works. Trane's non-traditional, employee-oriented philosophy sets the company—a leading manufacturer of heating, ventilating, air-conditioning, and building management systems and equipment—ahead of the competition. In Macon, The Trane Company is located at 7610 Industrial Highway, a 108,000-square-foot building where manufacturing began in 1988. Its parent company, American Standard, Inc., has housed other facilities there over the past 20 years.

What began as a small, family plumbing business in downtown La Crosse, Wisconsin, 110 years ago now boasts 16 manufacturing locations in the United States, and more than 100 sales offices throughout North America, with 7 locations overseas, including factories in Thailand, Malaysia, Taiwan, France, and the United Kingdom. The headquarters of the North American Commerical Group, of which the Macon plant is a part, are in La Crosse, where James Trane, a Norwegian immigrant, opened his first store in 1885.

Technological innovation marks Trane's worldwide success. Beginning in 1913 with the Trane Vapor Heating System, James Trane and his son, Reuben, devised such innovative systems as the convector radiator, leading to Trane's pioneering achievements in air-conditioning. Their first air-conditioning units were built in the 1930s, and worked by blowing air past convector coils through which cool well-water was circulated. The first commercial units were used in movie houses in Louisville, Kentucky, and Indianapolis, Indiana.

In 1938, Trane introduced the Turbovac, the air-conditioning industry's first hermetic centrifugal refrigeration machine and the predecessor of the modern CenTraVac®, which sets the industry standard for large, commercial air-conditioning systems. They introduced the first self-contained air-conditioning units in 1941.

In 1982, Trane acquired the central air-conditioning department of General Electric. In 1984, The Trane Company became a division of American Standard, Inc., an international leader in plumbing, air-conditioning, and automotive products. American Standard boasted sales of nearly $4.5 billion in 1994, with more than 90 manufacturing facilities and over 32,000 employees in 32 countries. Formerly privately held, American Standard returned to the New York Stock Exchange (ASD) in February 1995, following a successful initial public stock offering.

Today, Trane's innovative manufacturing system, "demand flow technology," incorporates a team approach that accounts for much of the company's continued success. In Macon, some 300 employees enjoy an open family environment marked by respect between management and employees. According to Trane Macon's Human Resource Philolophy, dress in the offices and the production floor is casual, and all employees are salaried and share common benefits, including educational opportunities. On the air-conditioned production floor, Trane's Team concept is in full force as employees quickly help others who have fallen behind. When production process problems arise, employees respond by identifying the problem and recommending a solution. This often requires gaining input from several co-workers.

The Trane Company expends a large investment in its diverse workforce, including many hours of training, to ensure the highest quality product for its customers and the most effective, enjoyable workplace for its employees.

Trane Macon marks a long term commitment to the Middle Georgia area by supporting various community activities, including the annual Cherry Blossom Festival held in Macon each March, the American Red Cross, and Volunteer Macon. ■

The Trane Company is located at 7610 Industrial Highway, a 108,000-spuare-foot building where manufacturing began in 1988.

ENGELHARD CORPORATION

Engelhard Corporation's Middle Georgia operations produce the finest kaolin products in the world with production facilities in Gordon and McIntyre, Georgia, and five major milling and mining

Engelhard has led the way in finding better methods of processing and purifying kaolin, in discovering new applications for this versatile mineral, and in producing high-quality new products.

sites and kaolin reserves in Wilkinson, Washington, and Twiggs Counties. Engelhard has led the way in finding better methods of processing and purifying kaolin, in discovering new applications for this versatile mineral, and in producing high-quality new products.

Kaolin has many industrial applications, including paper filling and coating and is widely used in paints, refractories, plastics, sanitary wares, fiberglass, adhesives, ceramics, and rubber products.

Engelhard's products for paper and paperboard coating and filling applications enhance brightness, opacity, whiteness, and printability. A commitment to products for the market led to the development of fine-particle, high-gloss, low-viscosity paper pigments designed to meet market-specific standards.

But the company doesn't stop at working with customers on product development. Engelhard technical teams work with paper-mill customers to analyze mill processes to achieve optimum pigment performance.

International Standardization Organization (ISO) certification is a requirement to do business with many European companies. In 1991, a team of employees were ISO trained and charged with the preparation, assembly, and submission of the appropriate documents for ISO registration.

In 1993, the Edgar Plant of Engelhard's Middle Georgia operations was the first domestic Engelhard site to receive ISO certification, and the first in the kaolin industry. The Gordon and Toddville plants were certified shortly thereafter. ISO certification has given the company a competitive edge with many of its customers.

Growth is essential to any company and Engelhard has demonstrated its desire and ability to invest the

necessary capital in the Middle Georgia operations to ensure its success and survival in tough economic times. Their $40 million plant expansion which started up in early 1995 included the installation of a new calciner which solidified Engelhard Corporation's premier position in calcined kaolin, and verified to its customers their continued support of growth.

As one of the largest employers in the region, Engelhard provides jobs for over 1,000 people at its various sites, with an annual payroll of nearly $52 million. Sales and property taxes paid by the Middle Georgia operations to five Middle Georgia counties are over $4 million each year with an additional $3 million paid directly to the state.

Engelhard's Middle Georgia operations are environmentally responsible. Hundreds of dry dust collectors capture usable kaolin rather than discharging it into the atmosphere. High-efficiency, wet scrubber systems also minimize air emissions. Water conservation receives a high priority with over 40 percent of the water used in the manufacturing process being recycled prior to treatment and discharging to local streams. The Middle Georgia operations have an extensive land reclamation program: Engelhard has won Georgia Mining Association's Land Reclamation Award for two years in a row, and received the President's Award of Excellence in 1992.

Being a good corporate citizen, Engelhard has established a partnership with the Wilkinson County school system consisting of financial aid and an ongoing personal involvement with the schools.

Through these actions and more, Engelhard Corporation makes clear its concern for its employees, the communities in which it operates, and its desire to be a good, cooperative corporate citizen. ■

Engelhard's Middle Georgia operations are environmentally responsible.

BUSINESS & FINANCE

Photography by Ken Krakow.

GREATER MACON CHAMBER OF COMMERCE

Established more than 130 years ago, the Greater Macon Chamber of Commerce is dedicated to the advancement of economic, civic, and cultural growth of Middle Georgia and to foster continuous improvement of the Greater Macon area as a place in which to live and conduct business. The Chamber represents the

The Chamber supports new local businesses as Chili's celebrates its grand opening. Photography by Ken Krakow.

business community and serves as the community touchstone for Macon and Bibb County. It is an organization where people come together to get information, share ideas, and develop solutions to improve the business environment and therefore the quality of life in Middle Georgia.

While the Chamber of Commerce does many things, its primary focus areas are Economic Development, Government Affairs, and Education. The Economic Development efforts include industry recruitment and support for existing industry. Existing industry creates more than 80 percent of all new jobs. The Greater Macon Chamber of Commerce funds two-thirds of the budget of the Macon Economic Development Commission, whose mission is to market Macon to industries that are considering relocation or expansion. Macon has seen a marked increase in economic development activity recently and consistently adds more

jobs than any other metropolitan area in Georgia outside of Atlanta.

The Governmental Affairs effort seeks to understand the needs of the business community and facilitate information exchange between the businesses and local, state, and federal government. This includes representation of the business community at public government meetings, communication of government developments to the business community, and support for public referendums that benefit business or help improve infrastructure for economic development. The Chamber's government effort was also instrumental in the implementation of the transportation improvements referendum and planning process for infrastructure improvements currently underway. Government Affairs also seeks to maintain a close relationship with Robins Air Force Base, which is the largest economic engine of the Middle Georgia area.

The Education effort supports the mission of the Macon 2000 Partnership which started as a focus area of the Chamber of Commerce to improve education in the Bibb County Public School System. The Chamber is committed to challenging business to become involved directly with the improvement of and support of education through partnerships with schools, classes, colleges, and universities.

In addition to the primary external objectives, the Greater Macon Chamber of Commerce offers many services to its membership. These services fall into the basic areas of Access, Information, Representation, and Solutions (AIRS). Business networking is a service provided through events such as Business After Hours, volunteer committees, new member breakfasts, and the monthly newspaper— *Business Macon*. Businesses also benefit from monthly professional development seminars and services on subjects such as customer service, legal issues facing businesses, management techniques, and marketing.

Special focus committees provide forums for exchange of information and solutions to industry-specific areas such as retail, medical,

The Red Carpet Tour provides prospective new industries an opportunity to view Macon. Photography by Ken Krakow.

The Greater Macon Chamber of Commerce Building. Photography by Ken Krakow.

forestry, mining, real estate development, and retirement. Another specific focus of the Chamber is to listen to the concerns of existing industry and look for solutions to mutually benefit the companies and the community. The Chamber also assists industrial parks in holding regular meetings to encourage neighboring industries to speak out mutual concerns and provide representation in the areas of policy development and infrastructure improvements. Other special events include industry recognition day, Macon Day in Atlanta to represent Macon to the legislature, annual meetings and planning retreats, legislative forums, and informational breakfasts. The Chamber also provides a multitude of information resources including membership directories, demographics information, mailing lists, legislative updates, transportation improvement updates, government meeting reports, surveys, and access to numerous other information and research organizations.

The Greater Macon Chamber of Commerce and Macon Economic Development Commission (MEDC) fulfills thousands of requests for information about Macon for individuals interested in visiting or moving to Macon. In addition, MEDC works with industries that are transferring employees by providing information about the move and the quality of life they can expect to enjoy in Macon and by helping the new families assimilate to the community after the move.

Throughout the years, the Chamber has been an incubator

for a number of organizations that have now grown large enough to support themselves. These organizations include the Macon/Bibb County Convention and Visitors Bureau, Career Women's Network, The Better Business Bureau, Macon Arts Alliance, Macon 2000 Partnership, Macon Progress, Leadership Macon, the Downtown Council, the Cherry Blossom Festival, and Southern Jubilee Street Parties held each year. The Chamber also provides substantial incubator support for the Georgia Music Hall of Fame and the Georgia Sports Hall of Fame that are now located in downtown Macon.

The Greater Macon Chamber of Commerce has been historically involved in many big projects for the Macon area, including the establishment of Robins Air Force Base in 1940 and the extensive defensive presentations on behalf of the base during the Base Closure and Realignment Processes of 1993 and 1995. The Chamber has been actively involved in the revitalization of the Downtown Business District and assisted with the development of all areas of Bibb County.

The Greater Macon Chamber of Commerce is a voluntary membership organization of the business community. It is a private, non-profit, tax-paying corporation that unites hundreds of businesses and professional firms. There are more than 1,400 member businesses with over 400 active volunteers working on 30 different committees that assist the Chamber in fulfilling its mission and plan of work each year. There are 15 paid staff members of the Chamber and MEDC to support the committee efforts and goals of the Chamber. The Greater Macon Chamber of Commerce is located at 305 Coliseum Drive in the parking lot of the Macon Centreplex (Coliseum) in a 13,000-square-foot building. The Chamber also provides space and services to four other community organizations. The Chamber acts as a central agency with the purpose of improving business, the business environment, and building a better community to serve the needs of the member businesses. ∎

Kurobe Chamber of Commerce & Industry dignitaries traveled from Japan to meet Macon's Chamber of Commerce leaders. Kurobe, Japan, and Macon are sister cities. Photography by Ken Krakow.

BANK SOUTH

In a message printed in Bank South's 1994 annual report, bank Chairman and CEO, Patrick L. Flinn, took a moment to remind everyone what a financial institution is all about—its customers.

"We must be more customer focused and conscious of our customers' needs," wrote Flinn. "We must push decision-making even closer to the customer and have the information and courage to make decisions faster."

In Macon, Bank South stands uniquely poised to carry out its mission of providing increased customer satisfaction. With 11 offices now located in Bibb County and another branch in Forsyth, the bank makes good its promise of customer commitment with convenient access, extended hours, and friendly service by more than 200 employees in the Macon branch system.

Bank South InStore branch. Photo by Horace Holmes Photography Studio.

Across Central Georgia, other Bank South locations include branches in Houston, Jasper, and Ben Hill counties.

The only financial institution in Macon to offer InStore banking, Bank South now features branch locations in five Kroger stores. The North Park Kroger and Baconsfield Kroger branches opened in 1988. The Wesleyan Station Kroger opened next. The newest InStore locations are at Plantation Centre Kroger on Zebulon Road, which opened in May 1995, and the Kroger store on Hartley Bridge Road, which opened in July. The Baconsfield

Bank South personal banker. Photo by Horace Holmes Photography Studio.

Kroger location was recently remodeled, and all future locations will boast the more up-to-date design.

To better serve its customers, the mid-size banking institution also maintains Georgia's largest ATM network, with 267 locations across the state. During 1994, all branch ATMs were upgraded to promote brand identity and create uniform deposit-taking capability.

Bank South of Macon initially opened as the Georgia Bank and Trust Company in 1960. Twenty years later, the Georgia Bank and Trust Company was purchased by Georgia Bancshares, Inc., which was in turn purchased by Bank South, N.A. in 1984.

Bank South Investment Services. Photo by Horace Holmes Photography Studio.

According to Flinn's comments in the latest annual report, the bank's net income for 1994 was a record $80.2 million, compared to $73.3 million in 1993. Consumer loan growth increased by 41.4 percent during 1994, while the average commercial loan growth increased 7.3 percent.

To be a leader as the industry continues to change, Bank South now offers investment products and services through Bank South Investment Services, Inc., utilizing branch offices, TeleServices areas, and other delivery channels. The service also features a full-service brokerage area with access to all financial markets and a wide variety of products. ■

GOVERNMENT EMPLOYEES INSURANCE CO.

In 1936, a brand new Pontiac coupe could be purchased for $585.00, and gas cost 18 cents a gallon. America was in the depths of the Great Depression, and Leo Goodwin, an insurance company accountant in Fort Worth, Texas, believed that automobile insurance was too expensive. After all, a typical 1-year policy might cost $30.00 or more.

Goodwin had an idea—a way to sell insurance at 20 to 30 percent below market rates. The concept: limit sales to preferred-risk customers (government employees seemed to be sober, stable, and reliable) and deal with them directly rather than through commissioned agents.

Leo and his wife, Lillian, put up $25,000 of their own capital and convinced Cleaves Rhea, a local Texas banker, to invest $75,000. The Government Employees Insurance Company was chartered on September 1, 1936.

GEICO Corporation assets now exceed $4.99 billion, with gross sales of almost half that figure annually. The company headquarters is now in Washington, D.C., and the company's regional office, its second, located in Macon celebrated its 20th anniversary in 1994.

Ross Pierce, regional vice president in Macon from 1974 through 1979, served as a member of the team that picked the Macon site. The committee was impressed with the city's infrastructure, he recalls, the site (once Camp Wheeler, a World War I and World War II army training camp), and the community reception.

"It appeared Macon had a tremendous reservoir of excellent people," Pierce says, "and we certainly weren't disappointed."

Some 1,330 associates now work at the Macon office. They provide sales, customer and claim services for a 15-state area. David Pushman has been regional vice president since 1989.

No longer does the company sell auto insurance only to government employees. Its policyholder base extends to most occupational groups. It offers its insurance through four separate companies: GEICO, for government employees who are considered a preferred risk; GEICO General, for preferred risks who do not work for the government; GEICO Indemnity, for standard-risk drivers; and GEICO Casualty, for non-standard-risk drivers.

Two of Leo Goodwin's principles remain firmly implanted at GEICO—keeping costs low by serving customers directly and providing the best customer service available.

GEICO uses direct marketing techniques—television, radio, and newspaper advertisements—to reach prospective customers. A 24-hour 800 number provides easy access for customers, and most sales and policy servicing is handled by telephone.

"Since we handle our transactions without agents, we cut the middlemen out and can save our policyholders money," said regional vice president Pushman. "Our customers find that having someone who can help them 24 hours a day, 7 days a week—and at a lower cost—is a big advantage."

GEICO takes full advantage of improved technology to serve its customers with quality and efficiency. A policy purchase or change takes minutes by phone, thanks to state-of-the-art computer systems and trained, helpful associates. File a claim in the evening, the next morning your car will be en route to a body shop, and a rental car will be awaiting you. Or drive a car in to a GEICO claim facility for an appraisal and you'll leave with a check for the repair.

"Customer satisfaction drives GEICO," said Pushman. "Associates here in Macon and throughout our company strive to give our customers the best possible product at the best price and with unsurpassable service. In short, we want to delight our customers." ∎

Insurance Sales Counselor Denise Grover and Insurance Service Counselor Lori Phillipy, with the Auto Sales Department, take all incoming sales calls using state-of-the-art computer systems. Photography by Ken Krakow.

Alice Rogers and Gerri Pauldo, with the Auto Service Department, take full advantage of improved technology to serve their customers with quality and efficiency. Photography by Ken Krakow.

GE CAPITAL CREDIT SERVICES

Established in 1876, General Electric Company is the parent Company of GE Capital Credit Services. Located on New Forsyth Road, the company employs approximately 500 men and women in its beautiful, modern, and spacious facility.

For processing services, customers can rely on the speed and reliability of a company that can deliver outstanding resources. GE Capital Credit Services offers technology, efficiency, and economics of scale beyond the reach of virtually any single company or in-house operation. Their advanced support in statement processing, remittance management, and card production helps customers meet their unique challenges and opportunities. They now serve over 75 million accounts for more than 300 clients, a few of which are Exxon, Home Depot, GE Capital Auto Lease, and Montgomery Ward.

GE Capital Credit Services leads the way in responsive, customer-focused service. Their resources include a 200,000 square-foot mailing facility, including 55,000 square feet of warehouse space; on-site U.S. Postal Service expediters; advanced telecommunications links and production equipment; and multiple sites in Arlington, Texas; Macon, Georgia; Edmonton, Alberta, Canada; and Leeds, England.

One of the largest centralized first-class mailers in the country, the organization processes 240 million statements and 1.1 billion inserts a year. The volume and resources of the company enable it to meet a variety of mailing and billing needs.

Equipped with the latest in printing, inserting, and sorting techniques, this company offers the speed, accuracy, and quality to maximize impact while controlling costs. Their state-of-the-art equipment helps customers manage mailing costs by leveraging optimum mailing discounts, and on-site U.S. Postal Service representatives keep 20 million mailings a month flowing smoothly.

GE Capital Credit Services can help any company build marketing muscle through creative statement design—or cut costs with integrated mailings. By utilizing their proprietary, sophisticated marketing software, they can include selective promotional messages to target specific customers and market segments.

Offering a complete, high-security printing function that employs the latest MICR technologies, they can print and disburse a customer's accounts payable, or EOB checks, and can provide electronic data interchange (EDI) as well. The result is a total solution for a customer's check disbursement needs.

At GE Capital Credit Services, 180 million payments are processed yearly. Offering quality performance you can rely on, they remain a recognized leader in remittance management with high-powered productivity, unsurpassed attention to detail and speed, and outstanding accuracy ratios. They convert customer payments into cash in as little time as possible, using resources

that include dedicated postal couriers, automated workstations, and advanced imaging technologies.

With GE Capital Credit Services as your remittance management outsourcer, you can keep close tabs on your transactions.

The company's beautiful facility is located on over 34 acres on New Forsyth Road.

All payments are automatically microfilmed and they also protect programs by offering the security of two processing centers—in Macon, Georgia and Arlington, Texas—with mirrored technologies, should the need arise.

GE Capital Credit Services is one of the largest credit card providers in the nation and produces more than 20 million cards a year. They have more than 300 clients. Speed and flexibility are essential to the way they do business.

They understand that any time customers are without your card—whether it be a credit card, membership card, or discount card—it costs you. That is why they respond so quickly with turnaround.

GE Capital Credit Services' operation includes one of the largest first-class sorting and mailing facilities in the country, assuring your card-mailing program of maximized postal-discount savings. And by leveraging their immense production efficiencies, you can realize some of the lowest plastic rates in the industry.

The company uses co-mingling and other proven techniques to minimize fraud and protect the integrity of your portfolio. They will design and implement a card production program that works for your business, built around a high level of security you can count on. With their services, you'll get speed, security, and flexibility for your card production.

The team at GE Capital Credit Services is an extension of your own organization. They are committed from the start to learning your needs and using all their resources to help your company grow and prosper. When you assign responsibility for processing services, you keep your focus where it really counts—on your business.

GE Capital Credit Services—through one of their Client Relations Managers, who understands their business and is dedicated to knowing yours—will provide you with the support you need. This Client Relations Manager will bring the entire team together to develop and run a program that meets your specific needs. Working closely with you, they'll assure that your needs are continually met, 24 hours a day, 365 days a year.

They also offer superior collection coverage, from early-stage collections and recovery management to aggressive bankruptcy services and specialized collections. When you outsource your collections services to this organization, the benefits are many: centralized recoveries, maximized profits, faster payments, reduced expenses, and higher recovery efficiencies.

GE Capital Credit Services is a leader and will continue to create new, leading edge solutions in processing and collections services. They are ready to show you how your company can tap their unmatched resources to inject new quality, efficiency, and value into every aspect of your credit services.

The Macon office of GE Capital Credit Services opened in April of 1991 with 85 associates. The number of associates has now grown to nearly 500.

"I was part of the team in search of a location for this business," says Bill Forget, Senior Vice President. "We decided on Macon because of its unique location in Central Georgia, the proximity to the airport postal facilities in Atlanta, and the quality of life necessary for our associates."

"We built our facility on sufficient property for planning future expansion," Forget says. "We have experienced substantial growth since 1991 and our outlook for future growth looks extremely positive. We're looking forward to growing with the Macon and Bibb County community and we will endeavor to be considered good corporate citizens."

The company's beautiful facility is located on over 34 acres on New Forsyth Road, just off Bass Road and close to I-75. ■

GE Capital Credit Services offers technology, efficiency, and economics of scale beyond the reach of virtually any single company or in-house operation.

GEORGIA FARM BUREAU

The Georgia Farm Bureau Federation is a non-profit service organization which represents its members in activities related to state and national legislation and commodity promotion. It also offers member services such as marketing, real estate, insurance, and the ability to purchase tires, batteries, and other goods at discount prices. Created by a small group of farmers in 1937, it is the state's largest farm organization, with over 260,000 member families. Georgia Farm Bureau is also affiliated with the American Farm Bureau Federation, comprised of over 4.4 million member families.

"The Georgia Farm Bureau is supported by its dues-paying membership and governed by a president and board of directors

As the state's largest general farm organization, the Georgia Farm Bureau Federation works for a better way of life for farmers and rural Georgians.

set by the membership. Farm Bureau lobbies for those issues born on the county level through a policy development process. Through the Farm Bureau, members have a powerful voice in local, state, and national affairs.

Farm Bureau members also have access to a complete range of competitively priced products and services, ranging from insurance, to commodity marketing, real estate, tax, financial and estate planning, and more.

The Georgia Farm Bureau Mutual Insurance Company was chartered in 1959 to provide needed insurance coverage to Farm Bureau members. It is now the largest domestic property and casualty insurer in Georgia. It is the third largest writer of automobile insurance, the third largest writer of homeowner coverage, and is first in farm owner coverage in the state. In 1993, it achieved ranking in "Ward's 50," which is comprised of the 50 top performing companies that have excelled at balancing safety, consistency, and performance. The Top 50 are chosen from among the more than 3,000 property and casualty companies in the United States. Insurance

coverage is also provided by the Georgia Farm Bureau Casualty Insurance Co. and Southern Farm Bureau Life Insurance Co.

who are elected by members of the federation," says Farm Bureau president, Wayne Dollar. "The farmers who created it almost 60 years ago saw a need to have input in the legislative process in Atlanta and Washington. They wanted their voices heard on legislation that would affect their lives and lives of their fellow Georgians," Dollar said. Later, economic services were added to ill member needs.

The Farm Bureau, which has an office in each county in the state, works for a better way of life for farmers and rural Georgians through a staff of full-time, registered lobbyists. It is truly a grassroots organization, since its governing policies are

Farm Bureau provides its members access to a team of tax and finance experts. The Farm Record Management department operates on a fee basis and provides a wide range of accounting services and filing of all state and federal income tax returns for clients.

The Georgia Farm Bureau Marketing Association provides members ready access to staff experts equipped to handle marketing of their farm commodities and livestock. Grain marketing, cattle marketing, and swine marketing are available.

The Marketing Association can also provide information relating to trend analysis, crop production, current local markets, supply and demand, and future pricing forecasts.

The Georgia Farm Bureau Commodities Department oversees State Commodity Advisory committees, composed of active producers of each major commodity grown in the state, who meet regularly to make recommendations to the Farm Bureau board of directors and staff. This helps Farm Bureau develop needed policy as it relates to each commodity.

The Georgia Farm Bureau Service Company sells tires, farm implements, filters, baler twine, fencing and posts, gates, fire extingushers, commodities, and other items throughout the state. Priced to save members money, the Service Company provides superior products and timely deliveries.

The Georgia Farm Bureau Real Estate Company provides a much needed service for rural Georgia: a statewide network for sales of rural and agricutural properties. While many real estate offices operate locally, Farm Bureau Real Estate operates collectively through branch offices on a statewide basis. The Forestry Division of the Farm Bureau's Real Estate company offers a statewide timber marketing service providing Georgia timber owners with professional forestry advice, a forestry plan, marketing expertise, assurance of highest price, protection from lost income and logging damage, and harvest supervision.

As the state's largest general farm organization, the Georgia Farm Bureau Federation seeks to represent and serve all of Georgia's argriculture industry. And a major industry it is.

According to a recent University of Georgia study, one in every six Georgians works in an argriculturally related sector of our economy. Georgia's agribusiness sector, or food and fiber industry, contributes $39.4 billion to our state's economic output. That's about 16 percent of Georgia's economic output. For comparison, that's larger than the contribution of the financial/real estate sector at $31.3 billion or the construction sector, at $20.3 billion.

Today's farmers are feeding twice as many people from the same amount of land as they did in 1960. The production of an average American farmer feeds about 128 people, 94 in the United States and 34 abroad. And we spend the least amount of money on food. Twelve percent of our disposable personal income is spent on food compared with Japan's 20 percent, Mexico's 37 percent, and India's 51 percent.

When you consider that Georgia has approximately 45,000 farms and 12.1 million acres of farm land, you can see that Georgia farmers are, in fact, helping to feed the world.

The Georgia Farm Bureau Federation and affiliates headquarters is located at 1620 Bass Road at Interstate 75 in Macon. The headquarters sits on 15 acres of land and has a square footage of 170,662. Approximately 500 employees work in the building; there are over 1,000 company employees statewide.

Today's farmers are feeding twice as many people from the same amount of land as they did in 1960.

The Georgia Farm Bureau facility was dedicated September 14, 1988. "We were one of the first major Macon businesses to come out here," says Dollar. "When the Farm Bureau moved to Macon in 1941, the assets of the company fit into the trunk of the president's car. Today, Farm Bureau consists of nine companies and a large number of employees. Starting with just a few farmers, the Georgia Farm Bureau Federation has grown into a large enterprise offering many advantages to many, many people." ■

FAIRFIELD FINANCIAL ASSOCIATES

Unassuming. He's the man in the business suit who walks past you on a downtown street, and you would never know the difference. He's the next door neighbor you see each day.

John W. Ramsey is the Clark Kent of Macon businessmen, and his company, Fairfield Financial, is the mortgage lending "superpower" in the Middle Georgia area.

This Macon native stepped into his hometown's business arena as early as 1968, but in 1985, on his return from Atlanta, he opened Fairfield Financial Corporation of Macon. In a typical, mild-mannered way, Ramsey has obtained consistent success through hard work, a keen marketing awareness, and dedicated service to his customers.

Referring to himself as a "committee of one," Ramsey and Fairfield Financial have been offering customers a faster, easier way of obtaining loans for 10 years. "The big advantage we've got over other lenders locally is that we can approve locally," Ramsey said. "That allows us to give the customer a little faster service. If I think we can make the loan work, I just make that decision immediately," Ramsey continues. "And if there's a problem with the loan's servicing, the customer knows where to find me."

Since graduating from the University of Georgia in 1965 with a bachelor's degree in finance and furthering his business knowledge with graduate work at the Columbia Business School in New York, Ramsey has known success in virtually every place he has worked.

He was hired by Macon's American Federal Savings and Loan Association in 1968 and within a year was the managing officer. At 30, he was president of the company. When Fulton Federal Savings and Loan bought American Federal in 1981, the new owners offered him a position. Ramsey rose from the chief of state branch operations to top mortgage lender and ultimately became senior vice president.

Ramsey was called to Atlanta in 1984 but the hustle and bustle of the Peach State's largest city wasn't for this Middle Georgia boy. In a daring move, he relinquished his lofty position with Fulton Federal and headed down I-75 south, toward home.

Not long after his return, Ramsey was introduced to Decatur Federal's Fairfield Financial network and "cold called" them. Within a month, he became a partner running its Macon mortgage loan office.

Fairfield grew quickly and expanded into eight South Georgia towns, Florida, and South Carolina. Ramsey's success landed him the 1990 Small Business Owner of the Year award presented by the Greater Macon Chamber of Commerce.

As captain of the Fairfield Financial ship, Ramsey was forced to take evasive action in 1992 and implement a new course in choppy waters. First Union Corporation bought out Decatur Federal and was not including Fairfield in its future plans. But Ramsey calmly made the adjustments needed and combined with Guaranty Bank from Milwaukee, Wisconsin.

Last January, Ramsey made another quiet move, promising big dividends for his company. He formed a partnership with Home Place, a home building company from Gainesville, Georgia. Now he has 23 offices in 6 states.

Even with the presence of his company being felt from North Carolina to Alabama, John Ramsey hasn't changed his tactics. He still relies on hard work and the principle of the customer coming first. Now it can be assumed that he and Fairfield Financial are one of the most prominent and profitable businesses in Middle Georgia and the Southeast. In keeping with his expanded trade area, Ramsey has changed the legal name to GROUP FINANCIAL SOUTHEAST. ■

Ramsey has obtained consistent success through hard work, a keen marketing awareness, and dedicated service to his customers. Photography by Ken Krakow.

Fairfield Financial is one of the most prominent and profitable businesses in Middle Georgia and the Southeast. Photography by Ken Krakow.

CIGNA Property & Casualty

Formerly the Insurance Company of North America (INA), CIGNA Insurance Company made its debut in Macon in the late 1940s as the Southeastern United States processing center. In the middle 1950s, INA built the facility which now houses Mercer University's Walter F. Georgia School of Law, at the top of Coleman Hill on Georgia Avenue. The building is a replica of Independence Hall in Philadelphia, Pennsylvania, the home of CIGNA's corporate headquarters.

INA continued to grow in the Macon area as a large underwriting and processing center for the Southeastern United States and the company continued to occupy the building until 1977, when they sold it to the City of Macon, which in turn sold it to Mercer University. At that time, the staff, which numbered approximately 300 men and women, moved into the multiple floor facility which is now the Liberty Bank Building at the corner of Walnut and Second streets. At this time, the company took on additional corporate responsibilities as one of three INA personal lines centers in the United States.

The company remained in the Liberty Bank Building until 1988, but in the interim, in 1981, it became, through a merger with Connecticut General Insurance Co., CIGNA Insurance Company. In 1988, CIGNA built its current location at 3920 Arkwright Road and moved into its new, modern facility with a staff of approximately 450 people.

"Through the years," says L. Ronald Peters, a senior vice-president of CIGNA, "CIGNA's staff has been very active in community affairs. One of the major activities we currently support is the conducting of four large blood drives a year for the American Red Cross. We are also a major participant in the American Cancer Society's 24-Hour Relay for Life. We're an active sponsor of the Museum of Aviation in Warner Robins efforts to educate the youth of Georgia and we also support *The Macon Telegraph* and Bibb County's Schools Newspaper in Education Program, as well as being involved in numerous other community activities."

In 1990 the CIGNA Insurance Company staff took on an entirely new role in the corporation. This new role consists of underwriting and servicing workers' compensation and commercial auto assigned risks policies for the entire United States. They currently employ about 350 people in their spacious facility on Arkwright Road.

One of Macon and Bibb County's largest office buildings, the approximately 185,000 square-foot, 4-floor facility also houses 11 other tenants. CIGNA occupies half the second and third floors and all the fourth floor.

CIGNA built its current location at 3920 Arkwright Road in 1988. The grounds and the building have both won numerous architectural and appearance awards and continues, along with the staff it houses, to highlight CIGNA's corporate citizenry.

"The physical structure," says Peters, "adds to the beauty of the Macon community. The grounds and the building have both won numerous architectural and appearance awards and continues, along with the staff it houses, to highlight CIGNA's corporate citizenry. Arkwright Associates, the building management firm, deserves accolades for their efforts ensuring the appearance of the facility."

In addition to the daily business activities of the entities located in the CIGNA building, there's a substantial amount of activity from local students attending the Macon campus of Georgia College in Milledgeville. Fort Valley State College in Fort Valley also holds night classes in the building. ■

TRUST COMPANY BANK OF MIDDLE GEORGIA

More than 100 years ago, a new bank opened its doors in the heart of downtown Macon, promising a firm commitment to financial stability, community involvement, and concern for its customers.

As the oldest bank in Macon, and with the second largest trust department in the state outside of Atlanta, Trust Company Bank has 11 branches in Macon. Photo by Horace Holmes Photography Studio.

Now known as Trust Company Bank of Middle Georgia, a continuing pledge to those same business ideas—coupled with a strong tradition of banking experience—will lead the bank into a new century of progress.

Chartered as Continental Trust Company Bank in downtown Macon in December 1890, the bank merged with Macon National Bank in 1930 to become what was then known as The First National Bank and Trust Company in Macon. After 51 years, the bank's name changed in 1981 to Trust Company Bank.

As the oldest bank in Macon, and with the second largest trust department in the state outside of Atlanta, Trust Company Bank boasts 11 branches in Macon, 3 in nearby Warner Robins, and 1 in Perry. Among other services—including numerous conveniently located ATM machines—the full-service bank offers special account services for senior citizens, investment services, and a leasing department to assist customers with new car purchases.

Additionally, Trust Company offers the new VISA debit card, used much like a credit card but with one important difference—purchases are not billed to the customer, but deducted from the cardholder's checking account at no additional fee.

The bank's president, John B. Frank, took over as President and Chief Executive Officer of Trust Company in April 1994. A second-generation banker, he brought to the company nearly 30 years of banking experience. A former Gwinnet county commissioner, Frank also has been an active member of various communities around Georgia where he and his family have lived.

As strong community advocates, Trust Company Bank's president, officers, and employees support numerous volunteer efforts within Middle Georgia. In addition to monetary support, employees participate and become active leaders in such charity organizations and civic endeavors as The American Heart Association, United Way, the Family Counseling Center, and the Greater Macon Chamber of Commerce. In addition, Trust Company has adopted the historic Fort Hill neighborhood on Macon's east side, where the bank will assist in redevelopment efforts and the building of new homes.

The fall of 1995 will bring a visible change to Trust Company Bank, when it and all of its subsidiaries will change their name to SunTrust Bank to reflect the name of its holding company, SunTrust Banks, Inc. Services in Macon will remain the same after the change, and the holding company's policy of a localized decision-making process will not be affected. The name change, however, will allow customers to more easily identify a SunTrust Bank wherever they travel in Georgia, Florida, Tennessee, and Alabama.

SunTrust Banks, Inc., is an Atlanta-based super-regional bank holding company with assets of more than $42 billion, ranking it among the nation's top 25 financial institutions. The company's 650 offices in 4 states provide a wide range of personal, corporate, and institutional financial services.

Stability and longevity have been the hallmarks of Trust Company Bank throughout its rich banking history. Since establishing its presence 105 years ago in Macon, the bank has relied upon its customers for success, and its customers have depended upon the bank for its dependable financial services and strong community presence.

With longtime employees and longtime customers, Trust Company Bank lives up to its motto of "Trust Company Bank Will Suit You to a T." ■

Stability and longevity have been the hallmarks of Trust Company Bank throughout its rich banking history. Photo by Horace Holmes Photography Studio.

Smith, Brown & Groover, Inc.

Smith, Brown & Groover, Inc., is the oldest and largest broker/dealer in the Middle Georgia area. First known as Brown & Groover, Inc., the company was formed by James F. Brown and T. Denmark Groover in 1933—the same year that the Glass-Steagal Act, separating banking from brokerage, was passed and implemented.

Company chairman Raymond H. Smith was once the largest shareholder in the old Clisby & Co. brokerage house. When Brown & Groover, Inc., was for sale in 1967, Smith sold his shares in Clisby & Co. to purchase it. The corporate name was eventually changed to Smith, Brown & Groover, Inc.

The elder Smith's son, Raymond H. Smith, Jr., now president, bought the company from his father in 1993 after having served for several years as vice president—and after having spent four years on Wall Street as an investment banker.

The younger Smith says that one of the primary components that makes Smith, Brown & Groover different from other broker/dealers is in the products that they do *not* handle.

"The difference is very important, too," Smith explains. "We have never offered limited partnerships and we don't trade future contracts or stock options," he continues. "Frankly, we have a history of turning down products that aren't in the best interest of the public."

"One of the most noticeable things that we feel really separates our firm from other broker/dealers is that we have never had a complaint filed with the SEC or NASD—and we've never had a lawsuit filed against us," Smith states proudly.

What they *do* handle is impressive, though. Smith, Brown & Groover manages mutual funds, common stocks, deferred annuities, tax free bonds, estate planning, life insurance, and health insurance. Moreover, they provide their clients with the products and information necessary to solve financial problems. In essence, they focus on making people money.

"We concentrate upon long-term growth with minimal trading activity," Smith explains. "This simply allows for minimal taxation during the holding period."

Previously located in the Southern Trust Building in historic downtown Macon for over 50 years, the elder Smith moved the company to a facility on Riverside Drive before relocating in 1991 to the current site. An attractive picturesque setting, the office is now located at 3496 Vineville Avenue in a former bank building. Over 1,000 square feet of additional office space, including a spacious conference room, was added to the structure in 1993.

"It truly is a superb location and we've been extraordinarily pleased here," Smith adds.

Significant growth has been achieved over the past decade. Currently, Smith, Brown & Groover manages over $200 million and handles fee-based and discretionary management accounts for all financial portfolios with a minimum of $1 million. However, Smith is quick to point out that the firm does not have a minimum account size for regular accounts. "We will help anyone that desires our assistance, that's our job," Smith states. It is not surprising that the firm's client base extends throughout Georgia, as well as in a number of other states, too.

Present licensed brokers at the firm include Raymond H. Smith; Raymond H. Smith, Jr.; Kathleen V. Smith; Dr. Joyce R. Shafer; Richard C. Keil; and Gerald Train.

"Unlike other broker/dealers, our company's representatives are triple licensed in securities, life and health insurance, and variable annuities," Smith says. "We work hard to give our staff the skills that are necessary to assist our clients in virtually any financial situation." ■

The staff of Smith, Brown & Groover, Inc.

President Raymond H. Smith, Jr. (standing) with his father, Raymond H. Smith, Sr. (seated). Photography by April Faith Copeland/Perdue Design Group.

NATIONSBANK

NationsBank has always been a leader in the banking industry and through insight, strong leadership, and a commitment to caring for their customers' needs they will continue to lead well into the next century.

NationsBank established itself on the corner of Third Street and Cherry in 1916, and the familiar red and blue name still proudly shines from the same corner. Photography by Ken Krakow.

NationsBank, formerly known as The Citizens and Southern National Bank, established itself on the corner of Third Street and Cherry in 1916, and the familiar red and blue name still proudly shines from the same corner. Rebuilding after a fire in 1932, construction of a larger building in 1967, and a $1 million renovation of the first floor in 1993 shows NationsBank's pride in downtown and their commitment to servicing the community by creating a bank that meets every individual's needs.

Through the introduction of a new delivery system, NationsBank offers their customers banking centers with "one-stop service." This state-of-the-art service allows busy customers the opportunity to conduct all aspects of their business, from opening an account to obtaining a loan, from one location and one associate.

Being the third largest banking company in the United States and the largest banking company in the Southeast, Southwest, and Mid-Atlantic regions with over $169 billion in assets doesn't keep NationsBank from being small enough to listen to their customers. Through customer-focus groups they succeed in staying one step ahead of the needs of their community, offering them fast, friendly, efficient, and accurate service.

NationsBank also provides commercial banking services to Middle Georgia companies with a commercial banking department that focuses on companies with revenues greater than $4 million and a small business banking department serving customers with revenues less than that amount.

Outside of the normal services offered by financial institutions, special services available through NationsBank include NationsCredit, cash management services, trusts, and investments.

In addition to caring for their customers' needs, community involvement is extremely important to the officers and employees at NationsBank. Whether it be repairing and rebuilding homes through the Christmas in April program, participating in March of Dimes fundraisers, being a part of the civic organizations in Macon, or sponsoring events during the annual Cherry Blossom Festival, NationsBank is a visible force within Middle Georgia. But they don't stop there. Following the decision to hold the 1996 Olympic Games in Atlanta, NationsBank, standing on its reputation of integrity and strength, was named by the Atlanta Committee of the Olympic Games to be the first corporate partner for the games. This agreement made NationsBank the official bank partner of the 1996 Olympics.

NationsBank's geographic presence extends to 9 states with over 2,100 banking centers throughout the Southeast. 177 full-service banking centers are in Georgia, with 11 of those in Macon and Warner Robins. Saturday drive-in banking is also available in Macon at the Westgate and Macon Mall locations and in Warner Robins at the Russell Parkway site and at North Highlands.

Regardless of their growth and technological advancement, NationsBank is fully aware of their most valuable asset—their customers. Keeping that in mind, they will continue to achieve excellence through understanding and fulfilling their customers' needs. ∎

Special services available through NationsBank include NationsCredit, cash management services, trusts, and investments. Photography by Ken Krakow

PROFESSIONS

Photography by Ken Krakow.

TRIBBLE & RICHARDSON, INC.

When Tribble & Richardson, Inc. was founded 25 years ago, the then small engineering company specialized in water and wastewater system design. Since that time, the company has greatly expanded its services and its staff to meet the ever-growing engineering challenges of the 1990s and of its clients.

Elmo Richardson, Jr., P.E., President of Tribble & Richardson.

"Throughout our 25-year history, we have maintained an environmental consciousness in providing design and engineering consulting services," said Elmo A. Richardson, Jr., P.E., president of Tribble & Richardson. "I feel that our mission to 'provide excellence in professional services to enhance the quality of life and protect the public welfare' is at the core of our success and longevity. We will continue to maintain careful attention to environmental protection, a person-to-person approach with our clients, and a philosophy of quality and timely service."

Tribble & Richardson was founded on February 1, 1970, by Elmo A. Richardson, Jr., and Hiram L. Tribble, Sr., and began operations in a small building on Ingleside Avenue with a staff of 6. In 1975, with 25 employees, the company moved to a new, 4,800-square-foot building on Pierce Avenue. In 1986, it moved to its current location, a 41,000-square-foot, breathtaking reflective glass office building at 4875 Riverside Drive.

Tribble & Richardson provides professional consulting services in the areas of environmental management, solid waste management, sanitary engineering, and general civil engineering and design to a broad range of clients. The company has the experience to design and implement a varied assortment of projects—small or large—industrial, commercial, residential, or civic development. A leader in environmental engineering, it has the ability to design, improve, or extend all aspects of a water-management system, from a single plumbing flow to distribution for an entire metropolitan area.

"We work primarily throughout the Southeast, providing civil, sanitary, and environmental engineering for local, state, and federal governments," said Richardson, "with most of our work being centered around city and county governments. We provide consulting and design services, water systems, water treatment facilities, water resources and sewerage systems, including sewers and treatment facilities."

Infrastructure planning is vitally important to maintain an adequate supply of potable water and adequate wastewater treatment capacity to satisfy the ever-expanding demands of the community. Tribble & Richardson's engineers are experienced in applying computer modeling techniques to project future demands and design water distribution and sewage collection systems.

"We also design roads and bridges, and we're involved in a number of road projects," Richardson said. "We're involved with Macon and Bibb County in the design of road and street improvements under the sales tax program."

In 1994, the company completed the planning, design, and construction of Town Creek Reservoir—a 640-acre water supply project—for the Macon Water Authority and a composting project for the City of Brunswick. The composting project is the state's first totally enclosed, agitated bed, municipal sludge and yard waste composting facility. The plant is a model for other Georgia communities looking for alternatives to landfill disposal for their municipal sludge and yard waste, and for this project, Tribble & Richardson received the Consulting Engineers Council of Georgia's 1995 Engineering Excellence Award. They are also currently designing a significant part of the relocation of Macon's water treatment plant project.

Tribble & Richardson is involved in numerous solid waste projects throughout the Southeast, including the construction of a solid waste co-composting facility for Cobb County.

The company has provided engineering services on more than 300 solid waste projects ranging from recycling studies to sanitary landfill design. These facilities varied in size, some receiving as little as 30 tons of waste per day to those receiving over 1,400 tons of waste per day. From 1989 to 1995, of the 42 authorized synthetically lined landfills in Georgia, Tribble & Richardson was responsible for the design of 14 of these landfills.

Over the years, this engineering firm has concentrated on working with local governments to plan and maintain suitable infrastructures, and its well-rounded staff of engineers and environmental professionals allows the company to provide total planning and design services to its clients. "We've been involved in the design and construction of major infrastructure improvements in the Macon and Bibb County area," said Richardson. "We've assisted local governments by providing them with design consulting services for various improvements."

Tribble & Richardson's broad range of services in the planning, design, and construction of transportation facilities include transportation planning, environmental impact statements, field surveys, utility relocation, roadway design, bridge design, construction observation, and intersection improvements. Successful projects are a direct result of the dedication of quality professionals in combination with the latest state-of-the-art production tools. The company's in-house computer capability includes computer-aided design and drafting (CADD) and the firm has 26 AUTOCAD systems used extensively in various types of design projects.

In 1989, in order to better serve clients throughout the Southeast, Tribble & Richardson established a branch office in Nashville, Tennessee. In 1993, the firm was instrumental in the development of Mercer University's School of Environmental Engineering. Members of Tribble & Richardson's staff often teach engineering related courses and have a close working relationship with professors there.

"We think we're very fortunate to have been a part of major developments in this area over the past 25 years," said Richardson. "I'm very excited about the future of this area and I have great expectations for the next 25 years. Changes in our world are visible, but our history attests that the need for quality and timely service to the client endures."

Richardson's firm and its staff are actively involved in various civic and community activities. They support the Museum of Arts & Sciences and the Greater Macon Chamber of Commerce and serve on the boards of various organizations. "We encourage participation in our professional and community activities. The community has given a lot to us, and we're trying to return this the best we can. We've been very active not only in local organizations, but also in state and national organizations."

Elmo A. Richardson, Jr., has served as Chairman of the Board of the Greater Macon Chamber of Commerce and serves as an Advisory Board member of the Georgia Environmental Facilities Authority. He has also served as past president of the Consulting Engineers Council of Georgia and president of the Museum of Arts & Sciences. A graduate of the Georgia Institute of Technology, Richardson is a registered Civil Engineer and Land Surveyor. With over 35 years of experience in all phases of civil, environmental, and sanitary engineering, he has been involved with the planning and design of water resource projects throughout the Southeast.

His company's history demonstrates its commitment to being accountable for long-term success of projects and they rely heavily on repeat business from satisfied customers. "Hiram Tribble and I . . . felt that our staff should be number one and should always be treated fairly. Our firm has retained these basic philosophies through the years." ■

Tribble & Richardson is a leader in environmental engineering.

CHRISTOPHER N. SMITH, ATTORNEY AT LAW

Christopher N. Smith maintains a general law practice with special emphasis placed on civil litigation, business law, personal injury, debt collection, and the preparation of wills. His offices are located at 3333 Northside Drive, Suite E.

A native of Middle Georgia, Smith was born in Macon and raised in Houston County, where he graduated from Warner Robins High School. A graduate of the University of Georgia, he holds a Bachelor of Business Administration degree with an emphasis in Marketing. Smith received his Juris Doctor from Mercer University's Walter F. George School of Law and has practiced in Macon since 1991.

He is admitted to practice law before the Court of Appeals of Georgia, the Supreme Court of Georgia, and the United States District Court for the Middle District of Georgia. Smith is a member of the State Bar of Georgia and the Macon Bar Association.

An interest in business law comes naturally for Smith, who at a young age began working in his family's automobile dealerships. Prior to attending law school, Smith served as vice president of Bob Lee Hyundai, Inc. As an attorney, he now represents small, medium, and large businesses, with whom he can empathize based on his own business experiences. In addition to the clients from Georgia, Smith represents international clients from such diverse places as the United Kingdom, R.S.A., and Bulgaria. He is a member of the International Law Section of the State Bar of Georgia.

Smith also pursues an interest in real estate development.

In an effort to conveniently serve a growing community, Smith chose to establish his practice on the north side of town. Several new businesses and residential developments are located in the area. The Arkwright Road exit off I-75 provides easy access for clients from Monroe, Jones, Houston, Peach, and Twiggs Counties, as well as metro Macon. Smith's practice, however, is not restricted to

Christopher Smith is excited and optimistic about the future and looks forward to playing a role in the area's development. Photo by Horace Holmes Photography Studio.

a particular geographic area; his clients and court appearances are spread throughout the state.

Smith is excited and optimistic about the future and looks forward to playing a role in the area's development. He enjoys practicing law in Macon and is pleased to provide services to businesses and individuals in such a dynamic region. ∎

(left to right) Abrie Bester, President of The Executive Group, R.S.A.; Lynn F. Sharpe, Legal Assistant; Christopher N. Smith. Photo by Horace Holmes Photography Studio.

Christopher N. Smith has given value for this communication.

CLIFTON, LIPFORD & TAYLOR, P.C.

Clifton, Lipford & Taylor, P.C. stands out as a leader in accounting firms in Central Georgia. The 50-year-old firm has built its reputation on providing a unique combination of services with emphasis on personal attention to its clients.

The firm serves a wide variety of clients in Macon and the surrounding area, with particular expertise in timber, mining, health care, lodging, hospitality, and government. Individual clients and businesses look to Clifton, Lipford & Taylor for tax services, auditing and accounting, management advisory services, and computer systems design and consulting. The company also offers financial planning advice, ownership transition planning, and other business services.

Located in its own 8,500 square-foot facility on Riverside Drive, Clifton, Lipford & Taylor currently employs 25 people. Four shareholders own the firm, which is managed through a president and management committee.

Clifton, Lipford & Taylor shareholders: (seated L to R) J. Russell Lipford, Jr., James O. Taylor, (standing L to R) Mark O. Hardison, Terry I. Parker. Photography by Horace Holmes Photography Studio.

The firm's tax department offers a variety of services to both personal and business clients that include tax preparation for corporations, partnerships, estates and trusts, retirement plans, and nonprofit entities. The department also works very closely with these clients in planning the tax aspects of proposed transactions and in their representation before the various taxing authorities.

The audit department provides services to a wide variety of private companies, nonprofits, and governmental entities. Services provided include audits, reviews, compilations, and other specialized engagements.

Governmental and nonprofit auditing and accounting have changed considerably during the last 10 years. Clifton, Lipford & Taylor has been on the forefront of this change and has developed a thorough understanding of the accounting and auditing problems of the governmental sector. The firm has assisted Bibb County and the City of Macon in obtaining the prestigious Certificate of Excellence Award from the Government Finance Officers Association for 12 fiscal years each.

The management advisory services department offers operational consulting and audits, systems reviews, assistance with special projects, litigation support, and financial planning for personal and business financial goals. One of the innovative services provided by Clifton, Lipford & Taylor is offered through its Systems Group, composed of a team of consulting professionals dedicated to assisting businesses with their computer systems. The group provides evaluation and selection services, advice about multi-user computer systems, installation and training for a number of accounting systems, recommendations for expansion and enhancements to in-place systems, and special services. The firm also has memberships in the AICPA Information Technology Section as well as the AICPA Management Consulting Services Division.

Clifton, Lipford & Taylor is committed to providing the best service and the latest in accounting information for its clients. It maintains a large tax and accounting library now utilizing the latest CD-ROM technology. The firm's CPAs and professionals frequently attend workshops and professional meetings to stay up-to-date on new developments in all areas of the practice.

Shareholders have recently developed a mission statement to lead Clifton, Lipford & Taylor into the second 50 years. The statement is as follows: "To continue to be a leading reputable firm, through both community and professional activities, providing quality (professional, competent, dependable, thorough, personal attention) services that help our clients grow and become more profitable while providing, to the members of the firm, a good stable standard of living and challenging professional work. Clifton, Lipford & Taylor will strive to enhance the entrepreneurial instinct throughout the entire organization, as well as position itself for the future through the exposure and expansion of its consulting expertise." ∎

McNair, McLemore, Middlebrooks & Co.

McNair, McLemore, Middlebrooks & Co. is distinguished as one of the preeminent accounting firms in Middle Georgia. As the region's largest local CPA firm, the 55-year old firm has built its reputation by offering a unique and comprehensive blend of services coupled with emphasis on personalized client attention.

Located at 389 Mulberry Street in Macon and at 1117 Morningside Drive in Perry, the firm has 14 partners, ranging in age from 52 to 33, and employs approximately 80 people. The diverse and varied professional strengths of the partners and professional staff supply the expertise necessary to provide a full range of accounting, tax, and financial services to a broad group of clients.

The firm serves a wide variety of clients located primarily in Georgia, South Carolina, Florida, and Tennessee with concentrated professional expertise in health care (including hospitals, nursing homes, and private physicians), banking, electric and telephone cooperatives, manufacturing, retail, insurance, and real estate development. Individuals as well as businesses rely on McNair, McLemore, Middlebrooks & Co. for auditing and accounting, tax services, and management advisory services. The firm also offers financial planning, business valuation, merger and acquisition consultation, litigation support, and other business and tax services.

The philosophy of McNair, McLemore, Middlebrooks & Co. is to provide its clients with the best personalized service possible. In the execution of this philosophy, the firm emphasizes the matching of its strengths with the needs of its clients. To achieve this goal, the firm is organized by departmental function, as follows: Audit and Accounting Department; and Tax and Private Business Department.

The Audit and Accounting Department provides attestation services to private and public companies as well as governmental organizations, including audits and reviews. A growing segment of the Audit and Accounting Department is management advisory and consulting services. The scope of each engagement is determined by the client's unique situation. These services generally fall into one of the following categories: information systems services; financial management; operations improvement; and, human resources management. The firm also provides consultation on internal controls and other business practices.

The Tax and Private Business Department works closely with business clients and individuals (as well as with the Audit Department) to develop appropriate tax planning strategies. This range of consulting services includes tax planning for all forms of business (corporations, S corporations, partnerships, and limited liability companies), as well as individual income tax and estate and gift planning. The firm's tax compliance services

include the preparation and review of all required tax filings, ranging from income tax and property tax returns to profit sharing reports and estate and gift tax returns. The firm also has extensive expertise in the area of tax controversy and routinely represents individual and corporate clients before the Internal Revenue

McNair, McLemore, Middlebrooks & Co. has 14 partners, ranging in age from 52 to 33.

Service at both the local and appeals levels. In addition, the firm offers a full range of computerized bookkeeping services, including general ledger, payroll, accounts receivable, inventory, billing, and special projects.

McNair, McLemore, Middlebrooks & Co. is committed to providing the best service and the most current accounting and tax advice to its clients. To ensure its partners and professional staff remain abreast of current developments, the firm requires each of its partners and professionals to obtain a minimum of 40 hours per year in continuing professional education. This educational requirement is generally met by attendance at seminars and professional meetings related to the individual's industry and/or functional area of specialization. The firm also maintains an extensive library which provides the necessary resources to provide clients with accurate, up-to-date advice.

McNair, McLemore, Middlebrooks & Co. is large enough to meet the needs of its clients, yet small enough to deliver responsive professional services. Personal attention and enduring client relationships have made the firm a leader among Georgia accounting firms. ■

The Center of Georgia

BUILDING GREATER MACON

Photography by Ken Krakow.

OCMULGEE FIELDS, INC.

Ocmulgee Fields, Inc., which is primarily involved in hotel/motel operations, also has numerous lease properties, including a number of major shopping centers. Most of the company's interests are located in Macon.

Ocmulgee Fields evolved from Charles H. Jones Enterprises and got its name from Jones' interest in the Creek Indians and their lives in this area hundreds of years ago. Some of the Creeks survived the terrible exile to a reservation in Oklahoma in the 1830s, along the infamous Trail of Tears; a number of their ancestors returned to

The Corporate office of Ocmulgee Fields, Inc., is located in a beautiful facility on Holiday North Drive in North Macon.

Macon in the early 1970s, partly to promote the Ocmulgee National Park in Macon as a tourist attraction, with the presence of the Indians and their exhibitions and other activities.

"In order to promote this project, Dad and several community leaders went to Oklahoma and convinced a number of the Creeks' descendants to come here where their heritage had been," Jeff Jones said. Ocmulgee Fields' name evolved from this interest that his father had in the Creeks and from the fact that the area around the Ocmulgee River in Macon was called Ocmulgee Fields.

The Macon Conference Center can host such events as conventions, proms, and weddings.

Charles H. Jones, who is chairman of Ocmulgee Fields, is currently serving a seven-year term on the Board of Regents of the University System of Georgia. A native of Thomaston and a graduate of the University of Georgia, Jones has been actively involved in many community and civic affairs. He has served as chairman of the Macon-Bibb County Hospital Authority and of the Macon-Bibb County Industrial Authority, and has been a member of the Board of Directors of Citizens & Southern National Bank and Family Federal Savings & Loan Association.

Charles H. Jones' many other activities in this community include serving as a member of the Board of Trustees of Mercer University and as a member of the Macon Economic Development Commission. He is an honorary member and honorary chief of the Creek Indian Nation (Tribe), Okmulgee, Oklahoma.

Ocmulgee Fields, Inc., is located in a beautiful facility on Holiday North Drive in North Macon. "Until we built this building, we never had a custom corporate office; instead, we had occupied some of our own speculative space. We've had an explosive growth since 1985 and as our company has grown, so has our staff. It came to the point that we had to consolidate our departments, including our corporate staff, our accounts receivable and accounts payable departments, and our maintenance department. We built this building so that we could have the facilities to have corporate control over our properties," said Jeff Jones.

In 1992 Ocmulgee Fields moved to its present location, in close proximity to two of its motels (the Holiday Inn and the Hampton Inn) on Riverside Drive and just around the corner from one of its prime business ventures, Rivergate Shopping Center on Tom Hill Boulevard. "With most of our newest assets being out here and with almost half of our employees being at the Holiday Inn and the Hampton Inn, we decided this is where we needed to be," Jones said. "The decision to come here has been extremely beneficial—both in economics and in the communications throughout our company, and the fact that we're now the center of the activity of our company, whose properties run from Middle Georgia to the Central Florida area. It's given us a presence among our employees. We came here to consolidate and to be more of a corporate support than we could in the past."

Ocmulgee Fields has a total employment of approximately 425 people, with over 40 of these being on staff in the corporate office supporting field activities. Their building has 8,000 square feet of office space upstairs, and 8,000 square feet downstairs used for maintenance and material warehouse and purchasing.

Jones said that he and his family are committed to a quality of life in Macon through their efforts in business and through community and state-wide involvement. "My dad; my brother, Dwight, who is Executive Vice President of the company; and I complement each other in the way we deal with local and state affairs we're involved in." Jeff Jones and his father are one of only two father-son pairs who have served on the Macon-Bibb County Industrial Authority since its inception; they served on the authority 20 years apart.

Ocmulgee Fields owner/development motel industry includes the following: Holiday Inn, Riverside Drive, and New Smyrna Beach, Florida; Hampton Inn, Riverside Drive, and Perry, Georgia; Inn Ambassador, Riverside Drive, Hartley Bridge Road, and Forsyth, Georgia; and Holiday Inn Express, Riverside Drive.

Located on 15 acres of property which formerly belonged to the Moose Club, the Holiday Inn at Riverside Drive and I-75 is a full-service hotel featuring 200 guest rooms with many amenities.

The Macon Conference Center, with approximately 25,000 square feet of space, can accommodate 1,000 people for sit-down dinners, has a full service kitchen, and hosts such events as conventions, proms, and weddings. In keeping with Macon's history as well as

The United States Government Office of Personnel Management houses the largest computer center in the Southeast, where all of the W-2 Forms are processed, even for the President.

Inn, is a limited service facility that meets the demands of today's business and leisure traveller.

The company's leasing assets include numerous restaurants— Applebee's, Hardee's, and the Food Court on Tom Hill, Sr. Boulevard, and Wendy's on Riverside Drive.

Ocmulgee Fields also owns Riverside Plaza Shopping Center, Rivergate Shopping Center, South Macon Shopping Center, Baconsfield Shopping Center, Wesleyan Station Shopping Center, Government Square Shopping Center, Baconsfield Piggly Wiggly Shopping Center, the Civil Service Building on Eisenhower Parkway, and other facilities.

Rivergate Shopping Center houses Regal Rivergate Cinema 14, which Jeff Jones says "is probably the largest theater center in Georgia," and the new Barnes and Noble Book Store opening in the fall of 1995. "This 22,000-square-foot, free-standing store," said Jones, "is a forerunner in the upper scale `book store/coffee shop' concept."

Jeff Jones has served on the Macon-Bibb County Industrial Authority, is a charter member of the Downtown Rotary Club, the Gridiron Secret Society— University of Georgia, past member of Leadership Macon, and has served as chairman of Governor Zell Miller's re-election campaign for the Middle Georgia area in 1994.

Dwight Jones, executive vice president of Ocmulgee Fields, is involved in Leadership Macon; a member of the board of directors of the Museum of Arts and Sciences, serves on the executive committee of the Macon-Bibb Convention and Visitors Bureau, and is a member of the Macon Sports Commission. ■

The Holiday Inn at Riverside Drive and I-75 is a full-service hotel featuring 200 guest rooms with many amenities.

Charlie Jones' interest in the Creek Indians, the meeting rooms of the center have varied Indian names such as the McIntosh Room and Treaty Hall.

The 150-room Hampton Inn, across the street from the Holiday

REEVES CONSTRUCTION COMPANY

Reeves Construction Company, the largest asphalt producer in the state of Georgia, is headquartered in Americus, Georgia. Other locations include Macon, Albany, Tifton, Dublin, Mount Vernon, Statesboro, and Millen. The Macon Division asphalt locations are in Monroe County and Jones County.

The company was founded in 1948 in Americus by two brothers, C.E. Reeves and Jake Reeves. C.E. Reeves' sons, Charles Reeves and Roy D. Reeves, later took over operations, with Charles serving as president and Roy serving as vice president. They held these positions until the company was sold in 1984, the company president is now Roger Dill. It is now owned by Hanson PLC of England, but Reeves corporate office is still located in Americus.

"Although we had been working in the Macon area in the early and middle 80s," says Chuck Reeves, Division Manager of Reeves Construction, "we really moved permanently into the Macon market in 1987 by buying an established business and expanding our work."

The company is involved primarily in clearing, drainage systems, miscellaneous concrete work, grading, base, and asphalt paving.

The Macon office, located at 2500 Gray Highway, handles projects within a 60-mile radius and maintains an employment force of approximately 120 people. The company's total employment

Work includes sections of the Fall Line Freeway, the Golden Isle Parkway, and the largest Department of Transportation project outside the Atlanta metropolitan area.

Parkway, and the largest Department of Transportation project outside the Atlanta metropolitan area. Some of the jobs in the Middle Georgia area include site work at the First Union Bank, Ryan's Family Steakhouse, Applebee's restaurant, the Culver Kidd Hospital, schools in Bibb, Peach, and Houston counties, and a number of shopping centers.

A large portion of the company's work in 1994 involved flood relief projects. Their crews worked 24-hour shifts for several weeks following the flood, and were still working on flood-related projects eight months later.

"We are very competitively priced and we place high emphasis on quality," says Chuck Reeves. "We are committed to the Middle Georgia area and our employees are involved in and represented in a number of local civic clubs, country clubs, and churches." They have also participated in many charity events involved in fund-raisers for such deserving organizations as the Children's Hospital at the Medical Center of Central Georgia, ARC (Association for Retarded Citizens), the Georgia Sports Hall of Fame, and Hospice, among others. The company is also a member of the Greater Macon Chamber of Commerce and the Better Business Bureau of Georgia.

"Our company employs highly qualified people," Reeves says, "and we were honored to be the feature story in *Dixie Contractors*, a magazine which features companies such as ours in the Southeastern region of the United States. We look forward to the future and to expanding with the Macon and Middle Georgia areas, as well as with other areas in the state." ■

Reeves Construction Company is involved primarily in clearing, drainage systems, miscellaneous concrete work, grading, base, and asphalt paving.

of approximately 490 people handles projects covering an area that includes over 50 percent of the state.

Chuck Reeves says that a large percentage of the work done by the company is in the commercial and private sectors. Work includes sections of the Fall Line Freeway, the Golden Isle

AMERSON CONSTRUCTION COMPANY

A glimpse nearly anywhere around the mid-state offers proof positive that over the years, the three-generation Amerson Construction Company has made a significant contribution to Macon and Middle Georgia.

From large historical renovations to construction of smaller building additions, projects completed by Amerson Construction affirm the continuing tradition of quality and excellence by the Amerson family for nearly 80 years.

Headquartered at 3184 Mercer University Drive, the company specializes in commercial, institutional, and industrial construction. A general contracting firm, Amerson handles competitive bid projects, negotiated contracts, design-build projects and historical renovations.

Recent projects include the $1.8 million construction and renovation of the Museum of Arts and Sciences on Forsyth Road. The 3-story project features 15,000 square feet in new construction, plus renovation of 10,000 square feet of the existing facility.

For F. Carl Amerson III, president of Amerson Construction, a self-appraisal of his successful contracting company proves modest. Over the past eight decades, the company has earned a reputation for executing their construction and renovation jobs in an efficient manner and with quality work. Now the only Amerson involved in the family business, the company president carries on the legacy created by his grandfather, Frank C. Amerson, Sr., since 1917.

A graduate of Mercer University, Carl Amerson began working for his father, Frank C. Amerson, Jr., at age 13, then later joined the company full time. He formed his own construction company, F. Carl Amerson III, in 1981, then in 1992, merged with Amerson Construction Company.

A major structural renovation project of the Bibb County Courthouse required gutting the entire fifth floor jail. A marble staircase was extended from the fourth to the fifth floor to reach the newly constructed offices and courtrooms.

Among the building and renovation projects completed over the years by the Amerson Construction family are the Charter Medical Building, the impressive Sports Medicine Center on Forsyth Street, Jones County High School in Gray, NationsBank, Robins Federal Credit Union, The Galleria in downtown Macon, a HUD project for the city of Macon, the Warner Robins Post Office, Northwest Common Shopping Center, and numerous Amoco stations.

Renovation of the Bibb County Courthouse proved to be a particularly involved and challenging project. A massive marble staircase was extended from the fourth to the fifth floors, and the old fifth-floor jail was converted to office and courtroom space. As construction progressed upstairs, county and court business proceeded as usual on the floors below.

The aesthetically-attractive Sports Medicine Center was structured as a total handicap functional facility. This state-of-the-art facility features a modern design of distinctive angles and high arches, which encompasses high-tech rehabilitation and examination capacities and a beautiful inner atrium. Photography by Ken Krakow.

Renovation and construction of the new museum addition in Macon proved to be similarly challenging. As construction progressed, youngsters continued daily visits to the facility for school tours and day camp sessions. Construction laborers also worked around other scheduled activities.

Amerson Construction enjoys a long history with the museum. In 1984, they completed a $500,000 museum project, which included finishing work on the interior of the facility.

Although the company frequently builds from a client's plans, Carl Amerson said he also enjoys design/build projects, which allow the construction company more latitude and control. Wachovia Bank building, which now also houses offices for the Bibb County Board of Education, was such a design/build project.

Comments from Amerson's clients leave no doubt about their satisfaction with their chosen contractor. For instance, Larry Justice, chairman of the Bibb County Board of Commissioners, applauds Amerson's proven tradition of flexibility on the job—a handy trait to have when retooling the entire fifth floor of a busy county courthouse.

Additionally, Jeffrey W. Johnson, president of First State Bank & Trust, lauds Amerson for building its single-story, red-brick bank branch under budget, and promises to include the contractor in any future projects.

Thus, Amerson Construction's proven tradition of stability and excellence not only hearkens back to its early beginnings, but also carries the company forward into new projects and accomplishments. Already a contributor to the area's history, the company will continue to make a lasting, visible mark on the landscape of Middle Georgia. ∎

EDUCATION & QUALITY OF LIFE

Photography by Paul Morris.

MERCER UNIVERSITY

Mercer Institute, the forerunner of Mercer University, was founded on January 14, 1833, by Georgia Baptists in Penfield, Georgia, as a manual labor school for boys. The legendary Jesse Mercer (1769-1841), esteemed Baptist preacher and one of the principal organizers of the Georgia Baptist Convention, is recognized as the founder of the University. The School's assets consisted of a red clay farm and two hewn log cabins, valued at approximately $1,933. The enrollment was 39 students and tuition was $25 per scholastic year and $35 for the collegiate year. Each student supplied his own bedding, candles, and furniture.

It was an inauspicious beginning in Penfield, and Jesse Mercer would be astonished to know that in 1995 Mercer is the second-largest Baptist-affiliated institution in the world and the only university of its size in the country to offer programs in liberal arts, business, engineering, medicine, pharmacy, and law. Approximately 7,000 students, who come from 44 states and 77 foreign countries, are enrolled in Mercer's seven schools and colleges in Macon and Atlanta.

The Georgia Baptist Convention in December 1870 passed a resolution to move Mercer from Penfield to Macon, and the School closed at the end of the year. Mercer re-located to Macon in 1871. On December 1, 1871, Macon's mayor presented to the Board of Trustees a deed for six acres of

land. Two years later, in 1873, a Law School was organized and classes began in February 1874.

The main campus in Macon, which is conveniently located one block off Interstate 75, now consists of a 130-acre tract with buildings that reflect a striking combination of tradition and progress. The centerpiece of this campus is the handsome and imposing Administration

R. Kirby Godsey has served as Mercer's 17th president since July 1, 1979. Photo by Paul Morris.

Building, of Victorian Gothic design, built in 1874 for $100,000 and now listed on the National Register of Historic Places. A few blocks away the Law School occupies an impressive building, a replica of Independence Hall, on Coleman Hill, overlooking downtown Macon.

The Cecil B. Day Campus in Northeast Atlanta serves as the University's Graduate and Professional Center. The beautifully wooded campus, which is home to the Southern School of Pharmacy and features programs offered by the Stetson School of Business and Economics, School of Engineering, College of Liberal Arts, and the School of Education, is conveniently located near the intersection of Interstates 285 and 85.

Through the years, Mercer has survived and overcome numerous obstacles and difficulties, including five very different wars, beginning with the War Between the States, which took the lives of 35 students. Mercer was one of the few colleges in the South and the only one in Georgia to remain open during the Civil War.

The Great Depression brought its own set of survival

Mercer's 7,000 students come from 44 states and 77 foreign countries. Photo by Paul Morris.

problems to Mercer. Only by much penny pinching, soul searching, and careful budgeting was the University able to survive when many institutions of higher learning, particularly private ones, succumbed.

Today Mercer occupies an enviable position. In 1994 *U.S. News and World Report* magazine ranked Mercer among the top four regional universities in the South. In addition, the magazine rated Mercer as the number one value among southern regional universities. The University's $120 million endowment ranks among the top 150 out of 3,400 colleges and universities in the country.

The College of Liberal Arts in Macon is the cornerstone of Mercer's academic programs. Presently, more than 1,800 students are enrolled, and a full array of baccalaureate programs in the humanities, sciences, fine arts, and social sciences is offered.

The Law School is recognized nationally for its innovative approach to legal education, and in 1987 received a major gift from the late George Woodruff that allowed the School to strengthen its curriculum and implement a multi-faceted plan to ensure that Mercer law graduates are among the best prepared in the country.

The Mercer School of Medicine's mission is to educate primary care physicians for rural and other underserved areas of Georgia. The youngest medical school in the country, Mercer began training physicians in 1982, and only Georgia residents are enrolled in the School. For the past three years the Medical School has had the highest percentage of graduates entering family medicine residencies of any medical school in the country. It also has the highest percentage of graduates going into primary care residencies of any medical school in the United States.

The Eugene W. Stetson School of Business and Economics opened in the fall of 1978 as a division of the College of Liberal Arts, and became a separate and independent school within the University in July 1984. Today both undergraduate and graduate degrees are offered on the Macon campus and on the Cecil B. Day Campus in Atlanta. The School recently began an Executive Master of Business Administration degree program in Atlanta, and offers undergraduate and graduate programs at Mercer's off-campus centers in Douglas County, Covington, Eastman, and Griffin.

The School of Engineering, one of only two schools of engineering in Georgia, admitted its first students in 1985. The bachelor of science in engineering degree is offered with various specializations, including biomedical engineering in conjunction with the Medical School. Master of science degrees in computer and information systems and technical management are also offered. The master of science in electrical engineering and engineering management are offered on the Atlanta campus.

Mercer's newest school, the School of Education, was established on July 1, 1995. The School offers bachelor of science in education, master of education and education specialist degrees, as well as degrees in fields such as criminal justice, communications, religious studies, applied sociology, and information systems. In addition to its programs on the main campus and the Cecil B. Day Campus in

Atlanta, the School of Education has off-campus centers in Douglas County, Covington, Eastman, and Griffin.

Started in 1987 as an operating unit of the University, the Mercer Engineering Research Center (MERC) provides engineering research and development services in the government and commercial sectors. MERC, headquartered in Warner Robins, employs more than 100 engineers, scientists, project managers, and technicians, and the client list includes customers in 11 states and Germany. MERC's current contracts exceed $40 million.

Mercer is the only Baptist-related university in the world with a full-fledged, functioning academic press. It is the fourth-largest university press in the Southeast and the nineteenth largest internationally. Mercer University Press was accepted into full membership in the Association of University Presses in 1982, at the earliest possible time of eligibility. The Press now has distributors in Canada and Belgium.

Mercer's beautiful 130-acre campus reflects a striking blend of traditional and contemporary features, from the majestic 125-year-old Administration Building to the modern Main Library. Photo by Paul Morris.

Rooted in the tradition of liberal education, Mercer continues to meet the changing educational needs of today's students, businesses, and communities, making the University a key player in ensuring tomorrow's leaders are ready to lead. ■

MOUNT DE SALES ACADEMY

Mount de Sales Academy, home of the Cavaliers, is nestled among the hills and white columns of Macon's downtown historic district where it has served since 1871.

Central Georgia's first academy and only private school to be recognized as a National Blue Ribbon School of Excellence,

Students enjoy a break on campus.

Mount de Sales has grown from a nationally renowned boarding school for girls to a nationally acclaimed co-educational college preparatory academy.

Known for its tradition of academic excellence in a disciplined and caring environment, the Academy stands clearly as a Catholic institution aimed at a Gospel values-oriented way of life. Each student at Mount de Sales Academy is nurtured as a whole person - spiritually, intellectually, socially, and physically, with the ability to make decisions based on beliefs and convictions. Serving students in the Middle School (grades 7- 8), and High School, (grades 9-12), the Academy is exclusively college preparatory. A Mount de Sales Academy education is an investment that pays rich dividends... for a lifetime!

Throughout its history, Mount de Sales Academy has consistently emphasized a strong foundation, preparing students for achievement both in college and throughout life. Both honors and advanced placement courses are offered. Mount de Sales students frequently receive both regional and state awards, honors and academic championships. A high percentage of our graduates regularly earn merit scholarships.

Fully accredited by the region's most prestigious accrediting body, the Southern Association of Colleges and Secondary Schools, Mount de Sales Academy is a member of the Georgia Independent Schools Association, and operates within the

framework of the Catholic Diocese of Savannah. The Academy is owned by the Sisters of Mercy and operated by a Board of Trustees. The Sisters of Mercy have a strong tradition of academic excellence in education, and service in many other world-wide ministries.

Serving as a community of faith as well as a community of learning, Mount de Sales Academy holds the following convictions to be at the heart of the educational endeavor: belief in a personal and loving God, belief in the value of life and dignity of the individual, and belief that each person must be aware of and responsive to obligations of their community. Mount de Sales Academy families appreciate the religious values and lessons that last a lifetime. Frequent school-wide service activities reinforce the theme that any definition of a successful life must include serving others.

Students at Mount de Sales Academy traditionally have come from varied religious, economic, racial, and ethnic backgrounds. Today, the student community is approximately half Catholic and half other faiths. The Academy's ecumenical philosophy has been central to its success. Students develop themselves through a wide variety of extracurricular activities including academic, social, and community service activities. Opportunities for leadership and involvement abound! Mount de Sales Academy prepares students for life, with lessons learned on the playing field as well as in the classroom. The competitive athletic program boasts many state championships! Cavaliers have distinguished themselves in both collegiate and professional sports...with the foundation of academics first!

The success of tomorrow begins today. The Mount de Sales Academy graduate joins a proud legacy of alumni. In partnership with student families and other members of the Cavalier family, Mount de Sales Academy continues its role as the area's benchmark in college preparatory education. ■

Mount de Sales Academy's Main Building overlooks Macon's downtown historic district.

TATTNALL SQUARE ACADEMY

Tattnall Square Academy, founded in 1969 by Tattnall Square Baptist Church, had an initial enrollment of 98 students in preschool through sixth grade. It is now the largest Baptist independent day school in the middle Georgia area, with more than 1,000 students in preschool through twelfth grade. The school's main objective is "to assure the school's continuing excellence in providing our children a well-rounded, Christian-oriented education."

Tattnall's reputation for excellence in academics, athletics, and other extracurricular activities has grown along with its enrollment. The Trojans and Lady Trojans sports teams have become very competitive on regional and state levels, with the Trojans winning the GISA (Georgia Independent School Association) state football championship four times since 1984 and the state track championship three times. The Lady Trojans have claimed five softball and two basketball state championships. Both teams have won numerous regional championships. The school also has soccer and baseball teams, a band, a drill team, and seven cheerleading squads.

Tattnall Square Academy has gained great success in areas such as oratorical competitions, acclaimed club presentations, and numerous musical accomplishments. Its dedication to excellence is evidenced by the students' enthusiasm for their studies and in the respect of students and teachers for each other.

The Academy continues to reinforce its mission of offering quality education in a Christian environment. This quality education is promoted through a gifted elementary program, advanced placement, honors classes, and international trips.

Fully accredited, Tattnall's curriculum is designed to provide foundations for learning in the lower school and preparation for college in the upper school, with the focus being on the individual student. Classes are kept small so that each student can have the personal attention needed to develop to his or her fullest potential.

The lower school offers a traditional, structured course of study, with strong emphasis placed on language and numerical skills. The curriculum of the upper school is designed to provide the students with the knowledge and skills to pursue successful college careers, to make responsible decisions, and to serve the community with their talents.

Tattnall's reputation for excellence has been enhanced by the administration's highly capable leadership. Walter Welsh, headmaster, has been at Tattnall since 1980, and Barney Hester, assistant headmaster and athletic director, has been there since 1982. Dr. Jeff Jackson, assistant headmaster and director of admissions, has been at Tattnall since 1992. Through sound financial management, maintenance of high academic standards, and Christian principles, this administration has made Tattnall Square Academy one of the finest independent schools in this area.

Tattnall is proud of the fact that almost 100 percent of its graduates continue on to colleges and universities. The school's alumni hold degrees from many respected institutions.

Educational excellence is enhanced by the Christian principles that underlie all endeavors at Tattnall and the atmosphere of honor and trust. In the required senior Christian Ethics course, students explore the meaning of Christian responsibility and service. Students actively

Aerial view of Tattnall Square Academy.

participate in service and leadership groups such as the Beta Club, Y-Club, Key Club, Student Council, Students Against Drunk Driving, and Fellowship of Christian Students. They also participate in such community service activities as Red Cross blood drives, Cystic Fibrosis Sports Challenge, Kids Yule Love and the Special Olympics.

All Tattnall parents are encouraged to participate in school activities through the Trojan Legion/PTO, the Gold Trojan Club, and the Band boosters. Tattnall Square Academy is located in North Macon off Wesleyan Drive. ■

HEALTHCARE

Photography by Ken Krakow.

COLISEUM HEALTHCARE SYSTEM

In February of 1994, HCA Coliseum Medical Centers was part of a bold step into the future. When Hospital Corporation of America (HCA) and Columbia Healthcare Corporation merged, they created the largest healthcare organization in the world, bringing Coliseum into the forefront of healthcare. With a network of over 300 hospitals nationwide, the newly combined Columbia/HCA Healthcare Corporation provides the community with more efficient and cost-effective services, as well as offering high quality treatment for healthcare needs.

a state-of-the-art critical care unit, diabetes management center, maternity center, a 13-bed neonatal intensive care unit, same day surgery center, physical rehabilitation center, laser surgery, and a breast health center.

The 375 physicians on the hospital's staff are supported by a strong and efficient nursing staff, and all hospital personnel are committed to community education in addition to caring for you when you are sick.

Coliseum Medical Centers' Day Hospital Center and Same Day Surgery Center offer surgical procedures on an outpatient basis, and Coliseum Primary Healthcare offers primary and ongoing care with a family physician or internist. The Primary Healthcare centers are located at 1560 Rocky Creek Road; 655 Baconsfield Center; 3200 Riverside Drive, Suite 210; and in Building D on the hospital's main campus.

The Stone Treatment Center was this area's first source for Extra-corporeal Shock Wave Lithotripsy, a non-surgical outpatient procedure that crushes kidney stones by low-energy wave impulses, reducing discomfort and shortening the recovery period. Coliseum Radiation Oncology Center's state-of-the-art equipment treats cancer with radiation, using a linear accelerator.

The Pain Care Center provides specialized medical services to individuals suffering from severe, disabling pain such as severe back pain, headaches, chronic joint pain, or pain caused by malignancies. Patients are seen on an inpatient and outpatient basis.

The Coliseum Maternity Center features all-private rooms, birthing options, prepared childbirth classes, and state-of-the-art equipment. Each of the LDR (labor-delivery-recovery) suites provides the comfort of home and enables parents to experience the entire birthing process in a single location. The neonatal intensive care unit provides specialized care for high-risk infants.

One of the main goals of Coliseum Healthcare System is to be the community's one source for all healthcare.

One of the main goals of Coliseum Healthcare System is to be the community's one source for all healthcare. With that in mind, they continue to set high standards. On their main campus, conveniently located off Coliseum Drive, stands a 258-bed medical and surgical hospital, a 92-bed psychiatric hospital, 4 medical buildings hosting doctors' offices, as well as an urgent care center, and a separate radiation/oncology center specifically built to treat cancer patients. In addition, there is a day care center, allowing parents to drop off their children when they have an appointment at the hospital. They also operate 5 physicians' offices in Bibb and Houston Counties as well as 6 outpatient mental health centers across the central portion of the state designed to meet the educational and emotional needs of the community.

Coliseum Medical Centers offers a wide variety of inpatient and outpatient services, including emergency and surgical care,

Coliseum Women's Center caters to the needs of today's woman by offering full diagnostic services, including mammograms, sonograms, and stereotactic breast biopsy. The Coliseum Breast Health Center is a centralized source for referral, education, and support regarding breast health.

Coliseum Rehabilitation Center is designed to help an individual who has suffered a disabling injury or illness return to the greatest possible level of independence. Inpatient and outpatient therapies help patients achieve maximum functional ability after strokes, orthopaedic injuries, and other debilitating conditions.

The Coliseum Prime Child Care Center, a day care center, is

open from 5:30 a.m. to midnight. The center provides a nurturing environment along with educational programs.

Coliseum Urgent Care, open 24 hours a day, 365 days a year, provides expert healthcare at a moment's notice on a walk-in basis. It is located on the hospital campus.

Health Care Finder, a free physician referral and health information service, provides information on various healthcare resources, including mental health services and support groups.

Other services provided by Coliseum Medical Centers include the Coliseum Diabetes Management Center, Coliseum Rehabilitation Center, Coliseum Occupational Medicine, Coliseum Weight Control Center, and A•P•P•L•E, a unique health and wellness program.

Through the Columbia/HCA merger, Coliseum Psychiatric Hospital has become a part of the largest healthcare company in the country and has joined this network of quality facilities that have made a new commitment to healthcare together. The hospital offers patients a comprehensive mental health system covering all aspects of inpatient and outpatient services.

Offering the highest level of care designed to meet each individual's needs, the psychiatric hospital treats all ages through community education, crisis intervention, and outpatient and inpatient care, as well as after-care. Families are encouraged to become involved in the treatment process from the beginning of care to after-care.

Inpatient treatment at Coliseum Psychiatric Hospital offers 24-hour nursing care for those who need to be in a supervised environment. The program involves individual, group, and family therapies for adults, youth, and children. Components of inpatient treatment include the Lifeworks Adult Psychiatric program, the New Life Recovery Addiction Program, Life Choices Adolescent Psychiatric and Addiction Program, and Kid's Place Child Psychiatric Program.

For those who do not need 24-hour nursing care, there are partial hospital programs that allow patients to experience an intensive, structured, therapeutic program during the day and then return home at night and weekends to apply their newly learned skills with their families. For other outpatient services, the six locations of the Coliseum Center for Families can provide individual and family therapy, psychological testing, and special programs for children and adolescents.

The program for adolescents in grades 7 through 12 who need help dealing with emotional and behavioral problems offers extensive outpatient treatment through individual counseling and group discussions, as well as spiritual and educational assistance. The program is available Monday through Thursday, 4:00 to 7:00 p.m.

Other intensive outpatient programs are available for adult psychiatric and addiction treatment. Coliseum Psychiatric Hospital's Life-Line, the only crisis intervention service of its kind in this area, is staffed by mental health professionals 24 hours each day. These professionals provide information, counseling, and assessments at no charge, offering the community a unique approach to help prevent small problems from becoming major crises. On-site intervention is available to businesses, physicians' offices, and social service agencies.

Coliseum Psychiatric Hospital provides mental health services throughout the community. Professionals from the hospital are available to speak on a wide variety of subjects to business, civic, and church groups.

With an emphasis on wellness, Coliseum is not only concerned with treating you when you are sick but also is committed to

Coliseum Psychiatric Hospital offers patients a comprehensive mental health system covering all aspects of inpatient and outpatient services.

educating the public on how to stay healthy. Monthly luncheon seminars are offered at no cost to the public with such topics as heart disease, breast cancer, addiction to drugs, and positive parenting.

According to Michael S. Boggs, chief executive officer of Coliseum Healthcare System, "It is our vision to be the healthcare provider of choice for patients, physicians, and employers. In the central Georgia area, we want everyone to 'Just think Coliseum' for all their healthcare needs." ■

MIDDLE GEORGIA HOSPITAL

Middle Georgia Hospital's commitment to quality has remained the same since it was originally founded in 1911 as Williams Private Sanitorium. Offering personal, high-quality health care to the citizens of Macon and Middle Georgia, the hospital's name was changed to Middle Georgia Hospital in 1937. Owned by Quorum Health Group, Inc., Middle Georgia Hospital has always been known as one of the finest health care facilities in this area.

Middle Georgia Hospital has been a leader in new technology for health care and was the first hospital in Macon to perform diagnostic testing with specialized heart catheterization equipment. State-of-the-art technologies and equipment are used by highly trained professionals striving to provide high-quality and individualized health care services for patients.

Middle Georgia Hospital's surgical suite includes cystoscopy and outpatient operating rooms and an intensive/coronary care unit staffed by teams of skilled nurses. Both units are equipped with the most modern equipment available. The hospital is proud to be a leader in the use of laser technology, and was the first hospital in this area to offer laser-assisted angioplasty.

In an effort to keep hospital costs down for its patients, Middle Georgia Hospital outpatient services allow many people to undergo tests and procedures without having to spend the night. The hospital's Surgery Today, Home Today wing offers private rooms with televisions and telephones.

Medical services at the hospital include echocardiography, a non-invasive procedure using high-frequency sound waves to take a picture of the heart; and heart catheterization, a sophisticated procedure used to locate any blockage around the heart. Other services include a pulmonary lab, respiratory therapy for treatments and diagnostic procedures to improve or maintain proper lung functioning, physical therapy for rehabilitation of injured or disabled patients, radiology, CT Scans and digital vascular imaging, ultrasound, and nuclear medicine.

Middle Georgia Hospital also has available the non-surgical Stereotactic Breast Biopsies, a procedure that enables the physician to identify with pinpoint accuracy a suspicious lesion in the breast and obtain a specimen. It enables the physician to bypass the initial surgical biopsy and is performed while the patient is awake. In addition, the patient is allowed to go home after the procedure.

Middle Georgia Hospital's Urgent Care Center, located across from the hospital, provides treatment for illnesses and injuries of all types. Open 24 hours a day, the center is backed by the full facilities of the hospital and is staffed and equipped like a traditional hospital emergency room.

The two Middle Georgia Family Health centers are full service family medical practices whose purposes are to provide personal

The 119-bed Middle Georgia Hospital is licensed by the Georgia State Department of Health, approved by Medicare and Medicaid, and is accredited by the Joint Commission on Accreditation of Healthcare Organizations.

physician care for patients. The goal of the staffs at the centers is to blend state-of-the-art medical knowledge with the traditional values of the old-fashioned family doctor.

Ask-A-Nurse, a service of Middle Georgia Hospital and Macon Northside Hospital, is a 24-hour telephone health information and referral service staffed by registered nurses who refer callers to appropriate health care services, physicians, community agencies, and other resources. You'll get accurate, confidential information in the privacy of your home . . . free of charge. ■

MACON NORTHSIDE HOSPITAL

Macon Northside Hospital is an all private, 103-bed, acute care hospital located on 40 beautiful acres in North Macon. Easily accessible from 2 major roadways, the hospital opened in 1984 with one adjacent medical office building. Since that time, the medical office building has nearly doubled in size and two detached office buildings have been added.

Macon Northside Hospital's 24-hour, full-service Emergency Room is staffed by highly trained emergency medical personnel. The Emergency Department boasts a Chest Pain Center staffed with physicians and support professionals specially trained to quickly pinpoint the causes of chest discomfort.

Staff radiologists are available 24 hours a day for consultation regarding interpretation and diagnosis. Services include state-of-the-art CT scan, ultrasound, radiography/fluoroscopy and MRI scans. Nuclear medicine examinations and physiological tests are also offered.

Macon Northside Hospital also has a state-of-the-art intensive care unit and operating rooms with the latest in equipment for performing laporoscopic procedures and other high-tech cases.

Macon Northside Hospital is an all private, 103-bed acute care hospital that is committed to improving the health of Middle Georgia residents.

Funds raised from gift shop profits are applied to scholarships for students in health-related careers.

A joint effort between area physicians and the hospital Emergency Department, the Night Call program, enables patients to access immediate care without paying emergency room prices. By consulting Emergency Room physicians, the patient's physician is able to monitor diagnosis and treatment.

Macon Northside Hospital's Day Surgery department is designed to accommodate patients requiring surgery without being admitted. The department staff prepares patients for their procedures, monitors them post-operatively, and then supervises their discharge when fully recovered from anesthesia.

One of the most popular programs at the hospital is Women's Health Services, designed to address the health issues of women over 40. A free monthly lecture series is held in the Conference Center where women are introduced to new technologies, procedures, and lifestyle changes that can help them lead longer and more productive lives.

In order to better serve the entire community, Macon Northside Hospital owns and operates Rutland Corners Family Healthcare Center and Northridge Family Healthcare Center. Both facilities are designed to care for the entire family and its health care needs.

A 24-hour telephone health information and referral service, Ask-A-Nurse, is a service of Macon Northside and Middle Georgia hospitals.

Macon Northside Hospital is accredited by The Joint Commission on Accreditation of Hospitals. The hospital is committed to improving the health of Middle Georgia residents by providing superior quality community education, preventive health care, and innovative patient care services. It boasts one of the finest medical staffs in the area; all of its physicians are board-certified or board-eligible in their specialty. ■

The mammogram unit, certified by the American College of Radiologists and Medicare, is now offering Sterotactic Breast Biopsies.

The hospital's Industrial Medicine Center helps businesses and industries control health care costs and reduces employee downtime through preventive programs and fast, cost-conscious treatment of work-related injuries and illnesses. An extensive referral network for specialists is also provided and rehabilitation programs are available through the Physical Therapy Department.

Macon Northside Hospital has a number of volunteers who operate and staff the hospital's unique gift shop, which offers flowers and gifts for all occasions—from personal gift items to wedding presents.

FORSYTH STREET ORTHOPAEDIC SURGERY & REHABILITATION CENTER

When members of the Macon Braves minor-league baseball team take a tumble on the playing field, they head to Forsyth Street Orthopaedic Surgery and Rehabilitation Center for help in recovering from their sports-related injuries.

Located at 1600 Forsyth Street, the complex offers passersby an impressive sight, with its jutting front columns and rows of glistening glass. Photo by Ken Krakow.

Athletes with the city's popular Sally League team aren't the only ones who can benefit from the center's staff of highly-trained doctors, physical and occupational therapists, and certified athletic trainers. Rather, the center's specialists stand ready to provide advanced, effective, and comprehensive care for sufferers of all types of orthopaedic injuries, athletic and non-athletic alike. Regardless of age or the origin of orthopaedic injuries, the center has complete facilities and expertise for treatment.

Located at 1600 Forsyth Street, the approximately 26,000-square-foot, state-of-the-art complex boasts examining rooms, x-ray equipment, plaster rooms, hydrotherapy facilities, and a gym complete with equipment for therapy, evaluation, and exercise. The center's four orthopaedic surgeons—Drs. Frank B. Kelly, Charles H. Richardson, Gary L. Hattaway, and Joseph E. Slappey—offer specialized treatment in total joint replacement, spinal disorders, and arthroscopic surgery.

The history of the center dates back to 1977 and 1978 when Dr. Richardson and Dr. Kelly opened their respective private practices. In 1980, the two physicians joined forces and introduced the practice of sports medicine, which had previously focused on athletes due to the frequency and intensity of their orthopaedic and muscular injuries. Kelly and Richardson, however, expanded the sports-medicine concept by employing successful treatment techniques on all types of orthopaedic injuries, and in 1987, opened The Sports Medicine Center on Northside Drive as a joint venture. That same year, Dr. Hattaway joined the practice, and in 1989, the doctors and rehabilitation team moved into the new facility on Forsyth Street. Dr. Slappey joined the practice in 1993 and became a partner the following year.

Tommy Williamson, P.T., was named medical director of the center's rehabilitation department in 1990. The rehabilitation team

The center's four orthopaedic surgeons (L to R); Drs. Charles H. Richardson, Gary L. Hattaway, Frank B. Kelly, and Joseph E. Slappey. Photo by Ken Krakow.

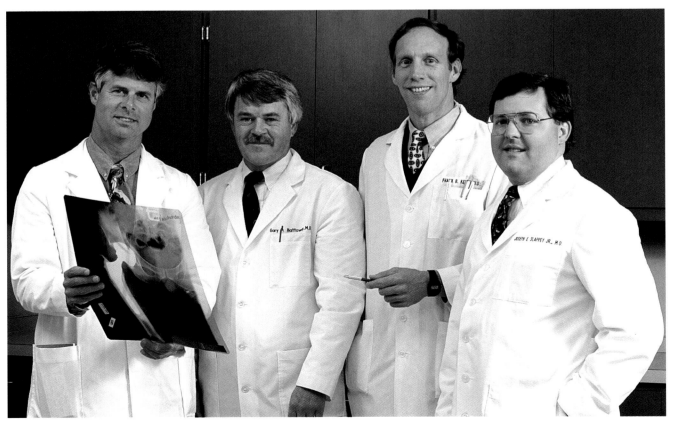

A glass-filled front atrium separates the doctors' offices and physical therapy sections, and features an open floor plan, streaming natural light, and an abundance of plants. Photo by Ken Krakow.

consists of experienced physical therapists, certified athletic trainers, and occupational therapists. The complex, which is completely handicapped-accessible, now has an assembled corps of 35 employees. In addition to serving as team physicians for the Macon Braves, the doctors perform similar services for Bibb County Public Schools, as well as several area private schools. The center—the first of its kind in Middle Georgia— features a convenient location near Interstate 75 and Interstate 16, affording easy accessibility to patients through Macon and the midstate area.

Architecturally, the complex offers passersby an impressive sight, with its jutting front columns and rows of glistening glass. Designed by the late Macon architect, Thomas Little, a glass-filled front atrium separates the doctors' offices and physical therapy sections, and features an open floor plan, streaming natural light, and an abundance of plants. The doctor's offices, measuring about 16,000 square feet, provide a more conventional medical atmosphere, while the 10,000 square-foot physical therapy building features a more open ambiance. The building, several years in the planning stages, took about a year to construct. Conveniently, patients may enter the building through either the front or back doors.

The doctors' philosophy of orthopaedic treatment and rehabilitation is simple: To provide Central Georgians suffering from orthopaedic injuries the most advanced, effective, and comprehensive treatment available, thereby ensuring patients a complete recovery and quick return to their active lifestyles.

Diversity in training allows the center's specialists to treat a full range of orthopaedic injuries, and each of the doctors brings a

particular area of expertise to the medical practice. Dr. Kelly, a Phi Beta Kappa graduate of the University of North Carolina at Chapel Hill, completed his medical training at the Medical College of Georgia and served his orthopaedic surgery residency at the University of Tennessee. Board certified by the American Board of Orthopaedic Society, Dr. Kelly also teaches at Mercer Medical School. He specializes in joint replacement and arthroscopic surgery. His affiliation with Wright Medical Technology, Inc., accords him invitations from around the country to speak to other doctors on his surgical techniques.

Dr. Hattaway, a graduate of Emory University in Atlanta, studied medicine at the Medical College of Georgia in Augusta, where he received his medical degree with honors. Board certified by the American Board of Orthopaedic Surgery and a member of AOA Medical Honor Society, he completed his orthopaedic surgery training at Georgia Baptist Medical Center. His specialty is joint replacement and arthroscopic surgery.

Dr. Slappey graduated from Georgia Southwestern College in Americus. He completed a six-year residency and one-year internship at Georgia Baptist Medical Center in Atlanta. His specialty is general orthopaedics.

A graduate of Vanderbilt University, Dr. Richardson earned his medical degree from the Medical College of Georgia in Augusta and completed his orthopaedic surgery training at The Johns Hopkins Hospital in Baltimore, Maryland. On the faculty at Mercer Medical School, he is board-certified by the American Board of Orthopaedic Surgery. Dr. Richardson specializes in the treatment of spinal disorders and problems of the lower extremities.

No surgical procedures are performed at the complex. Drs. Richardson, Slappey, Hattaway, and Kelly are affiliated with all local hospitals, primarily using The Medical Center of Central Georgia, HCA Coliseum Medical Centers, and Middle Georgia Hospital. ■

The center's specialists stand ready to provide advanced, effective, and comprehensive care for sufferers of all types of orthopaedic injuries. Photo by Ken Krakow.

THE MACON ORTHOPAEDIC AND HAND CENTER

The physicians and staff at Macon Orthopaedic and Hand Center care about what they do. Letters and success stories adorn the hallways and walls of the doctors' offices. Smiles and friendly greetings welcome patients as they enter the waiting room and shelves of literature and medical information are at your fingertips as the doctors and staff know that an informed patient is always the best patient.

Seated from left to right - Waldo E. Floyd, Jr. M.D., Alexander H. S. Weaver, Jr. M.D. Standing from left to right - Waldo E. Floyd, III M.D., C. Emory Johnson, Jr. M.D., John W. Sapp, M.D. Photography by Ken Krakow.

It all began with Dr. Waldo Floyd, Jr. Born and raised in South Georgia, Dr. Floyd followed in the footsteps of his father, and numerous others in the Floyd family tree, in becoming a doctor.

After completing advanced training at Grady Memorial Hospital, Georgia Baptist Hospital, and hospitals at the Medical College of Georgia, Dr. Floyd received his medical degree from The Johns Hopkins Medical School in Baltimore, Maryland. In 1961 he settled in Macon and founded the practice.

His compassion and skill as a physician quickly spread throughout Middle Georgia as he pioneered the development of reconstructive hand surgery in the region. The growing practice led to the addition of another skilled Georgian physician, Dr. A.H.S. Weaver, Jr.

Dr. Weaver joined Dr. Floyd in 1967 after graduating from Mercer University and receiving his doctorate at The Medical College of Georgia where he also completed his orthopaedic training. He was an orthopaedic surgery

instructor at Talmadge Memorial Hospital in Augusta, Georgia, before serving in the United States Army for two years at Martin Army Hospital, during which part of the time he was Chief of Orthopaedic Surgery.

The practice continued to grow and flourish as patients came, not only from Macon, but from the surrounding areas as well. In 1974, native Maconite, C. Emory Johnson, Jr., joined the staff after finishing his education at Emory University and receiving his medical degree at the Medical College of Georgia. He trained in orthopaedic surgery at both Georgia Baptist Hospital and the Scottish Rite Children's Hospital in Atlanta. He returned to Macon after a two-year stint in the United States Air Force where he served as the Chief of Orthopaedic Surgery at Shaw Air Force Base in Sumter, South Carolina.

The three doctors were busy, with Dr. Floyd specializing in reconstructive hand and upper extremity surgery, and Drs. Weaver and Johnson specializing in general orthopaedic surgery with a particular interest in foot and ankle disorders, arthroscopy, joint replacement, and children's orthopaedic problems.

In 1987, Macon Orthopaedic and Hand Center proudly opened its arms to another doctor. Dr. Waldo Floyd III joined his father and Drs. Weaver and Johnson. Dr. Floyd III received his medical degree from Emory University and further training in surgery at The Johns Hopkins Hospital. He completed residency in orthopaedic surgery at Harvard Medical School, a fellowship in hand surgery at Roosevelt Hospital in New York City, and managed a practice in Boston treating patients from all over the world.

Dr. Floyd III specializes in surgery of the hand and upper limbs. He is among a limited number of microhand surgeons in the region and has received widespread recognition. He has published numerous articles and book chapters dealing with hand and orthopaedic surgery and is Clinical Instructor in Orthopaedic Surgery at Emory University School of Medicine and

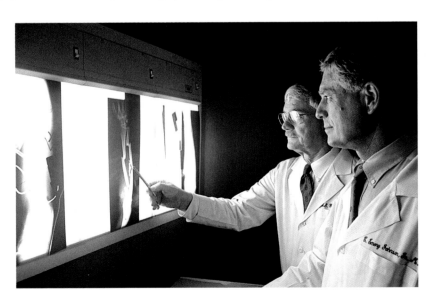

Dr. Alexander Weaver and Dr. Emory Johnson review a patient's x-rays. Photography by Ken Krakow.

Clinical Associate Professor of Surgery at Mercer University School of Medicine.

The doctors were working continuously as their reputation continued to spread across the state. In 1992, Dr. John Sapp joined the team after graduating from The Medical College of Georgia, completing his residency in general surgery at the Medical Center of Central Georgia, and plastic surgery at Louisiana State University in New Orleans. After spending an additional year at the University of Florida as a fellow in hand and microsurgery, he came to Macon and specialized in hand surgery and microsurgery—the transfer of tissue from one area of the body to another and replantation following amputations—as well as arthroscopy of the wrist.

In addition to memberships in professional medical organizations, Dr. Sapp is also on the faculty of Mercer University School of Medicine as Clinical Assistant Professor in the Department of Surgery.

In 1994, the practice saw over 17,000 patients and is still growing. To continue to be able to care for the medical needs of the people of Georgia, Macon Orthopaedic and Hand Center will be welcoming two new doctors into the practice in the fall of 1995.

Native Georgian, Dr. Robert Thornsberry, attended Davidson College and The Medical College of Georgia, completed residency in orthopaedic surgery at the University of Kentucky College of Medicine, and will complete his fellowship in sports injuries at The Hughston Clinic before joining the practice. Once in Macon, he will specialize in general orthopaedics, sports injuries, and total joint replacement to complement and expand the work already being performed by the current doctors.

Shortly after Dr. Thornsberry's arrival, Dr. Guy Foulkes will join the staff. A graduate of Mercer University School of Medicine, he did his internship in general surgery at the Medical Center here in Macon. He completed his orthopaedic residency at the University of Hawaii, and will complete his fellowship in hand surgery at UCLA before arriving in Macon. An accomplished writer, he has published and presented numerous papers on orthopaedic surgery, specifically hand surgery.

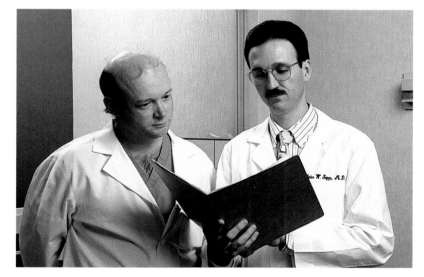

Dr. Waldo Floyd, III, and Dr. John Sapp discuss a patient's chart. Photography by Ken Krakow.

The physicians at Macon Orthopaedic and Hand Center want their patients to be the best that they can be and they realize that supervised therapy is the answer to most of their patients' needs. Therapy can be an alternative to surgery or the only way to recover fully after

These four employees have 106 years experience with Macon Orthopaedic and Hand Center. Photography by Ken Krakow.

having surgery. With that in mind in 1988 they started their own therapy department.

Beginning with a part-time therapist three days a week, the therapy department has expanded as the practice has. Now with four full-time Certified Hand Therapists and their trained support staff, the therapy department treated over 12,000 patients in 1994.

The therapists complete a computerized evaluation of each patient and, working closely with the doctors, determine the best treatment plan and appropriate modalities in which to use. Then, using high-tech equipment intertwined with understanding and patience, they work one-on-one with the patient to increase strength, mobility, and a return of function to the affected limb.

The logo for Macon Orthopaedic and Hand Center is the symbol for orthopaedics—that of a bent tree being supported and straightened—and since Dr. Floyd Jr.'s humble beginning in 1961, Macon Orthopaedic has been supporting the people of Middle Georgia.

When Dr. Floyd III was asked why he thought the practice his father started 34 years ago was so successful, he smiled and quietly answered, "The bottom line is, the gentleman who founded this practice cares a lot about people."

That statement is evident today and it applies to each doctor, therapist, nurse, x-ray technician, and the entire support staff—Macon Orthopaedic and Hand Center cares about people. ■

THE MEDICAL CENTER OF CENTRAL GEORGIA

In the 1880s, a group of women belonging to a philanthropic organization known as the King's Daughters became concerned about the need for a hospital in Macon. They enlisted their husbands and friends for assistance in raising money to build a hospital.

In 1895, their dream came true and a small hospital, then known as Macon Hospital, was established in a converted school building. From these small beginnings, Macon Hospital has grown into the dynamic organization now known as The Medical Center of Central Georgia. Standing proudly on Hemlock Street, The Medical Center was recently named one of the 100 top-performing hospitals and one of the top 20 teaching hospitals in the country.

Standing proudly on Hemlock Street, The Medical Center was recently named one of the 100 top-performing hospitals and one of the top 20 teaching hospitals in the country. Photo by Bill Lisenby.

This not-for-profit, 518-bed, full-service, acute-care facility employs approximately 3,300 people and is the single largest plant employer in Bibb County. Over 375 physicians are affiliated with the hospital.

For the past 100 years, The Medical Center has continued to add new programs and services, creating a complete healthcare system.

The Georgia Heart Center provides comprehensive diagnostic, surgical, and rehabilitative heart services and includes a cardiac critical care unit.

The Cancer Life Center offers services ranging from comprehensive oncology treatment programs to outreach programs on cancer prevention.

The Children's Hospital functions as a "hospital within a hospital" and features a pediatric intensive care unit, intensive care nursery, and pediatric heart center.

The Critical Care Center provides skilled medical care for the most serious of illnesses and injuries and is equipped and staffed to provide minute-by-minute monitoring and care for trauma, cardiovascular surgery, and neurosurgery patients.

The Medical Center's Surgery Center houses 18 operating rooms and 4 floors of medical office space and cost $27.5 million to construct and equip.

The Emergency Center offers the most complete emergency service within an 85-mile radius and operates a fully-equipped, state-licensed ambulance service.

The Medical Center's four urgent care centers provide quick, convenient care for most illnesses and injuries.

The Pavilion provides patients with intensive and supportive psychotherapy, group therapy, and individually prescribed activities, as well as occupational and recreational therapy, addictive disease educational programs, stress management training, and a special group dealing with women's issues.

Beginnings, The Medical Center's prenatal education program, offers classes on every aspect of pregnancy and a special siblings class that helps future brothers and sisters adjust to the new arrival.

The Family Birth Center offers 22 private birthing suites and offers a pleasant "home-like" environment while providing a safe hospital delivery.

Other services provided by The Medical Center include the Regional Imaging Center, Lifelink, the Diabetes Treatment Center, the Family Health Center, the Neighborhood Healthcare Centers, Sleep Lab, and Focal Pointe Women.

The Wellness Center and Macon Health Club, operated by the hospital, offer a wide range of exercise options, and Partners in Health offers health education programs and support groups to the community. The Occupational Health Center offers a variety of occupational medicine programs to business and industry.

Licensed by the Georgia Department of Human Resources, The Medical Center is approved by Medicare and Medicaid and is fully approved by the Joint Commission of Accreditation of Healthcare Organizations.

A teaching hospital, The Medical Center is affiliated with many Georgia universities and colleges. Its residency programs are approved by the AMA Council of Education. ∎

CENTRAL GEORGIA REHABILITATION NETWORK

The Central Georgia Rehabilitation Network offers a broad range of treatments and settings to meet the individual needs of patients and families. The network consists of the Central Georgia Rehabilitation Hospital and the Macon Rehabilitation Center, both in Macon, Georgia—and Central Georgia Rehab at Fort Valley.

The rehabilitation process for the program areas is the same throughout the network. The process includes referral, evaluation, treatment, discharge, and follow-up. At each Central Georgia Rehabilitation Network facility, a team of professionals works together to develop the most effective program of care.

At the initial patient evaluation, a facility and a program of care are recommended. Patients and family members participate in the early decision-making process and learn about the treatment and care that will restore the patient to the highest level of function.

Employees at the Network facilities work closely with employers and insurance providers to assist family members and patients with the legal and financial matters involved with injuries and diseases, allowing them to better concentrate on the rehabilitation process.

Central Georgia Rehabilitation Hospital at 3351 Northside Drive in Macon offers the following program areas: brain injury, stroke/general rehabilitation, orthopedic/neuromuscular, spinal cord injury, amputation, general weakness/deconditioning, pain management, and pediatric rehabilitation. After discharge, outpatient services are available if needed.

This hospital, a 50-bed facility which opened in 1988, uses a personalized treatment approach to help patients build upon their strengths and compensate for weaknesses in physical, self-care, communication, and psycho-social skills.

Central Georgia Rehabilitation Hospital accepts patients immediately after medical stabilization. By starting the comprehensive rehabilitation process as quickly as possible, patients have a greater opportunity to regain functional skills.

Upon admission, each patient is assigned a case manager who serves as a patient advocate and acts as the liaison for the patient, family, treatment team, referral source, and payer. Throughout the healing process, the team of rehabilitation professionals meets regularly to review progress and determine effective methods for continuing rehabilitation.

Central Georgia Rehabilitation Hospital is the only CARF-accredited rehabilitation facility in the Macon area.

The Macon Rehabilitation Center, located across the street from the hospital, at 3330 Northside Drive, opened in 1991. It provides a continuum of care for inpatients being discharged who need further treatment to functionally improve. Individuals who may not require an inpatient stay, but who have suffered an injury or impairment of function, may also benefit from the outpatient services. Some of the conditions seen at the center include orthopedic, stroke, musculoskeletal, and neurological disorders.

By starting the comprehensive rehabilitation process as quickly as possible, patients have a greater opportunity to regain functional skills.

The Brain Injury Program at the Macon Rehabilitation Center targets neurologically impaired adults with the potential to return to maximum independence and function. The Functional Restoration and Chronic Pain Program is directed by the center's physiatrist and is designed to help restore individual function.

Central Georgia Rehab at Fort Valley, a 25-bed sub-acute facility, offers both inpatient and outpatient rehabilitation services. Established in 1992, its programs are designed to help patients regain the physical, emotional, social, and communication skills needed to function at home, at work, and in the community—skills which have sometimes been temporarily lost due to an illness or injury.

In 1994, Central Georgia Rehabilitation Hospital was awarded the prestigious "CARF" (Commission on Accreditation of Rehabilitation Facilities) accreditation for three years for its comprehensive general rehabilitation services and both its brain injury and spinal cord programs. Central Georgia Rehabilitation Hospital is the only CARF-accredited rehabilitation facility in the Macon area. The Central Georgia Rehabilitation Network is part of the Birmingham, Alabama based HEALTHSOUTH Corporation, the nation's largest provider of rehabilitation services, with approximately 450 locations throughout the United States and Canada. ■

THE MARKET PLACE

Photography by Ken Krakow.

ACME BUSINESS PRODUCTS

In 1972 Earl Benson had a dream . . . he borrowed $10,000 against his personal life insurance policy and took a gamble. In 23 years he took his fledgling business venture with $10,000 in capital to $90,000,000 in sales. Such an undertaking takes vision and determination.

Originally opening the doors under the name of Acme Business Machines in his home town of Macon, Georgia, he used the borrowed $10,000 to purchase the inventory of Smith Corona Marchant (SCM) Corporation's Macon location which was closing its branch. Using this small customer base as his cornerstone, he was able to acquire the dealership for Sharp Calculators as the main product line.

Armed with this state-of-the-art equipment, he made his way to banks and other financial institutions, pushing the APR program which was programmed into this new-age equipment. Since these units could be programmed, he immediately acted on his next idea, which was to create a program that could be used by peanut growers, tobacco buyers, and other agricultural enterprises. Armed with this futuristic equipment, he headed for South Georgia, calling on the agricultural market and selling the benefits of his machine.

With all this modern equipment, Benson knew he had to establish a state-of-the-art service department which could provide the support the equipment would need. Benson called on his long-time friend and business acquaintance, Gary Peacock, to head up the needed technical support staff. Peacock joined Benson in the new venture and eventually became his partner, where he served as vice president until he retired in 1985.

Peacock was unrelenting in his quest to provide quality service and insisted that all Acme technicians be factory-trained. Twenty-three years later, Acme's service department still triumphs with factory-trained technicians who have earned numerous awards for their superior customer service.

Thus, Acme Business Machines was on its way to success. Fortunately, Benson did not stop dreaming when Acme recorded $90,000 in sales and $8,000 in income during the first year of operation.

A new "gadget" appeared on the scene, making its cut into the pathway of the future—the Savin

E-Stat Copier—providing businesses with copies without the use of carbon paper or a mimeograph machine. Even though it was a little messy to run the original through the fluid and the paper was coated and slick, it was a time saver.

In 1975 Savin introduced the Savin 750 Plain Paper Copier. Acme's foresight had ensured them a dealership with Savin for this extraordinary new machine. This unit, the Savin 750, revolutionized the copier industry and led the company to where it is today, providing the paradigm on which modern copying applications are developed.

The Savin 750 Plain Paper Copier earned Acme Business Machines the reputation of being "the leader" in technologically advanced equipment, a reputation the company enjoys to the present day. Acme is always prepared to meet customer needs, whether they be color, digital, engineering copiers, high volume, or connectivity. They are there and ready to serve customers, providing the most proficient equipment, unsurpassed customer support, factory-authorized supplies, and innovative financing.

Acme continues to go the extra mile for customers, taking pride in its claim: Our Customers Are Our Future. Competition is stiff in the copier industry, and the one asset that makes Acme different from the competition is quality customer service. The company recently invested in Total Quality Management (TQM) training for all employees, empowering them to satisfy customers, no matter what it takes!

Acme Business Products offers its customers a unique advantage by combining quality Ricoh products with the strength of Acme. Photography by Hood & Associates.

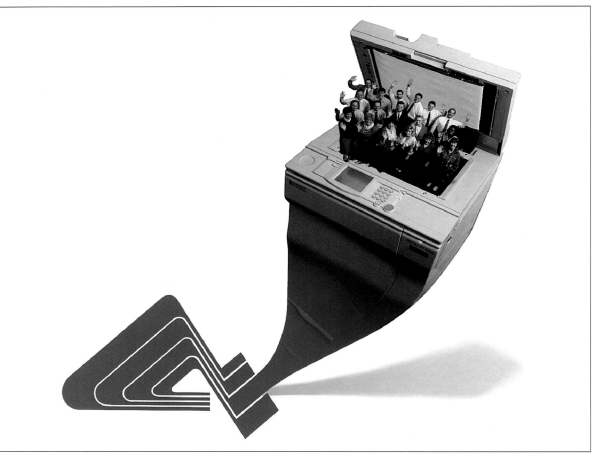

Based on the phenomenal growth they have enjoyed since joining forces with Alco Standard Corporation in 1983, Acme now provides about 250 Macon and Middle Georgia residents with jobs. This growth is scheduled to continue at approximately the rate of 20 new jobs each year. Acme believes in investing in the community and encourages all branch offices to do business with their local merchants.

In 1983, Acme was acquired by Alco Standard Corporation of Valley Forge, Pennsylvania. It was the first of many acquisitions for Alco Office Products, a division of Alco Standard Corporation. Alco has developed into a $9 billion network sales organization with over 60 Alco Office Products dealers across the United States and Europe. Acme is now the nation's second largest Ricoh dealer.

Acme Business Products offers its customers a unique advantage by combining quality Ricoh products with the strength of Acme. That means the customer receives personalized service from an extensive network of local offices plus the resources of one of the largest office products dealers in the nation, all backed by the financial stability of Alco Standard.

Acme has 35 branch locations throughout the South, assuring convenient support. This personalized service is backed up by the expertise and resources of Acme Business Products and Alco. There are more than 650 Acme employees and each has a single goal: customer satisfaction. All employees are stockholders in the company, giving them another reason to ensure that each customer is happy.

Many customers choose to lease their office products because of the flexibility, financial benefits, and convenience leasing offers. Acme has its own in-house leasing company, Alco Capital Resource, which leases equipment sold exclusively by Alco Office Products dealers. Leasing with Acme eliminates unnecessary delays and red tape; in addition, credit decisions are usually made within a matter of hours.

The company's complete product line allows them to meet the needs of any business, large or small, whether it needs the most technologically advanced office solution or reliable, cost-effective facsimile or copier equipment. However, quality differentiates Acme Business Products from its competitors—the quality of its products and the quality of its people. The company's TQM program plus the superiority of Ricoh office products combine to create an outstanding product that is backed by dedicated employees and a wide range of services.

As over 25,000 satisfied customers throughout the Southeast can attest, Acme Business Products has provided the peak of excellence to thousands of people throughout the Southeast.

Today, the company is at the forefront of technological development, with integrated, multi-functional imaging equipment that satisfies a wide range of needs. But what puts Acme at the peak is not only the quality of its products, but the quality and level of service it provides each customer.

Acme Business Products is committed to ensuring customer satisfaction and will do whatever it takes to make it right. ■

There are more than 650 Acme employees and each has a single goal: customer satisfaction.

ALCO CAPITAL RESOURCE, INC.

Macon is headquarters for two premiere companies, Acme Business Products and Alco Capital Resource. Both of these companies are owned by Alco Standard Corporation (a New York Stock Exchange company which is headquartered in Valley Forge, Pennsylvania, with annual revenues in excess of $8 billion) and fall under the Alco Office Products (AOP) division.

Acme Business Products was purchased by Alco Standard Corporation in 1983. One of the services that set Acme apart from its competition was the ability to offer customers leasing through their in-house leasing arm, Metro Leasing Company. Through Alco's vision of offering leasing to its growing network of office products dealers, Alco Capital was formed from Metro Leasing in 1987 and became Alco Office Products' captive leasing company. Today, Alco Capital serves more than 65 dynamic Alco dealers who comprise the largest network of office products dealers in the United States.

Alco Capital Resource began in a back office of Acme Business Products on Eisenhower Parkway, with a small nucleus of Acme employees, including Alco Capital's President, Rick Maier, who was then Vice President of Acme. The company soon outgrew a 10,000-square-foot facility behind Acme and in 1990, moved to its present location on Bass Road in North Macon. Originally a 19,000-square-foot-building, an 18,000-square-foot addition was completed in September 1994. The modern facility houses Alco Capital's 150 customer care and support team employees, a state-of-the-art data center, and a first class training/conference center.

Alco Office Products gave Alco Capital the freedom to locate anywhere in the United States, but according to Rick Maier, President, Macon was the ideal location. "People in the Macon area have a strong work ethic and form an ideal pool from which to draw enthusiastic, quality employees," said Maier. "The close proximity to the Atlanta airport is important, as we hold many meetings and training sessions for our dealer representatives from all parts of the United States."

The 65-plus Alco Office Products dealers lease nearly 60 percent of their business through Alco Capital, and this figure is increasing monthly. Maier says that "leasing is becoming a more attractive alternative to buying office equipment because companies don't have the money up front for a new piece of equipment. Leasing gives the customer flexibility. Alco Capital is successful because we offer a very high level of service to our dealers and great convenience for their customers. We are family to our dealers and together we do whatever it takes to ensure that our customers are satisfied."

Maier also says "because 80 percent of Alco Capital's business comes in during the first four days of the month and must be processed within a short time frame, it challenges our people to handle the large volume of business we receive. We keep our employees motivated to handle this volume by doing our best to keep them happy. Happy employees equal happy customers. We try to make this the best place to work in Middle Georgia by focusing on the internal customer—the employee. The spirit, productivity, and enthusiasm of our people is remarkable."

Alco Capital employees' participation in Alco's 401K stock plan is 100 percent. No one cares like an owner, and the return for

Alco Capital serves more than 65 dynamic Alco dealers who comprise the largest network of office products dealers in the United States.

employees is extraordinary. Stock price has risen from $20.00 in March 1988 to $78.00 in June 1995. The total shareholder return has been over 19 percent for the last 20 years.

In 1994, Alco Capital transformed from functional departments to cross-functional, customer-focused teams to serve their customers

The benefits of leasing with Alco Capital include convenience of one-stop-shopping, income tax advantages, protected lines of credit, hedge against inflation, and affordability.

from the beginning to the end of a lease. To prepare for future growth, their philosophy was to have the same skill and spirit that made them so successful with 20 employees and 1,000 customers. How? Break into small, empowered, motivated teams; develop leadership skills; and cross-train. Most importantly, measure and reward. The early results were phenomenal, and the rapid increase in lease volume has far exceeded the steady increase in employees.

A portfolio of more than $950 million and over 115,000 customers throughout the United States are the results of a focus on quality by Alco Capital, a company which is sharing its growth with Macon and Middle Georgia. What does the future hold? By the year 2000, Alco Capital's portfolio is expected to increase to $2 billion. The company will employ over 200 skilled and spirited employees whose focus will remain, as now, on exceeding customers' expectations. ■

CROWNE PLAZA MACON

The merging of the past and the present is evident in every aspect of the Crowne Plaza Macon. Located in the historic downtown area, the hotel was built in the early 1970s as a Hilton Hotel and became part of the Crowne Plaza Macon chain in 1995.

With major renovations taking place in 1995, the hotel has upgraded its more than 300 traditionally decorated rooms and modernized many aspects to better suit customer needs. A new telephone system with voice mail for each room, a two-floor executive level geared toward the corporate traveler, and a new exercise room are just some of the enhancements the hotel has received. The new executive level boasts such modern elements as facsimile machines, data ports, and two telephones in each room.

The exterior of the hotel has received a recent facelift with complete repainting, landscaping, three-tiered water fountain, and cobblestone circular drive entrance. Inside, lush gardens and flowing fountains have been added to the lower lobby area.

Other features the hotel offers include a swimming pool overlooking the city, a four-level parking garage, state-of-the-art security cameras, 24-hour security, room service, and a gift shop. Groome Transportation, housed in the hotel, allows convenient transportation to and from Atlanta.

First Street Grille featuring American fare, cafe-style Park Place, and the elegant four-star Paul's Restaurant make dining at the Crowne Plaza Macon a pleasure. Located in the lobby, the High Street Piano Bar offers a relaxing, cozy atmosphere in which to unwind.

With over 20,000 square feet of flexible meeting space, the hotel can accommodate groups of 10 to 1,000. Whether its a business meeting, a lunch for 20, an extravagant wedding reception or a sit-down dinner for 500, the hotel's banquet staff stands ready to provide the finest food and highest quality service available. The Preservation Hall Ballroom, with its multiple chandeliers, offers big-city elegance. The hotel also pays tribute to Macon's history through such names as the Lanier Room, named for famed Macon poet Sidney Lanier, and the Mercer and Wesleyan rooms, named for the city's two historic colleges.

The hotel's proximity to the many downtown historic sites and the new Georgia Music Hall of Fame, makes it a likely destination for travelers to Macon. Also, with just over an hour's drive from Atlanta, the hotel hopes to attract the many visitors traveling to the 1996 Olympic games.

From the fresh flowers in the lobby to the smiling face of the hotel employee serving complimentary coffee from a silver coffee service each morning in the lobby, the hotel strives to offer the best in Southern hospitality, blended with the modern amenities today's busy traveler deserves. ∎

From the fresh flowers in the lobby to the smiling face of the hotel employee serving complimentary coffee from a silver coffee service each morning, the hotel strives to offer the best in Southern hospitality.

MACON MALL
COLONIAL PROPERTIES

The Macon Mall serves customers not only from Macon and Central Georgia, but also from a 32-county area. Its convenient location on Eisenhower Parkway makes it easily accessible to travelers on both I-75 and I-475.

The largest retail center outside Atlanta, the Macon Mall is a 1.2 million square-foot facility and is located on 85 acres of land. It was built in 1975 and underwent a $6 million renovation in 1988.

Owned and operated by Colonial Properties of Birmingham, Alabama, the Macon Mall features a mixture of some of the country's leading retailers and continues to set the retailing standard of excellence in Central Georgia. Anchored by Belk Matthews, Macy's, JC Penney, and Sears, it features over 120 specialty shops and restaurants, as well as a food court which offers shoppers an opportunity to sit down, eat, and relax.

The merchandise variety available at the many stores and shops offers something for everyone. Merchandise categories include apparel, gifts, accessories, shoes, jewelry, music/entertainment, hobby, athletics, food, home furnishings, and appliances.

The selection of national, regional, and local merchants, along with the various special events and exhibits hosted by the mall each year, attracts over 10 million visitors annually.

The Macon Mall also offers a variety of programs and services, as well as numerous events and exhibits throughout the year. Although events which have been offered for the past 20 years are too numerous to name, they have included the circus, life-size robotic dinosaurs, sand sculptures, spring gardens, and concert series.

Each year the mall hosts 3 arts and crafts shows and 3 antique shows. Exhibitors throughout the Southeast participate and the mall draws from a pool of over 500 artisans and crafters in producing these popular events.

The Macon Mall has an information center which offers gift-certificate sales, wheelchairs, and customer assistance. Ticketmaster services at the information center sell tickets to sporting events and concerts in Macon and Atlanta.

The Macon Mall has a strong sense of community and offers several pro-

The Macon Mall has a strong sense of community and offers several programs which provide service to the community.

grams which provide service to the community. It is a participant in the Bibb County Board of Education "Adopt a School" program; presents two community expos each year as fund-raising events for area non-profit organizations; and is an annual supporter of the Salvation Army Angel Tree program. The mall also sponsors two blood drives yearly for the American Red Cross; hosts a walkers' club with over 500 members, providing a safe, pleasant place to walk, and hosts monthly programs presented by members of the medical community. The mall also hosts two events each year for the residents of Macon's four children's homes.

The Macon Mall's convenient store hours are from 10:00 a.m. to 9:30 p.m. Monday through Saturday and from 1:00 to 6:00 p.m. on Sunday. Special holiday hours are offered during the Christmas season. ■

Owned and operated by Colonial Properties of Birmingham, Alabama, the Macon Mall features a mixture of some of the country's leading retailers and continues to set the retailing standard of excellence in Central Georgia.

Macon Coliseum & City Auditorium

The Macon Coliseum, built in 1968, was the first multi-purpose facility of its kind in the state, and with its new addition now offers more flat floor square feet and more exhibition space under one roof than any other facility in the state.

The City Auditorium has a seating capacity of 2,688, is fully carpeted, and offers 14,000 square feet of exhibition space and 3 meeting rooms. Photography by Ken Krakow.

"The expansion puts us in an excellent position," says Gary Desjardins, General Manager of the Coliseum and the Macon Auditorium. "No one can compete with the amount of space we have now."

The Coliseum's recent expansion more than doubled its square footage to over 86,000 square feet. The facility can operate as one large complex or two separate facilities and can host events such as a circus or concert in the arena and at the same time host a convention, civic function, or banquet in the convention center.

Together, the Coliseum and the Auditorium have close to 600 use days a year for all kinds of events—an economic impact close to $20 million on the local economy, with the expansion adding an additional $11 million impact. This state-of-the-art facility will not only have a big economic impact on the area, but will serve two main purposes. It will bring conventions into Macon and Bibb County, and it will help existing businesses expand their operations. An article in Parade magazine listing places to hold a convention cited Macon as the least expensive and the most economical, as far as restaurants, motels, and other facilities.

The new expansion, named the Edgar H. Wilson Convention Centre (after one of Macon's former mayors) is a part of the Macon Centreplex, which includes the convention center, the coliseum, and the auditorium. The convention center offers 10 meeting rooms, a 9,100 square foot ballroom, and 30,800 square feet of exhibition space. It offers a business center complete with fax and copy machines, as well as the facilities to mail packages overnight. The utility grid in the exhibition hall floor has electrical power, water, compressed air and data communications, along with satellite down-link communications.

The third facility of the Macon Centreplex, the City Auditorium, was designed after the Mormon Tabernacle and built in 1925. It's seen many big events, including basketball tournaments, concerts from every genre, as well as conventions, consumer shows, and civic functions. The auditorium has a seating capacity of 2,688, is fully carpeted and offers 14,000 square feet of exhibition space and 3 meeting rooms.

The Macon Coliseum offers a 42,000-square-foot space and can seat 7,600 for basketball and hockey games and up to 9,200 for concerts. "We had Elvis here three times," says Desjardins, "and many well-known artists and groups have played here, but country is our biggest entertainment." The Coliseum not only has concerts but hosts the state basketball championships and is the home of the Mercer University basketball team.

Gary Desjardins, who majored in sports administration and minored in business at Tulane University, interned at the Louisianna Superdome and came to the Macon Coliseum in 1987 as a building supervisor. "I really enjoy my job," he says, "It's a great place to work, and Macon is a great city to live in." ∎

The City Auditorium was designed after the Mormon Tabernacle and built in 1925. Photography by Ken Krakow.

BIBLIOGRAPHY

Books

Anderson, Nancy. *Macon: A Pictorial History.* Virginia Beach: The Donning Company, 1979.

Butler, John C. *Historical Record of Macon and Central Georgia.* Macon: J.W. Burke Company, 1879; rpt. Macon: Middle Georgia Historical Society, 1969.

Escott, Paul D. and David R. Goldfield, eds. *The South for New Southerners.* Chapel Hill: University of North Carolina Press, 1991.

Freeman, Scott. *Midnight Riders: The Story of the Allman Brothers Band.* Boston: Little, Brown and Company, 1995.

Jones, Bill Walker. *Vocational Legacy: Biography of Dudley Mays Hughes.* Dry Branch, 1976.

Simms, Kristina. *Macon, Georgia's Central City: An Illustrated History.* Chatsworth: Windsor Publications, 1989.

Periodicals

Multiple articles from *The Macon Telegraph, Business Macon,* and *Macon Magazine.*

HERE Magazine. 7th ed. Macon: *Macon Magazine,* 1994.

Other Printed Materials

A Story of Progress in Macon: Yearbook 1940, Macon Chamber of Commerce. Macon: J.W. Burke Company, 1940.

Destination Macon. Annual Report. Macon: Macon-Bibb County Convention and Visitors Bureau, 1994.

Discoveries: 1994-1995 Research Update. Macon: Mercer University Office of University Relations, Alumni Services and Development, 1995.

Georgia—The State of Business Today. Atlanta: Georgia Department of Industry, Trade and Tourism, 1992.

Glenn, Helen. "*And So It Began...*" Bulletin of Wesleyan College April 1958; rpt. Macon: Wesleyan College (undated pamphlet).

Macon Technical Institute 1994 Annual Report. Macon: Macon Technical Institute, 1994.

Niemi, Albert W. Jr. *Macon—Middle Georgia Economic Yearbook.* 1993 ed. Athens: Simon S. Selig, Jr. Center for Economic Growth, Terry College of Business, University of Georgia, 1993.

The Partnership Press. Newsletter, vol. 3, numbers 4, 5 and 6. Macon: Macon 2000 Partnership, 1994.

Tubman News. Newsletter, vol. 4. Macon: Tubman African American Museum, Winter 1994-95.

Numerous brochures, press releases, and flyers.

MACON'S ENTERPRISE INDEX

INDEX

INDEX